JUNIOR LEAGUE
COOKBOOK COLLECTION

Classic

Virginia
Hospitality

Hospitality in eighteenth century Virginia gained the state her reputation as "the land of hospitality." The colonists in the English custom displayed pineapples as a sign of welcome on doorways, gateposts and gardenwalls. Fresh pineapples were used as the center of table arrangements and as a main feature of Christmas decorations. The tradition of warm hospitality is cherished and continued by today's Virginia hostesses.

Junior League of Hampton Roads, Inc.
729 Thimble Shoals Blvd., Suite 4D
Newport News, Virginia 23606

Favorite Recipes® Press

Executive Editor: Sheila Thomas
Project Editor: Tanis Westbrook
Classic Junior League Cookbook Collection Cover Design: Starletta Polster

Library of Congress Control Number: 2011924415
ISBN: 978-0-87197-552-2

Manufactured in the United States of America

One of the criteria to be considered for the Classic Junior League Cookbook
Collection is the original publication date; the cookbook must be at
least 25 years old. As a result of the length of time in print, some titles have
gone through revisions and updates; others have been intentionally
left in their original context in order to preserve the integrity and authenticity
of the publication. This printing has been taken from the most recent
edition. We hope you enjoy this American icon.

For more than 70 years, Junior League cookbooks have been sought out and collected by both novice and seasoned home cooks. Turned to again and again for their tried-and-true recipes, these cookbooks are a testament to the Junior League volunteers who dedicate themselves to improving the quality of life within their communities. These treasured cookbooks have played a significant role both in raising funds to help fulfill the organizations' missions and by documenting and preserving regional culinary traditions.

Favorite Recipes® Press, a longtime friend and partner of the Association of Junior Leagues International, is proud to present the *Classic Junior League Cookbook Collection*. The inaugural collection is comprised of six Junior League cookbooks that define all that is *Classic;* each serves as a standard of excellence and is considered an authentic and authoritative work on the foods and traditions of its region.

Enjoy,

Sheila Thomas

Executive Editor
Favorite Recipes Press

CONTENTS

Appetizers

Appetizers, as we think of them, are strictly a twentieth-century innovation which skyrocketed to importance as the cocktail party became a favorite means of entertaining. Prior to the 1900's, guests were invited for dinner instead of just for drinks, and appetizers or canapés were seldom served.

The one possible exception to this rule might be the half dozen oysters or the bluepoint clams so popular in the 1800's which were frequently served before the soup course. Even our colonial forefathers enjoyed a plate of raw oysters as an appetizer before the meal, and anecdotes recorded by the Virginia settlers reveal that great sport was derived by forcing a plate of them upon unsuspecting English and European visitors.

The term "appetizer" is derived from the word appetite, and the product—a small tasty portion of food served in advance of the meal—was originally intended to stimulate the appetite. Such foods may be served as the first course of the meal or by themselves. Currently, appetizers used as party fare have become so popular that they now form the complete menu for festive occasions such as open-houses, holiday parties, receptions, and cocktail buffets.

Although cocktail parties do not enjoy the popularity abroad that they do in America, the appetizer course is by no means limited to the American menu. Special traditional dishes to stimulate the appetite are also prepared by the French, the Slavs, the Scandinavians, and the Italians. Best known to us and adapted by us are the French hors d'oeuvres—small pieces of meat, cheese or fish served with an elegant flair—and the Italian antipasto—a tangy assortment of olives, sliced sausages, artichoke hearts, cheese and fish.

The Slavic counterpart of the hors d'oeuvres is known as Zaskouska and was formerly served with generous quantities of wine and liquor in an anteroom outside the dining room. Nowadays, however, this course may be served on trays at the dining room table. In Scandinavia, the first course is known as the smorgasbord, traditionally meaning the "bread and butter table." The modern smorgasboard, in addition to a variety of breads, cheese and butter, also includes many hot and cold delicacies, such as smoked and pickled fish, salads and meats. Many times the smorgasbord is so lavishly spread that it is used as an entire meal.

Anchovy Puffs

¹/₂ cup butter, softened
3 ounces cream cheese, softened
1 cup flour

1 tube anchovy paste
¹/₂ cup pecans, chopped

Blend butter and cheese, add flour. Chill. Roll very thin and cut with small biscuit cutter. Spread each with a dab of paste and nuts. Fold over, pinch edges. Bake at 400 for 10 minutes. Serve hot. Yields 45.

Note: For variation, omit paste and use a small piece of anchovy fillet in each puff.

Artichoke Puffs

30 Melba toast rounds
2 tablespoons butter, melted
¹/₈ teaspoon salt
2 egg whites
²/₃ cup mayonnaise

¹/₄ teaspoon Worcestershire
¹/₃ cup sharp Cheddar cheese, grated
15 ounces artichoke hearts,
*   drained and quartered*

Spread rounds with butter. Add salt to egg whites and beat until stiff. Fold in mayonnaise, Worcestershire and cheese. Place artichoke quarters on toast, cover with cheese mixture and broil one minute or until golden brown. Yields thirty.

Note: Cherry tomatoes, shrimp or cocktail onions may be substituted for artichokes.

Cheese and Bacon Puffs

1 cup mayonnaise
½ cup Cheddar cheese, grated
2 teaspoons horseradish, drained

1 tablespoon sherry
½ cup cooked bacon, crumbled

Combine all ingredients; spread on party-size bread, toast cut outs or crackers and broil until golden bubbly brown. Yields 2 cups.
"Serve while hot!"

Cheese Canapés

1 egg, beaten
½ teaspoon mustard
salt and pepper to taste
3 ounces sharp cheese, grated

2 teaspoons cream
6 slices bread
6 slices bacon, chopped

Combine first 5 ingredients. Trim crusts from bread and cut into 4 squares or triangles. Spread with mixture. Top with small pieces of bacon. Broil until bacon browns.
"Cheese mixture keeps well."

Crabmeat Bacon Rounds

½ cup sharp Cheddar cheese,
  grated
6½ ounces crabmeat, canned or
  fresh
2 egg whites, stiffly beaten

20 (2-inch) toast rounds, buttered
3 strips bacon, diced
7 stuffed green olives, sliced in
  thirds

Fold cheese and crab into egg whites. Pile on toast rounds. Top with bacon and broil until cheese melts and bacon is crisp. Top with an olive slice. Yields 20.
Note: The mixture can be prepared ahead and assembled just before serving.

Crabmeat Rounds

15 (2-inch) bread rounds, toasted
  and buttered
1 cup crabmeat
4 tablespoons sauterne

½ teaspoon salt
1 cup Swiss or Gruyère cheese,
  grated
1 tablespoon mayonnaise

Preheat oven to 450. Prepare bread and reserve. Mix other ingredients; pile high on rounds, bake until cheese melts and is lightly browned.
"Nice and cheesy!"

"Mushrooms were once thought magical since they appear overnight."

Hot Mushroom Turnovers

9 ounces cream cheese, softened
½ cup butter, softened

1½ cups flour

Mix cream cheese and butter. Add flour and blend until smooth. Chill 30 minutes. Preheat oven to 450. Roll dough ⅛ inch thick on lightly floured board and cut into 3 inch rounds. Place 1 teaspoon of filling on each and fold dough over. Press edges with a fork and prick top. Bake on ungreased cookie sheet for 15 minutes or until lightly browned. Yields 50.
Note: Can be frozen before baking; bake frozen as needed.

Filling:

3 tablespoons butter
1 large onion, minced
½ pound mushrooms, chopped
¼ teaspoon thyme

½ teaspoon salt
pepper to taste
2 tablespoons flour
¼ cup sweet or sour cream

Brown onions lightly in butter. Add mushrooms and cook for 3 minutes. Add thyme, salt, pepper and sprinkle with flour. Stir in cream and cook gently until thickened.

Parmesan-Onion Canapés

36 (1-inch) bread rounds or
   party rye or pumpernickel
1 large onion, grated

1 cup mayonnaise
5-6 tablespoons Parmesan cheese

Toast one side of bread. Spread the other side with onion. Mix mayonnaise and cheese. Place a small teaspoon of the cheese mixture over the onion. Broil 3-5 minutes.

Note: A small olive hidden under the cheese provides a pungent surprise!

Cocktail Pizzas

1 pound hot sausage, crumbled,
  fried and drained
1 cup onion, chopped
1/2 cup sharp cheese, grated
1/2 cup Parmesan cheese

1 1/2 teaspoons oregano
1 teaspoon garlic salt
8 ounces tomato sauce
6 ounces tomato paste
3 cans refrigerated flaky biscuits

Combine all ingredients except biscuits. Separate each biscuit into 3 pizza rounds. Spread with mixture and place on cookie sheets. Freeze. Store in plastic bags until ready to use. Bake in preheated oven at 425 for 10 minutes. Yields 90. "Always waiting for unexpected guests.!"

Sausage Rolls

2 cups flour
1/2 teaspoon salt
3 teaspoons baking powder
5 tablespoons shortening

2/3 cup milk
1 pound of mild or hot sausage,
  uncooked

Preheat oven to 400. Sift dry ingredients together and cut in shortening. Add milk and mix. Divide dough into 2 rectangles 1/4 inch thick. Spread dough with sausage and roll "jelly-roll" style. Chill until firm. Slice 1/4 inch thick and bake 10 minutes. Yields 30.

Note: The rolls may be wrapped and frozen before slicing.

Individual Shrimp Quiches

½ cup butter, softened
4 ounces cream cheese, softened
2 tablespoons heavy cream
1¼ cups flour
½ teaspoon salt
2 cups shrimp, cooked and chopped
1 teaspoon fresh dill, snipped or
  ½ teaspoon dried dill

1½ cups heavy cream
3 eggs, slightly beaten
¼ cup Gruyère or Swiss cheese,
  grated
salt and pepper to taste
⅓ cup Parmesan cheese, freshly
  grated

Cream butter and cream cheese well. Beat in cream and work in flour and salt to make dough. Wrap in wax paper and chill several hours or overnight. Before rolling pastry, preheat oven to 425. Roll out ⅛ inch thick, and cut to fit miniature muffin tins. Fit in tins. (Instead of rolling dough, bits can be pinched off and pressed thinly into each tin.) Evenly distribute shrimp in tins and cover with a mixture of all remaining ingredients except Parmesan cheese. Sprinkle with Parmesan and bake 5 minutes. Reduce temperature to 350 and bake 15 minutes longer. Quiches should be set and lightly browned. Serve immediately. Yields 48.

Note: To prepare ahead, cool on rack at end of baking time. Chill. Pack in boxes lined with foil. Cover with foil and freeze. To serve, remove ½ hour before serving. Preheat oven to 375. Place quiches on baking sheet and bake 15-20 minutes until heated thoroughly.

"This is one of those little goodies that an interested cook will enjoy doing because her guests will consider her a gourmet cook."

Cape Fear Canapés

36 (1½ inch) bread rounds
1 pound fresh shrimp, cooked and
  chopped
1 tablespoon onion, minced
1 teaspoon green pepper, minced
2 teaspoons fresh lemon juice

1 teaspoon celery, minced
½ teaspoon lemon rind, grated
¼ teaspoon salt
4-5 drops Tabasco
2-3 grinds of whole pepper
¾ cup mayonnaise

Lightly toast rounds. Reserve. Mix all ingredients and pile one heaping teaspoon on each round.

"All your guests will want more!"

La Fonda del Sol

1 pound ground beef
½ cup onion, chopped
½ cup extra hot ketchup
4 teaspoons chili powder,
  or to taste
1 teaspoon salt

2 cups kidney beans, undrained
1 cup sharp cheese, shredded
½ cup onion, shredded
½ cup stuffed green olives,
  sliced

Brown meat and ½ cup onion in skillet. Stir in ketchup, chili powder and salt. Mash kidney beans and liquid, and combine with meat mixture. Pour into chafing dish and top with an outer ring of chopped onions, a middle ring of shredded cheese and inner ring of sliced olives. Serve hot with broken taco shells, corn chips or Doritos.

Chafing Dish Crab

8 ounces cream cheese
6½ ounces crabmeat, fresh or
  canned
1 tablespoon crab or clam juice
2 tablespoons onion, grated

½ teaspoon horseradish
salt and pepper to taste
sliced almonds, toasted
paprika

Mix first 6 ingredients well in small bowl. Chill at least 1 hour. Bake at 375 for 15 minutes in a covered casserole. Serve in chafing dish with toasted sliced almonds and paprika on top. Serve with crackers. Yields 1½ cups.
Note: A 6½ ounce can of crabmeat equals ¾ cup.

Cocktail Meatballs

1 pound ground pork
1 pound ground veal
2 cups soft bread crumbs
2 eggs
½ cup onion, chopped

2 tablespoons parsley, chopped
2 teaspoons salt
2 tablespoons margarine
10 ounces apricot preserves
½ cup barbecue sauce

Preheat oven to 350. Combine first 7 ingredients and shape into meatballs. Brown in margarine and place in casserole. Combine preserves and barbecue sauce; pour over meat. Bake for 30 minutes. Serve in chafing dish. Yields 80.
"Can be cooked, frozen and re-heated."

Sweet and Sour Meatballs

2 pounds ground chuck
1 onion, chopped
3 eggs
2 slices bread, crumbled

12 ounces chili sauce
10 ounces orange marmalade
1 lemon, juiced

Combine meat, onion, eggs and bread to form 1½ inch meatballs. Make sauce from remaining ingredients. Simmer in the sauce for 1 hour. Serve from chafing dish. Yields 36.

Note: The beauty of this dish is the fact that the meatballs do not have to be browned. Be sure to use very lean meat. Chilling after they have been simmered allows fat to harden and be easily removed. Warm gently at serving time. Cook and freeze meatballs in the sauce.

Hot Oyster Cocktail
(Courtesy of The Tides Inn, Irvington, Virginia)

1 pint select oysters
½ teaspoon Worcestershire
¼ teaspoon Tabasco
2 tablespoons butter

pinch of seafood seasoning
salt and pepper to taste
crisp toast points

Combine all ingredients except toast points; bring them to a slow boil. Simmer until edges curl. Drain slightly and serve hot with crisp toast points in a cocktail cup. As an appetizer this recipe serves 6-8.
"Don't overcook."

Cocktail Sausages

2 pounds hot sausage
½ cup ketchup
½ cup wine vinegar

½ cup brown sugar
1 tablespoon soy sauce
½ teaspoon ginger

Form sausage into 1½ inch balls and fry. Drain and marinate overnight in sauce made from the remaining ingredients. Heat in chafing dish and serve hot.
"These are favorites of men because they are very hot."

Cottage Cheese Dip

2 cups cottage cheese
2-3 tablespoons sour cream
1/4 teaspoon onion, grated
2 teaspoons lemon juice

1/4 teaspoon salt
2 ounces blue cheese
1/4 teaspoon parsley flakes
1/4 teaspoon chives

Mix all ingredients in blender. Use to dip raw vegetables or to dress a salad. Yields 1 pint.

Dill Sauce

1 1/2 cups mayonnaise
1 cup sour cream
1 teaspoon garlic salt
1 teaspoon Maggi (liquid)
1 teaspoon Ac'cent
1 teaspoon dry mustard

1 tablespoon dill weed
1/2 cup parsley, chopped
2 shakes Tabasco
2 tablespoons olive oil
1 lemon, juiced

Blend well. Use as a dip for vegetables. Yields 1 pint.
"Will keep a month in the refrigerator."

Curried Herb Dip

1 cup mayonnaise
1/2 cup sour cream
1 teaspoon herb seasoning
1/4 teaspoon salt
1/8 teaspoon curry powder

1 tablespoon parsley, snipped
1 tablespoon onion, grated
1 1/2 teaspoons lemon juice
1/2 teaspoon Worcestershire
2 teaspoons capers (optional)

Blend and chill. Serve with fresh vegetables. Yields 1 pint.
Note: McCormick makes the seasoning. Also use in shrimp salad or potato salad.

Hot Clam Dip

5-8 ounce cans minced clams
5-8 ounce packages cream cheese,
    softened
1 large onion, grated

3 tablespoons Worcestershire
    sauce
1 teaspoon Tabasco

Drain clams, reserving juice. Melt cheese in top of double boiler. Add clam juice as needed for consistency. Add seasonings and clams. Place in chafing dish over low heat. Serve with crackers. Serves 40.
Note: Seasonings may be varied according to taste. Make it good and spicy!

Hot Crab Dip

1 pound crabmeat
1 tablespoon horseradish
¼ bottle capers
2 cups mayonnaise
1 teaspoon lemon rind, grated

½ teaspoon Ac'cent
½ teaspoon garlic powder
2 dashes of Tabasco
1 teaspoon Worcestershire

Preheat oven to 350. Mix and pour into greased 2 quart casserole. Bake 20-30 minutes. Serve from chafing dish on Melba rounds or toast.

"Marinate cooked shrimp and sliced onions overnight in a spicy oil and vinegar dressing to serve cold with toothpicks."

Shrimp Dip
(Courtesy of The Columns, Lynchburg, Virginia)

16 ounces cream cheese, softened
½ tablespoon onion, grated
1 teaspoon lemon juice
1 cup medium shrimp, cut in several pieces

3 tablespoons chutney, finely
    chopped
2 dashes curry powder
Ritz crackers

Mix first 6 ingredients well. Serve on Ritz crackers.

Hot Virginia Dip

1 cup pecans, chopped
2 teaspoons butter
16 ounces cream cheese, softened
4 tablespoons milk

5 ounces dried beef, minced
1 teaspoon garlic salt
1 cup sour cream
4 teaspoons onion, minced

Saute pecans in butter. Reserve. Mix all ingredients thoroughly. Place in 1½ quart baking dish, top with pecans. Chill until serving time. Bake at 350 for 20 minutes. Serve hot with crackers or small bread sticks.
"Everybody's favorite!"

Beer Cheese

12 ounces stale beer
2 cloves garlic, minced
½ medium onion, diced
1 teaspoon Worcestershire

¼ teaspoon cayenne pepper
¼ teaspoon Tabasco
salt to taste
2 pounds sharp cheese, grated

To make stale beer, boil and cool. Mix all ingredients. Add beer until spreadable. Fills 4 8-ounce crocks.
Note: Store in refrigerator.
"Keeps for several weeks."

Cheddar Ball

2 cups sharp Cheddar cheese, grated
3 ounces cream cheese, softened
3 tablespoons mayonnaise
½-¾ teaspoon Worcestershire
celery salt to taste

garlic salt to taste
2-3 ounces olives, green or black,
*   chopped*
¼ cup pecans, chopped

Mix all ingredients except nuts with mixer. Form ball, chill and roll in nuts. Serves 10-12.
Note: Can be made several days ahead.

Herb Butter

"A delicious recipe from the extensive herb gardens of Muskettoe Pointe Farm."

1 teaspoon basil	*1 teaspoon chives*
1 teaspoon thyme	*1 teaspoon rosemary*
1 teaspoon tarragon	*1 cup butter*

Chop herbs. Cream these into butter. Serve as an hors d'ouevre on freshly baked bread.

Curried Chutney Cheese Spread

4 ounces sharp Cheddar cheese, grated	*¼-½ teaspoon curry powder*
6 ounces cream cheese, softened	*2 ounces chutney, minced*
2 tablespoons dry sherry	*1 tablespoon green onions, including tops, minced*
¼ teaspoon salt	

Blend cheeses, sherry, salt and curry powder well. Add chutney. Chill. At serving time, top with onions. Yields 1 ⅔ cups.
Note: Serve with crackers or fresh fruit.
"Curry lovers will use ½ teaspoon of curry and savor every bite!"

"Always serve cheese at room temperature."

Islander Cheese Ball

16 ounces cream cheese, softened	*¼-½ cup green pepper, chopped*
8 ounces crushed pineapple, drained	*2 teaspoons seasoned salt*
2 tablespoons green onions, including tops, chopped	*2 cups pecans, chopped*

Mix cheese and pineapple with mixer. Stir in onion, green pepper, salt and ½ cup pecans. Roll into one large ball, 2 logs or fill a scooped-out fresh pineapple half. Roll or top with remaining pecans.
Note: Serve with bacon-flavored crackers.
"Delightfully refreshing!"

Muskettoe Pointe Farm

This frame house of wonderful proportions, interesting tilts and angles, has tiny dormers tucked between the graceful brick chimneys. It is surrounded by the same gnarled mulberry trees that were planted in vain by Virginia colonists dreaming of a native silk industry. Part of this riverfront house, located in Lancaster County, dates back to the seventeenth century. Facing Lawson Bay on the Rappahannock River, it was built by the Lawson family for whom the bay is named. The present owners, Mr. and Mrs. James Northern Carter, discovered the house after it had been unoccupied for almost ten years. During their occupancy, they have restored and enlarged the house, its dependencies, and the gardens for the enjoyment of the entire Carter family.

Crab Spread

1 pint mayonnaise
4 tablespoons ketchup
1 tablespoon Parmesan cheese

2 teaspoons A-1 sauce
½ teaspoon curry powder
1 pound crabmeat

Mix well and chill. Serve with crackers.
"Guests will rave over this!"

Cocktail Hour Crab Mold

1 pound crabmeat
8 ounces cream cheese, softened
few dashes of Tabasco

grinding of whole black pepper
1 teaspoon chives
dash of Worcestershire

Mix ingredients and mold, leaving a well in the center. Chill. At serving time, fill center with cocktail sauce. Serve with crackers to 8-10 guests.
"Superbly delicious."

"Mound chicken salad on a silver tray, garnish with toasted almonds and white grapes, and let guests stuff miniature hot rolls."

Chicken Liver Paté

½ pound chicken livers
1 medium onion, chopped
¼ cup butter
2 eggs, hard-boiled

2 lemons, juiced
salt and pepper to taste
2 tablespoons parsley, chopped

Sauté liver and onions for 20 minutes. Cool. Place liver mixture and eggs in blender, a little at a time; add lemon juice; salt and pepper. Blend until smooth. Remove and garnish with parsley. Yields 1 pint.
"Rave notices accompany this dish!"

Liverwurst Spread

16 ounces liverwurst
3 ounces cream cheese, softened
1 tablespoon sherry

1½ teaspoons curry powder
1 tablespoon sour cream
1 tablespoon onion, grated

Blend first 4 ingredients. Form into ball. Chill. Frost with sour cream and onion. Garnish.

Zesty Olive and Beef Spread

1 teaspoon dry minced onion
1 tablespoon dry sherry
8 ounces cream cheese, softened

2 tablespoons mayonnaise
3-4 ounces dried beef, minced
¼ cup stuffed green olives, chopped

Soak onion in sherry to soften. Blend cheese and mayonnaise. Add onion, beef and olives. Serve on whole wheat crackers. Serves 15-20.

Smoked Oyster Cheese Ball

1 can smoked oysters, drained
    slightly
8 ounces cream cheese, softened

1 tablespoon Worcestershire sauce
curry powder, to taste
½ cup pecans, chopped

Combine all ingredients except pecans. Form into ball and roll in pecans.
Note: Do not omit the curry powder. It's a must!

Shrimp Louis

1 pound shrimp, cooked and cut
¾ cup mayonnaise
8 ounces cream cheese, softened
1 medium onion, minced

½ cup celery, minced
3 tablespoons ketchup
½ lemon, juiced
crackers

Mix together all ingredients. Chill. Mound on tray and surround with crackers. Serves 35.

19

Shrimp Mold

1 tablespoon gelatin
3 ounces cream cheese
10¾ ounces condensed tomato soup
½ cup celery, chopped
½ cup onion, chopped

½ cup green pepper, chopped
1 cup mayonnaise
1 cup shrimp, cooked and cut or
    4½ ounces canned medium shrimp,
    chopped

Soften gelatin in ¼ cup cool water and save. Melt cheese and soup in saucepan. Pour into mixing bowl, add gelatin and beat until smooth. Add remaining ingredients and pour into lightly-greased 6 cup mold. Serve with Triscuits to 12-15 for cocktails.

Note: Other seafoods can be substituted for shrimp. Lobster is lovely and elegant! This can be cut in squares for a luncheon dish.

Bacon Roll-Ups

¼ cup butter
½ cup water
1½ cups herb stuffing mix

1 egg, slightly beaten
¼ pound sausage, hot or mild
8-12 ounces bacon

Melt butter in water, remove from heat; add stuffing, egg and sausage. Chill 1 hour. Preheat oven to 375. Shape into pieces the size of pecans. Divide bacon strips into thirds. Wrap around mixture and secure with toothpicks. Bake in shallow pan for 35 minutes, turning once. Drain on paper towels. Serve hot. Yields 30.

Note: Can be made a day ahead, or frozen before baking.

Hot Cheese Balls

1½ cups sharp Cheddar cheese,
   grated
1 tablespoon flour
¼ teaspoon salt

2 egg whites, stiffly beaten
dash of cayenne
¾ cup fine cracker crumbs
oil for frying

Mix cheese, flour, salt and cayenne. Add egg whites. Shape into balls and roll in crumbs. Place 2 inches of oil in a 1 quart saucepan. Heat and fry balls until brown. Drain and serve immediately on toothpicks. Yields 20-24.

Note: Balls may be prepared and kept in refrigerator until time to fry.

Corbin Hall

Corbin Hall, situated on the Eastern Shore, has a magnificent view of Chincoteague Bay from its terraced lawns. Built in the 1700's of hand-burned bricks, it is a classic example of Georgian architecture. Original interior details feature handsome paneling, hand-carved mantels and fine wooden floors. During a recent renovation of a wing, a petrified rat was found sealed in the wall. This may have been intentionally placed there to scare off witches, according to an old British custom. This curious memento of three centuries ago is now displayed for Garden Week visitors to view.

My Mother's Cheese Straws
(Courtesy of Corbin Hall)

1 cup flour
1 teaspoon baking powder
½ teaspoon salt
dash of cayenne

2 tablespoons butter
3 tablespoons cold water
⅓ pound sharp cheese, grated

Blend all ingredients thoroughly. Roll thin and cut in narrow strips about 4 inches long. Bake on cookie sheet at 475 until crisp.

Cheese Crisps

1 1/2 cups sharp cheese, grated
1/2 cup butter, softened
1 cup sifted flour

1/2 teaspoon salt
1 teaspoon red pepper
1/2 cup pecans, chopped

Cream cheese and butter. Add flour, salt and pepper. Mix well. Stir in pecans. Flour hands and shape into 2 rolls, 1 inch in diameter. Wrap in wax paper and chill overnight. Preheat oven to 350. Slice thin and bake for 10 minutes on an ungreased cookie sheet. Cool. Yields 70.

Cheese Puffs

2 cups Cheddar cheese, grated
1/2 cup butter, softened
1/4 teaspoon paprika

1 cup sifted flour
1/8 teaspoon salt

Soften cheese and work all ingredients together with hands, and roll into balls the size of marbles. Bake at 350 for 15 minutes. Yields 6 dozen.
Note: To freeze, place on cookie sheet, freeze and store in plastic bag. Bake when needed.
"These can be kept in the freezer for months."

"Clams are found all over the world . . . however, they were so prolific in the waters of Virginia in 1616 that Captain John Smith enthused: 'You shall scarce find any bay or cove of sand where you may not take any clampes, or lobsters or both at your pleasure.'"

Clams Casino

2 dozen small clams
salt to taste
pepper to taste
oregano to taste

2-3 cloves garlic, minced
1/4 cup butter, cut in 24 pats
1 cup Sauterne
4-6 strips bacon

Open clams and remove; reserve juice and half of the shells. Place shells on baking sheet. On each, place a clam, small amount juice, salt, pepper, oregano, dab of garlic, butter, capful of wine and a square of bacon. Broil until bacon is crisp. Serves 4-6.
"The best ever!"

Crabmeat en Brochette

2 pounds fresh crabmeat
2 cups bread crumbs, seasoned
1/3 cup dry sherry

1 teaspoon dry mustard
2 teaspoons frozen chopped chives
20 slices bacon, halved

Combine all ingredients except bacon. Shape into balls the size of walnuts. Wrap in bacon and fasten with toothpicks. Chill until ready to serve. Bake at 400 for 15 minutes or until well-browned.

Note: This recipe is delicious for stuffing a flounder or flounder fillets.

Chicken Liver Hors D'Oeuvres

1 pound chicken livers
1/2 cup soy sauce

1 teaspoon ginger
bacon strips

Marinate livers in soy sauce and ginger in a covered dish for 6-8 hours. At serving time, wrap each liver in half strip of bacon. Secure bacon ends with a toothpick. Broil 20-25 minutes, turning once, until bacon is well-cooked. Serve hot. Yields 24.

Note: A variation of this dish is called Rumaki. A slice of water chestnut is placed inside the liver before rolling.

Marvelous Marinated Mushrooms

3 pounds fresh button mushrooms
1/2 ounce package garlic
   salad dressing mix
1 1/2 cups oil
1/2 cup lemon juice

salt and pepper to taste
2 tablespoons Ac'cent
2 tablespoons parsley flakes
2 tablespoons garlic powder
   (optional)

Wash and cap mushrooms. Cover in salt water and boil 1 minute. Drain. Prepare marinade from rest of ingredients. Pour over caps and chill minimum of 24 hours. Drain and serve cold. Yields about 36.

Note: Garlic powder gives them a very strong taste.

"A big hit at every party!"

Stuffed Mushrooms

36 small fresh mushrooms
1/2 medium onion, chopped
1/2 cup butter

2/3 cup dry bread crumbs
1/2 teaspoon salt
1/8 teaspoon pepper

Wash mushrooms, remove stems and save. Chop stems and sauté with onions in butter for 10 minutes. Add remaining ingredients, and use mixture to stuff mushrooms. Broil 5-8 minutes. Yields 36.
Note: To accompany rare roast beef, fill 12 large caps for 6 servings.

Mushrooms Stuffed with Crab

36 fresh medium mushrooms
1/2 pound fresh crabmeat
1 tablespoon parsley, chopped
1 tablespoon pimento, chopped

1 teaspoon capers, chopped
1/4 teaspoon dry mustard
1/2 cup mayonnaise
Parmesan cheese

Preheat oven to 375. Remove stems and discard. Mix other ingredients, stuff caps and sprinkle with cheese. Bake for 10 minutes. Yields 36.

"Combine mayonnaise, Worcestershire and lemon juice to use as a sauce for fresh picked crab."

Sausage-Stuffed Mushrooms

36 medium mushrooms
1/2 pound sausage
4 ounces herb stuffing mix,
   crumb type

mayonnaise to moisten
1 large onion, or
3 green onions, including tops,
   chopped

Wash mushrooms. Remove stems and chop. Brown sausage, stems and onions. Drain well. Mix sausage mixture and stuffing with enough mayonnaise to hold together. Place caps in baking dish, fill with sausage mixture. Cover and chill. These can be made a day ahead. At serving time, preheat oven to 450. Bake 10 minutes.
Note: To accompany steak, use 8 very large mushrooms. Bake 15 minutes.
"Fix twice as many as you think you'll need. Guests gobble them up."

Swiss Stuffed Mushrooms

12 large mushrooms
2-3 tablespoons butter, melted
salt and pepper
2 tablespoons shallots, minced
2 tablespoons butter

½ tablespoon flour
½ cup heavy cream
3 tablespoons parsley, minced
¼ cup Swiss cheese, grated
1-2 tablespoons butter, melted

Preheat oven to 375. Remove mushroom stems and reserve. Wash and dry caps. Brush with melted butter, arrange hollow-side up in baking dish. Season lightly with salt and pepper. Chop stems, and squeeze in towel to remove as much juice as possible. Sauté with shallots in butter for 4-5 minutes. Lower heat, add flour and stir for one minute. Stir in cream and simmer until thickened. Add parsley, salt and pepper. Fill caps with mixture. Top each with 1 teaspoon cheese and drizzle with melted butter. Bake 15 minutes. Yields 12 servings.
"Messy, but yummy."

Curried Nuts

8 tablespoons butter
2 tablespoons curry powder
1 tablespoon powdered ginger

2 tablespoons brown sugar
1 pound pecans
2-3 tablespoons chutney

Preheat oven to 300. Melt butter; add curry powder, ginger and brown sugar. Remove from heat; add pecans; toss. Drip chutney about; mix. Place nut mixture on cookie sheet, covered with paper towels. Place in oven and turn *off* heat. Leave in oven to dry 10-15 minutes. Salt and cool. Store in jar.

Cherry Tomato Appetizers

40 cherry tomatoes
7½ ounces tuna
4 ounces cream cheese, softened
2 tablespoons onion, grated

salt and pepper to taste
2 tablespoons lemon juice
heavy cream to moisten
(about 1 tablespoon)

Cut a thin slice from stem end of each tomato. Remove pulp, and invert on paper towel to drain. Combine all other ingredients to form a creamy consistency. Stuff tomatoes using a small spoon. Garnish with parsley. Make ahead and chill. Yields 40.

Appetizers

The Gracious Virginia Hostess Would:

. . . cover a large block of cream cheese with crabmeat, top with cocktail sauce and serve with crackers.

. . . wrap half slices of bacon around an assortment of livers, oysters and water chestnuts to bake in a hot oven or broil 'til crisp. Guests love the variety!

. . . top a block of cream cheese with chutney and toasted almonds to spread on crackers.

. . . broil smoked oysters on a chicken flavored cracker until lightly browned.

. . . add sliced raw squash, zucchini, turnips and mushrooms to a vegetable tray.

. . . mix three cups of mayonnaise and one cup of horseradish to always have on hand to dress rare roast beef.

. . . marinate canned mushrooms in Italian dressing overnight and serve with toothpicks.

. . . wrap melon balls in thin strips of Smithfield ham and secure with picks.

. . . top party rye bread with tomato sauce, oregano, pizza fixin's and grated mozzarella to broil golden brown.

. . . roll a cocktail onion in a small ball of cream cheese, wrap in dried beef and spear with a pick.

. . . steam artichokes and allow guests to pick and dip in choice of dressings.

. . . arrange a tray of luscious fruits and cheeses for guests to slice and serve.

. . . always serve one sweet with cocktails; a tray of petite chocolates is an elegant touch.

. . . use a pineapple boat to fill with a cheese ball.

. . . serve beach guests a platter of sardines, chopped onion, lemon wedges and saltines to assemble themselves.

. . . fill miniature cream puff shells with any meat salad one or two hours ahead and garnish lavishly with fresh parsley.

. . . place washed cherry tomatoes in a jar and cover generously with Lawry's Seasoned Salt to be served with picks and nibbled all day. Keep cold!

. . . boil a pan of water containing cloves and cinnamon sticks to make her house smell divine for guests.

Beverages

All recorded history points to one fact: drinking was a favorite indoor and outdoor sport in the budding Commonwealth. The sluggish, humid weather—enhanced by tradition and natural aptitude—made sipping and toasting a logical source of amusement and refreshment in a setting of gracious living and languid movement.

Having once subdued the wilderness, the thirsty Virginia settlers vigorously applied their skills with true American ingenuity to brewing beer from potatoes, pumpkins, persimmons, Jerusalem artichokes, green cornstalks and other available materials. Later, as life in the colony became more sophisticated, there was keen competition among planters to see who could produce the best cider and brandies from the abundant orchards, and experimentation with recipes for homemade liqueurs and cordials knew no bounds. To enhance the reputation of domestic beverages even further, Thomas Jefferson strove diligently to produce superior wines at his plantation, Monticello.

Rum, imported from the nearby Indies, was another favorite drink of the emerging patriots, and during the early stages of American politics it was frequently used to influence voters. In keeping with this early campaign technique, when George Washington ran for State Legislature in 1758 his agent furnished 160 gallons of rum, beer, wine and cider to the voters of Frederick County (roughly equivalent to one and a half quarts a voter).

Other spirited imports of high esteem among the colonists were sack, acquivate and Madeira; however, arrack (a liquor produced in the East Indies) was *the* favorite ingredient of Colonial punches. So popular was the drink, in fact, that William Randolph transferred 200 acres of land to Peter Jefferson in "consideration of Henry Wetherburn's biggest bowl of arrack punch." This land later became the birthplace of Thomas Jefferson.

27

On less festive occasions—when not toasting their fellow man, the weather or a fleeting fad—the colonists enjoyed a rousing cup of coffee in the early morning. Hot tea in the English tradition was enjoyed at all times; however, a strictly American variation was developed on the eve of the American Revolution, when sassafras was substituted for tea leaves imported from England. Tea, as a favorite drink in Virginia today, again varies from the English manner and is most often served on ice with a touch of mint or lemon.

Best of all, though, Virginians—as most Southerners—have remained true to the favorite local product, corn whiskey, and its more refined relative, bourbon. For pure drinking pleasure, bourbon and water has become the undisputed "State" drink although bourbon is also still used as the base for many other more elaborate and delicious concoctions including the most famous of all Southern drinks—the Mint Julep.

Easter Bonnets

1 1/2 ounces vodka
1 1/2 ounces apricot brandy
1 1/2 ounces peach brandy

1/4 lemon, juiced
champagne
slice of orange, cherry or pineapple

Place the first 4 ingredients in a tall glass. Add ice to top of glass and fill with champagne. Garnish with slice of orange, cherry or pineapple. Serve with a straw.

"A smooth, delicious drink, but guests must be warned, two is the limit."

Grasshopper

1 1/2 ounces green crème de menthe
1 1/2 ounces brandy

1 scoop French vanilla ice cream

Put ingredients in blender for couple of seconds. Serve in champagne glass. Serves 1.

"It is better to serve a good drink in the wrong glass, than a bad drink in a proper glass; but best of all, serve the right drink in the right glass!"

Sangria

1 banana	*¼-½ cup brandy*
1 lime	*½ cup club soda*
1 orange	*2 tablespoons sugar*
1 fifth burgundy wine	

Fill large pitcher half-full of ice. Slice banana and rub on inside of pitcher. Slice lime and orange; prick with fork to allow juices to seep into drink. Place all fruits in pitcher; add other ingredients. Stir well. Serves 6-8.
Note: Fruit-flavored brandy is best!

Southern Mint Julep

2 sprigs fresh mint	*½ cup ice, crushed*
1 tablespoon water	*1½ ounces bourbon*
1 teaspoon confectioners' sugar	*1 sprig fresh mint*

Place mint in blender; add water and sugar. Blend until leaves disappear, add ice and bourbon; blend a few seconds. Pour into frosted glass or julep cup which has been filled with finely chopped ice. Stir and decorate with a sprig of mint. Serves 1.
Note: Serve with a short straw that is no taller than the mint, so one enjoys the aroma as well as the taste.

The following account was written by a Lieutenant-General in the Confederate Army of a mint julep served him on a June morning in the midst of the war at Barboursville.
"The white-headed butler, face beaming hospitality, advanced, holding a salver, on which rested a huge silver goblet filled with Virginia's nectar, mint julep. Quantities of cracked ice rattled refreshingly in the goblet; sprigs of fresh mint peered above its broad rim; a mass of white sugar, too sweetly indolent to melt, rested on the mint; and, like rose buds on a snow bank, luscious strawberries crowned the sugar. Ah! that julep!"

After Dinner Coffee

¾ ounce brandy
¾ ounce coffee liqueur (Kahlua)

black coffee
whipped cream, sweetened

Place brandy and coffee liqueur in cup. Fill with black coffee. Top with dollop of cream. Serves 1.

Quick and Easy Irish Coffee

6-8 cups coffee
6-8 ounces bourbon

½ pint heavy cream, whipped
and sweetened

To be made at table:
Put coffee in silver pot. Pour bourbon in decanter. Put cream in a silver bowl. Pour coffee into cups about ⅔ full (no more). Add 1 ounce of bourbon and top with couple of dollops of cream. Cup should be completely filled. Serve as it is made. Do not stir. Serves 6-8.
"Serve from coffee table."

Luncheon Cocktail

2-4 tablespoons rum
2 cups cranberry juice

pineapple sherbet

Mix rum and cranberry juice. Pour into stem glass. Top with small scoop of sherbet. Serves 2.

Frozen Daiquiri

6 ounces frozen limeade concentrate
6 ounces of light rum

crushed ice

Put limeade and rum in blender. Fill blender with crushed ice. Blend at high speed. Serve in stem glass. Garnish with cherry, mint sprig or fresh strawberry. Serves 8.
Note: A Pink Lady is made by using gin and pink lemonade.

Pina Colada

1 ounce Coco cream   3 ounces pineapple juice
2 ounces white rum   1 cup crushed ice

Mix thoroughly in blender. Serve in stemmed glasses. Yields two drinks.
Note: Coco cream is sold in stores by the brand name, Coco Lopez.

"Sugar does not dissolve in alcohol. Always add sugar to water or fruit juice before adding alcohol."

Hot Toddy

2-3 ounces rum, light or dark   1 slice lemon
1 ½ teaspoons sugar   boiling water
2 whole cloves

Place a silver spoon in a heavy Old Fashion glass or heat-proof mug to prevent cracking. Add rum, sugar, cloves and lemon slice. Fill with boiling water. Stir and serve. Serves 1.
Variation: Hot Buttered Toddy
                Add 1 tablespoon of butter before pouring in boiling water.

"Rum in your toddy is good for a cold,
Or whatever else ails you—or so I am told."

Sherry Sours

1 fifth dry sherry   2 tablespoons lemon juice
6 ounces frozen lemonade
  concentrate

Mix in blender. Store for 3-4 days. Serve chilled in wineglasses, garnished with cherries or strawberries. Serves 10-12.

Sherry Cobbler

For individual serving:

1 tablespoon sugar   *2 ounces dry sherry*
1 ounce fresh lemon juice

Dissolve sugar in lemon juice. Add sherry. Mix well, and add crushed ice. Garnish with slice of orange and cherry.

For larger quantities:

³/₄ cup plus 1 tablespoon sugar   *1 fifth dry sherry*
1 ¹/₂ cups plus 2 tablespoons
fresh lemon juice

Serves 12.
"May be made several days ahead. A favorite with ladies!"

Bloody Marys for Brunch

46 ounces tomato juice   *¹/₂ teaspoons Tabasco, or to taste*
1 ¹/₂ cups vodka   *¹/₂ teaspoon cracked pepper*
¹/₄ cup Worcestershire   *1 teaspoon salt*
¹/₃ cup lemon juice

Combine ingredients and serve over lots of ice. Garnish each drink with lemon or lime squeezed in the top of each drink. Serves 12.
Note: You may prefer less Tabasco. These are wonderfully spicy!

Poor Charlie

1 ¹/₂ ounces vodka   *2 ounces Fresca*
3-4 ounces orange juice

Combine ingredients and serve over ice.

Note: To prepare a delicious variation of a Harvey Wallbanger, float 1 tablespoon of Galliano on top. DO NOT STIR!

*"This drink is a favorite of both men and women. Great for brunches, lun-
cheons or midnight breakfasts."*

32

Whiskey Sour

6 ounces frozen orange juice
  concentrate
6 ounces frozen lemonade
  concentrate

6 ounces blended whiskey
3 ounces club soda
cracked ice

Fill blender with all ingredients and cracked ice. Blend until smooth. Serves 12.
Note: Keeps indefinitely in freezer.

Golden Champagne Punch

46 ounces pineapple juice
6 ounces frozen orange juice
  concentrate
1 cup lemon juice

1 cup sugar
1 fifth sauterne
2 fifths champagne

Mix juices and sugar; chill. Pour juice mixture over block of ice in punch
bowl; add wines. Stir. Serves 15-18.

Holiday Punch

1 fifth sparkling burgundy
1 fifth champagne

orange liqueur (Cointreau) to taste
strawberries

Mix burgundy and champagne, add orange liqueur to taste. Garnish with
strawberries. Serves 12.
"Easy and delicious."

Spiked Cranberry Punch

1 quart cranberry juice
18 ounces pineapple juice
1 cup orange juice
½ cup lemon juice

1 cup bourbon
1 cup rum
2 quarts ginger ale, chilled

Combine fruit juices and liquors in punch bowl. Chill. Pour in ginger ale just
before serving. Serves 15-20.
Note: Use some punch and freeze in ice cube tray; float cubes in punch bowl.

Christmas Egg Nog

7 eggs
¾ cup sugar
1 pint heavy cream
2 cups milk

1 pint blended whiskey
3 ounces dark Jamaican rum
grated nutmeg

Beat separately yolks and whites of eggs. Add ½ cup sugar to the yolks while beating, and ¼ cup sugar to the whites after they have been beaten very stiff. Fold the egg whites into the yolks. Fold in cream and milk. Slowly add whiskey and rum. Stir thoroughly and serve cold with dash of nutmeg on top of each cup. Serves 10.

"Can be kept in refrigerator or cool place for several days or weeks."

Egg Nog

6 eggs, separated
½ gallon French vanilla ice
    cream, softened
1 quart milk

1 cup bourbon
½ cup rum
½ cup apple jack brandy

Beat egg yolks, add ice cream and milk. Slowly add bourbon, rum and brandy. Beat egg whites and fold in carefully. Serve with nutmeg. Serves 10.

"During the eighteenth century Virginia was famous for egg nog, New York for brandy punch, South Carolina for milk punch and the frontier for corn liquor. Bourbon whiskey was developed in the last part of the century."

Longwood House Milk Punch
(Courtesy of Longwood House)

1 gallon milk
1 gallon vanilla ice cream
2 fifths bourbon

1 fifth rum, medium dark
1 cup creme de cacao
1 quart vanilla ice cream

Mix first 5 ingredients one day prior to serving and refrigerate. At serving time, place the remaining ice cream in punch bowl. Pour punch mixture over ice cream and sprinkle with freshly grated nutmeg. (Nutmeg may also be sprinkled over individual servings, if desired.)

Longwood House

This lovely white frame house with its rolling lawn serves as the home of the President of Longwood College in Farmville. It was built in 1815 and is the site of the birthplace of Confederate General Joseph E. Johnston. Having once been a tea room where students, faculty and townspeople could meet, it now serves as the scene of many college functions. Thus its charm and beauty have been shared by many young ladies during their scholarly pursuits at this traditional Virginia school.

Rosé Punch

3 fifths rosé wine
6 ounces frozen pink lemonade
   concentrate

46 ounces fruit punch
1 quart club soda

Combine the wine, lemonade and punch; add 2 quarts water. Just before serving, add the ice mold and soda. Serves 25.

Ice Mold:

1 orange
1 lemon

1 bunch green grapes

Slice one orange and one lemon in round slices. Put in 8 inch round cake pan. Fill pan with water. Top with green grapes. Freeze until ready to use.
"Great for ladies' luncheon."

> *The Cook, 1885:*
> *There's a little place just out of town*
>   *Where, if you go to lunch,*
> *They'll make you forget your mother-in-law*
>   *With a drink called Fish-House Punch.*

Fish House Punch

1 ½ cups sugar
2 quarts water
1 quart lemon juice

2 quarts Jamaican rum
1 quart cognac
4 ounces peach brandy

Dissolve sugar in water; add all other ingredients. Allow ingredients to mellow for 2 hours, occasionally stirring to insure a perfect blend. Pour over ice in punch bowl. Serves 30.

"Flip was a very popular drink of colonial times. It was made with two thirds pitcher of beer, enough molasses to sweeten, rum to suit your preference and stirred with a hot poker from the fire until foamy."

Fourth of July Rum Punch

1 quart rum
¼ cup brown sugar
¾ cup strong cold tea, strained

juice of 10 lemons, strained
peels of 5 lemons, thinly sliced
approximately 2 quarts ginger ale

Mix first 4 ingredients. Add lemon peels. Let stand overnight. Keep in a warm place the first night, then remove peels and put punch in bottles until used. Serve with equal parts cold ginger ale. Pour over ice. Serves 20.
Note: After bottling, the punch may be chilled or allowed to mellow from seven to ten days at room temperature.

Rum Punch

4 fifths rum
2 quarts pineapple juice,
    unsweetened

2 fifths sauterne
2 quarts ginger ale
1 ounce bitters

Place ingredients in a large punch bowl. Garnish with pineapple rings or cut citrus fruits if desired. Float ice ring in the bowl. Serves 35-40.
Hint: Make ice in 9 inch ring mold with strawberries or cherries added.

Vodka Punch

1 fifth vodka
1 quart ginger ale
46 ounces apple juice

3 ounces concentrated lemon juice
orange slices

Mix together all ingredients, add orange slices frozen in ice block and serve. May be prepared 1 day ahead. Serves 15.
"Good for ladies' daytime tea."

"In the eighteenth century drinking was a pastime of great magnitude. Non-intoxicating drinks, like coffee, tea, chocolate, water and milk, were called 'Small Drinks.' The gentlemen enjoyed rum, brandy, Portugese and Spanish wines, and punch. Many of the colonial towns had a problem with their water supply, but the residents drank for the love of drink."

Coffee Punch

1 gallon strong coffee
1 stick cinnamon
2 quarts French vanilla ice cream

1 quart heavy cream
5 tablespoons sugar
5 teaspoons vanilla

Perk coffee with cinnamon stick in water; cool thoroughly. Whip cream, adding sugar and vanilla gradually while beating. Place ice cream and whipped cream in punch bowl. Pour in coffee; mix well. Serves 50-60.
Note: Rum, brandy, or coffee liqueur may be added to taste.

Frozen Patio Punch

1 cup sugar
2½ cups crushed pineapple and
  juice
2 cups banana, mashed
2 cups orange juice

2 tablespoons lemon juice
dash of salt
10-12 maraschino cherries
4 quarts ginger ale

Combine ingredients and beat until fluffy in blender. Freeze in ice cube trays. Pour room temperature ginger ale over punch cubes. Serves 20.
Hint: For variation, use 2 cubes per 8 ounce glass. Pour ginger ale over cubes and add 1 ounce rum.

Golden Tea Punch

2 cups water
2 rounded tablespoons instant tea
½ cup sugar
3 cups orange juice

1 cup lemon juice
1 cup pineapple juice
¼ cup grenadine
1 quart ginger ale

Stir tea into water until dissolved, add sugar and stir until dissolved. Add juices and chill. Place ice mold in punch bowl. Pour punch mixture in bowl and add ginger ale. Serves 18.

Russian Tea

6 cups water
12 whole cloves
6 teaspoons tea leaves
2½ cups pineapple juice

2 lemons, juiced
1 teaspoon lemon rind, grated
2 oranges, juiced
sugar to taste

Boil water and cloves for 15 minutes. Add tea and steep for 2-4 minutes. Strain.
Add remaining ingredients. Serve HOT.

Spiced Tea Mixture

18 ounces orange breakfast drink
    powder
1 cup sugar

½ cup instant tea
1 teaspoon ground cinnamon
½ teaspoon ground cloves

Place ingredients in blender, a little at a time, until blended into fine powder.
Store in jar and use as needed. Use 2 teaspoons per serving. Serve hot or cold.
Note: Makes a nice gift at Christmas.

Spiced Tomato Juice

⅔ cup sugar
½ teaspoon nutmeg
½ teaspoon cinnamon
several whole cloves

1 quart tomato juice
½ cup lemon juice
2 cups hot water

Mix first 4 ingredients. Add to juice. Simmer until sugar dissolves. Add lemon
juice and water. Simmer until flavors blend. Serve cold in wineglasses or gob-
lets. Serves 15.

Soups, Chowders and Stews

Originally, soups were extremely thick, like present-day stews, and were made of fresh ingredients. Stewing meat was popular with all classes of Virginia's young society because of its simplicity and tastiness. The most commonly used stew meats were joints of Virginia ham, veal or lamb, though fowl of all kinds were prepared similarly. Unsurprisingly, *the* most popular standing dish of the day was that of boiled or stewed joint of Virginia ham, seasoned imaginatively with cider, wine, beer or spices.

Fish stews had been great favorites of the English, and this inclination was transferred to the Virginia colony. Great pains were taken in dressing fish and shellfish for such a recipe, which might for a special occasion substitute wine for water. A special delicacy, turtle soup, was produced in Tidewater, but its preparation was so tedious and time-consuming that it was eventually dropped from the cookbooks.

Undoubtedly, the best known and favorite of all Virginia stews is Brunswick stew, thought to have originated in Brunswick County in 1720 when a hungry hunter supposedly concocted the dish, using freshly killed squirrels and rabbits as the main ingredients. Since then the dish spread rapidly throughout the South; consequently, every place along the East Coast named Brunswick lays claim to the original recipe. Today chicken serves as the main meat of the stew, and sometimes beef and ham are used as supplements. But to be authentic, Brunswick stew should be thick enough to eat with a fork, and it should be cooked the old way—simmered all day in a black iron kettle.

The ever economical and resourceful colonial housewife utilized excess cooking liquids from stews for broths, soups, gruels, pottages, porridges and for seasoning sauces and gravies. Early soups were basically broths seasoned with herbs, onions, carrots and turnips.

When Mrs. Mary Randolph, considered Richmond's best cook, published *The Virginia Housewife or Methodical Cook* in 1824, her preference for cream soups and tomato seasoning greatly influenced the cooking trends and left an indelible impression on contemporary Virginian taste.

Interestingly, the first known clam chowder was cooked by French immigrants to America. The name "chowder" is derived from the French word "chaudiere," which was the kettle in which stews and soups were cooked.

The importance of soups two centuries ago was so great that soup tureens graced every table, and the wise traveler often journeyed with a flask of soup in his pocket. During the eighteenth century, soup tureens became status symbols and were produced in ceramics and silver—sometimes of enormous proportions. Often the tureen was the central part of the table setting, and the designs (which were not always appetizing) ranged from ships and fish to animals, fowl, fruits and vegetables.

It seems strange, on reflecting, that an item once so significant to the American diet has become of so little consequence!

Yorktown Crab Soup

¼-½ cup butter	½ teaspoon fresh parsley (optional)
1 tablespoon flour	½ pint milk
½ teaspoon salt	2 cups crabmeat
⅛ teaspoon red pepper	¾ pint cream
⅛ teaspoon mace	¼ cup sherry, regular or dry
⅛ teaspoon nutmeg	

Melt butter in top of double boiler. Add flour, seasonings and milk. Stir constantly until thick. Add crabmeat and stir. When ready to serve, add heated cream and sherry. Serves 6.

Hampton Crab Soup

2½ cups chicken broth	½ cup cream
½ pound fresh crabmeat	white pepper and salt to taste
2 tablespoons bread crumbs	parsley

Heat the chicken broth; add crabmeat and simmer for 7-8 minutes. Add bread crumbs to thicken soup. Pour in cream, heat and season to taste. Garnish with a little parsley. Serves 4-6.

Crabmeat Soup

*10¾ ounces condensed green pea
   soup*
10¾ ounces condensed tomato soup
¾ cup water
1 cup half and half cream

dash of Tabasco (optional)
1 teaspoon sugar
2 teaspoons Worcestershire
1 pound fresh crabmeat
5 tablespoons sherry

Combine and heat all ingredients except sherry. Remove from heat and add sherry. Serves 6.

Navy Bean Soup

16 ounces dried navy beans
ham bone
2 medium onions,chopped
2 cups celery, diced

1½ teaspoons Italian seasoning
salt and pepper
1½-2 cups condensed tomato soup

Soak beans overnight; drain off water. Fill ½ Dutch oven with water. Add ham bone, beans, onions, celery and seasonings. Simmer for at least 4 hours. Remove ham bone; cut up ham and return to soup. Continue to simmer; after it has thickened, add tomato soup and water to desired consistency. Serves 8-10.
Note: This soup can simmer all day; it enhances flavor and thickens soup.

Chili Soup

1 pound ground beef
1 onion, chopped
1 tablespoon chili powder
16 ounces canned kidney beans

16 ounces canned tomatoes
1 quart water
1 cup spaghetti, cooked

Brown beef and onion. Stir in chili powder; add kidney beans, tomatoes and water. Bring to a boil; reduce to simmer and cook covered for 1½ hours. Fold in cooked spaghetti and simmer 15 minutes more. May be prepared ahead and refrigerated. Serves 10.

Frito Salad

1 pound ground round steak
1 onion, minced
1 green pepper, diced
7 ounces enchilada sauce
8 ounces tomato sauce

chili powder, salt and pepper to taste
Fritos or broken tacos
sharp cheese, grated
lettuce, shredded
tomatoes, diced

Brown meat, onion and pepper; drain. Add enchilada and tomato sauces. Season to taste with spices. Simmer 40 minutes. At serving time, place a layer of Fritos in the bottom of each bowl; top with hot meat mixture, cheese, lettuce and tomatoes.

"A mexican variation of chili. Especially good for a winter supper."

Cajun Gumbo

2 tablespoons salad oil
1 onion, chopped
2 whole scallions, chopped
1/2 green pepper, chopped
2 cloves garlic, minced
3 ribs celery with leaves, chopped
1 pound canned tomatoes
8 ounces tomato sauce
1 1/2 cups water
1 tablespoon salt

1 1/4 teaspoons pepper
1/4 - 1/2 teaspoon chili powder
1 tablespoon sugar
1 tablespoon Worcestershire
10 ounces frozen or 1 pound fresh
  okra, sliced
1 pound shrimp, uncooked
2 teaspoons gumbo file
1 cup rice, uncooked

Sauté onion, green pepper, scallions, garlic and celery in oil until tender. Add remaining ingredients except for shrimp, gumbo file and rice. Cover and cook slowly for 30 minutes. Add shrimp and boil gently for 10 minutes or more. Remove from heat and add gumbo file. Let stand until ready to serve. Cook rice according to package directions. Place a scoop of rice in large soup bowls and ladle gumbo over rice. Serves 4 generously.

Note: For variation, crab may be substituted for shrimp. Also for that summer casual gathering, drop cooked, clean crab bodies into gumbo when adding shrimp. Guests will scoop up and pick out meat.

"Best made a day ahead."

43

Yorktown Onion Soup

¼ cup butter
3 cups onions, thinly sliced
3-10¾ ounce cans beef bouillon
1½ cans water
1 tablespoon sugar

1 tablespoon cornstarch
¼ cup water
¼ cup sour cream
6 toast circles
Parmesan cheese

Melt butter in 2 quart pot and sauté onions until translucent. Add bouillon, water and sugar; cover and simmer ½ hour or until onion is soft. Mix cornstarch and water to make a thin paste; add to simmering soup to thicken slightly, stirring constantly with a whisk. Simmer on low heat for 10 minutes or longer, if not serving immediately. Remove soup and cover. Before serving add sour cream to soup and reheat while blending with whisk. Place very crisp toast rounds in soup bowls, sprinkle with Parmesan cheese and ladle hot soup over all. Serves 6.

French Onion Soup

3 tablespoons butter
1 tablespoon salad oil
5-6 cups onions, sliced
1 teaspoon salt
½ teaspoon sugar
3 tablespoons flour
3-10¾ ounce cans beef
* bouillon*

3 soup cans water
1 cup dry red or white wine (optional)
1 bay leaf
½ teaspoon sage
salt and pepper to taste
French bread
1½ cups grated Swiss and
* Parmesan cheese, mixed*

Melt butter and oil in a heavy 4 quart pan or casserole. Add onions and stir; cover and cook over medium heat for 15 minutes, stirring occasionally. When onions are tender and translucent, uncover, raise heat to medium high and stir in salt and sugar. Cook for 20-30 minutes, stirring frequently until onions turn golden brown. Lower heat to medium. Stir in flour; cook and stir for 2 minutes. Remove from heat. Heat bouillon and water and stir 1 cup into onion mixture with a whisk. Add rest of bouillon, wine, bay leaf, sage and simmer slowly for 3-4 minutes. Season with salt and pepper. If not serving immediately, cool uncovered and refrigerate. At serving time, toast 1 inch slices of bread in a 325 oven for 20 minutes. Ladle soup in individual crocks or use casserole. Place bread on top of soup, closely packed if in casserole. Sprinkle cheese on top and bake at 350 for 30 minutes until soup is bubbly and cheese melted. Serves 6-8.
"Great winter supper with a large tossed salad, red wine and a light dessert!"

Split Pea Soup

1 pound dried split peas	*¼ teaspoon marjoram*
2 quarts cold water	*1 clove garlic, minced*
1 ham bone	*dash cayenne*
1½ cups onion, diced	*¼ teaspoon thyme*
1 teaspoon salt	*1 cup celery, diced*
½ teaspoon pepper	*1 cup carrots, diced*

Cover peas in water and soak overnight. Next day, add ham bone to same water. Add onion and all seasonings; bring to boil. Reduce to simmer, cover and cook for 1½ hours. Remove bone and dice meat remaining on it. Add meat, celery and carrots. Cook slowly, uncovered, for 1 hour. Will thicken in storage; add water to reheat. Serves 8-10.

"Hale and hearty."

Cream of Peanut Soup
(Courtesy of Evans Farm Inn, McLean, Virginia)

2 ribs celery, chopped	*1 cup milk*
¼ cup butter	*1 cup light cream*
1 small onion, chopped	*1 cup peanut butter*
2 tablespoons flour	*salt and pepper*
2 cups chicken broth	*paprika*

Brown celery and onions in butter. Add flour and chicken broth and bring to a boil. Add milk and cream. Strain. Add peanut butter and simmer for 5 minutes. Season to taste. Yields 6 servings or 8 cups.

Colonial Vegetable Soup

2 large soup bones	*6-7 large celery ribs*
5½ cups water	*5-6 medium potatoes, cubed*
1 pound stew beef	*20 ounces frozen green beans*
2 pounds canned tomatoes	*20 ounces frozen corn*
1½ tablespoons salt	*10 ounces frozen lima beans*
1 teaspoon pepper	*½ cup barley*
1 large onion, sliced	*1 teaspoon sugar*
1 tablespoon Worcestershire	*½ medium head cabbage, sliced*
5 medium carrots, thinly sliced	

In a large soup pot, place bones, water, beef, tomatoes, salt, pepper and onion. Bring to a boil, reduce heat and simmer for 2 hours or until meat begins to fall apart. Remove soup bones and add all ingredients except cabbage. Cook until potatoes are just tender. Add cabbage and cook until cabbage is tender. Yields approximately 6 quarts.

Note: Vary barley according to taste.

"Freeze several quarts for later use."

Gazpacho

2 large tomatoes
1 large cucumber, seeded and
    quartered
1 medium onion, peeled and
    quartered
½ medium green pepper
24 ounces tomato juice

¼ cup olive or salad oil
⅓ cup red wine vinegar
¼ teaspoon Tabasco
1½ teaspoons salt
⅛ teaspoon pepper, coarsely ground
¼ cup chives, chopped

In blender, combine tomatoes, cucumber, onion and green pepper. Grind coarsely; do not let vegetables get to purée stage. In a large bowl, mix vegetables with the tomato juice, oil, vinegar, Tabasco, salt and pepper. Cover and refrigerate until well-chilled, about 2 hours. Sprinkle with chives before serving. Serves 6-8.

Garnish:

1 cup tomato, chopped
1 cup onion, chopped
1 cup cucumber, chopped

1 cup green pepper, chopped
1 cup croutons

Place each ingredient in separate bowls to serve as accompaniments for this cold soup.

Note: The garnishes make the dish superb!

"Not an authentic Old Virginia dish, but loved by all on a hot summer day."

Vichyssoise

4 spring onions, thinly sliced
½ cup butter
2 pounds potatoes, peeled and
    thinly sliced

1 teaspoon salt
2 cups milk
1 teaspoon chives, chopped
pepper, freshly ground

In deep saucepan, sauté onions in butter. Add potatoes, salt and water to barely cover. Bring to a boil, reduce heat and cover; simmer for 45 minutes. Press through food mill. Cool and chill for at least 1 hour before serving. Stir in chilled milk. Sprinkle with chives and pepper. Serves 10.

Chesapeake Clam Chowder

1 1/2 quarts water
2 medium potatoes, diced
1 medium onion, minced
2 tablespoons bacon drippings
1 tablespoon salt

1 tablespoon sugar
1/2 teaspoon pepper
2 dozen fresh clams, drained
1 pint milk

Boil water and add potatoes and onion. Cook until tender. Add bacon drippings, salt, sugar and pepper. Cut up clams and add. Cook 10 minutes. Slowly pour in milk and stir until soup begins to thicken. Serves 6.

Clam Chowder Au Vin

2 cups potatoes, diced
1/2 cup onions, chopped
1/2 cup celery, chopped
1/4 teaspoon salt
1 cup water
*10 3/4 ounces condensed Manhattan
    clam chowder*

7 ounces minced clams, drained
1 cup milk
3 tablespoons dry white wine
1/2 cup heavy cream, whipped
salt and pepper
2 tablespoons parsley, snipped

Put potatoes, onion, celery, salt and water into large saucepan and cover. Cook 10 minutes or until potatoes are tender; mash slightly. Add chowder, clams, milk and wine. Heat, but do not boil. Stir cream into chowder and season to taste. Sprinkle with parsley. Serves 4-6.

Fish Ragout

4 medium potatoes, thinly sliced
1 small bay leaf
2 1/2 teaspoons salt
1 1/2 cups water
*12 ounces frozen perch fillets,
    thawed*

1/3 cup onion flakes
dash cayenne
1 tablespoon butter
1/2 cup sour cream

Cook potatoes with bay leaf and salt in water until tender. Add fish and onion flakes; cook 10 minutes until fish is tender. Add cayenne, butter and sour cream; heat for 3-4 minutes. Serves 4-6.

Fish Chowder

(Courtesy of Deep Creek Plantation)

2-3 pounds fish	*2 bay leaves*
3 cups potatoes, diced	*6 fresh basil leaves*
1 cup onion, diced	*small handful parsley*
1 cup celery, diced	*salt and pepper to taste*
3 chicken bouillon cubes	

Scale and clean fish. Place in a large pan and cover with water. Bring slowly to a simmer and poach gently for 4-5 minutes. Remove the fish carefully. Strain the stock into another large saucepan. Add all other ingredients. While this simmers for 30 minutes or so, remove the fish from bones and skin. Add to the soup when the vegetables are well cooked. The head, bones, skin, etc. may be reboiled in a little water and strained and the stock added to the soup for additional flavor.

Note: This recipe is a delicious way to use an assortment of fish—small bluefish, trout, croaker and rockfish.

Shrimp Chowder

5 large onions, peeled and diced	*1 pound Velveeta cheese*
¼ pound butter	*1½ pints milk*
4 large potatoes, peeled and diced	*1½ pounds shrimp, cooked*
2 cups boiling water	*fresh parsley*
salt and pepper	

Lightly cook onions in butter. Add potatoes and boiling water. Simmer until potatoes are tender and season to taste. Melt cheese in milk and add to potatoes and onions. Add shrimp and simmer gently for 20 minutes or more; do not boil. Place a little snipped parsley in bottom of each bowl and fill with chowder. Serves 8.

"A truly gourmet meal in itself!"

Deep Creek Plantation

This Eastern Shore plantation was begun in the mid 1700's but was developed and beautified over a period of a hundred years. The house suffered many years of neglect and abuse until about twenty-five years ago when the owners did extensive repair work to preserve the home for ultimate restoration. Under the present ownership of Brigadier General and Mrs. Chester B. deGavre the house and gardens have taken on new life with reconstruction of many dependencies and the addition of a rose garden which is a delight to all. The house is handsomely furnished with family heirlooms, English and American antiques, and reproductions of museum pieces made by General deGavre from measured drawings.

Creamy Oyster Stew

1 1/2 pints oysters and oyster
    liquor
5 tablespoons butter
2 cups heavy cream

1 cup milk
salt and pepper to taste
cayenne to taste
chopped parsley or paprika

Combine oysters and butter in a skillet and cook until the edges curl. Add hot milk and cream; and heat to the boiling point. Season, ladle into bowls and garnish with parsley or paprika. Serves 4-6.

Note: You decide on the richness. Try it with milk, with milk and cream, or, to be absolutely fabulous, with heavy cream.

Brunswick Stew

1 whole chicken, cut up
1 onion, quartered
2 ribs celery, diced
1 teaspoon salt
1/4 teaspoon pepper
16 1/2 ounces white shoepeg corn
10 ounces frozen small butterbeans
1 pound canned tomatoes

2 small potatoes, cubed
1/3 cup ketchup
2-3 tablespoons vinegar
1 tablespoon brown sugar
1 teaspoon Worcestershire
1/2 teaspoon Tabasco
1/4 teaspoon marjoram
2-3 tablespoons butter

Place chicken in Dutch oven and add enough water to cover well. Add onion, celery, salt and pepper. Boil until chicken comes off bones easily. Remove chicken to cool and add corn, butterbeans, tomatoes, potatoes, ketchup and vinegar; cook 2 hours or until tender. Remove chicken from bones and add to vegetables along with Worcestershire, Tabasco, marjoram and butter. Serves 6-8.

Note: Vary amount of water for thick or soupy stew. Add a cup of chicken bouillon after the first or second serving.

Quick and Easy Corn Beef Hash

Prepare in any quantity desired. Brown potatoes and onions in a little cooking oil; add a few tablespoons of water and cook until tender. Season to taste with salt and pepper; stir in one or more cans of corn beef and cook in a covered skillet for 15 additional minutes.

"Serve with sliced tomatoes and a green salad for a quick and easy supper that tastes great."

Stifado

3 pounds lean beef, 1 1/2 inch cubes
4 tablespoons butter
1 tablespoon salt
3 ounces tomato paste
2 3/4 cups condensed beef broth
1 bay leaf

1 clove garlic, split
2 tablespoons wine vinegar
2 pounds small white onions,
   peeled
1 cup walnuts, chopped
1/2 pound Feta cheese

Brown beef in butter. Add remaining ingredients except onions, nuts and cheese. Add water to cover and boil for 1 1/2 hours. Add onions and cook until tender. Put in nuts and bring to boil. Add cheese just before serving. Serves 6.
Note: Feta cheese may be purchased at a cheese or gourmet shop.

Confederate Beef Stew

2 pounds stew beef
2 tablespoons salad oil
1 large apple, pared and shredded
1 medium carrot, shredded
1/2 onion, sliced
1/2 cup water
1/3 cup dry red wine
1 clove garlic, minced
2 beef bouillon cubes

1 small bay leaf
1/8 teaspoon thyme
4 teaspoons cornstarch
1/4 cup cold water
1/4 teaspoon Kitchen Bouquet
2 1/2 cups medium noodles, cooked
   and drained
1/4 teaspoon poppy seed

Cut meat into 1 inch cubes and brown in hot oil. Add apple, carrot, onion, water, wine, garlic, bouillon cubes, bay leaf and thyme. Cover and cook over low heat for 2 hours or until beef is tender. Remove bay leaf. Combine cornstarch and cold water; add to beef mixture. Cook and stir until thickened. Stir in Kitchen Bouquet. Serve over noodles and sprinkle with poppy seed. Serves 6.

Seafood

" . . . No country can boast of more variety, greater plenty or better of their several kinds," wrote Robert Beverley of Virginia's fish and shellfish in 1705. Rivers so teemed with herring, he exclaimed, that boats could hardly make their way without treading on them and sturgeon leaped into the boats. Other early Virginians wrote of oysters thirteen inches long and crabs so large that one would feed four men.

Whereas the accuracy of such exuberant accounts is a bit dubious, the abundance and excellence of the seafood inhabiting the waters of the Old Dominion cannot be questioned. It was this plentifully available source of food, along with acorns, wild fruits and vegetables, that enabled the colonists to survive in the new world.

One specially delectable species, renowned for its roe and its barbecuing properties, is the shad, which was so plentiful during colonial times that it became unfashionable. Selling for the modern day equivalent of only one or two cents apiece, shad were often thrown back after other fish were gleaned from the net. The wealthy ate them on the sly for fear someone might think they didn't have pork.

Nevertheless, baked shad was one of George Washington's favorite meals, and in spite of local taboos it remained popular at the capital where numerous parties were held for the purpose of eating shad and enjoying drinks. Even today gourmets across the land still turn to Virginia in the spring for the prized delicacy—shad roe.

Another staple fish of the area, especially along the Potomac river, was herring. When salted, herring had marvelous keeping powers and provided an important food item to the poor—especially during the winters. Because of this

George Washington appropriated one of his best herring stations to the poor with all necessary apparatus for catching the fish.

The Tidewater area has held a notable wealth in shellfish and mussels; during the summertime Virginia's tables are graced with luscious sweet white crab meat. Moreover, along with the shad bake, Virginia oyster roasts have long been events of much acclaim, especially on the Eastern Shore.

Roast fish garnished with a simple oyster, lobster or shrimp sauce was popular during the infancy of the Commonwealth. However, the favorite technique for preparing fish, large and small, was stewing; an elaborate display of special utensils for handling stewed fish was found in the better equipped kitchens of colonial vintage.

Smaller fish were sometimes fried, as were oysters; but the attitude of the colonial cook was that frying in general was a "coarse and greasy kind of cookery," not practiced often by the genteel families.

Shellfish were frequently used in sauces and stuffings, and such delicacies as oyster stuffing for turkey and capon were not uncommon. However, most often shellfish were stewed or boiled; and buttered shellfish was then, as now, a favorite.

Baked Fish and Rice Dressing

3 pound fish
2 tablespoons butter
salt and pepper
1/2 tablespoon onion, chopped
1/2 pound mushrooms, chopped

1/4 cup butter
1 cup rice, cooked
1/2 teaspoon poultry seasoning
2 eggs, beaten

Place fish in shallow pan and dot with 1 tablespoon butter. Broil for 15 minutes; turn; dot with 1 tablespoon butter and cook 10 minutes more. Season with salt and pepper. Sauté onion and mushrooms in butter until tender. Add the rice, seasoning and eggs. Mix well and cook over low heat until the eggs are set. Mound stuffing in center of baking dish and place fish, skin side up, over stuffing. Bake at 350 for 45 minutes. Serves 4 generously.

Boneless Baked Shad

4 pound shad
salt and pepper to taste

3 slices bacon
green onions (optional)

Preheat oven to 250. Salt and pepper the fish and place it in a greased roasting pan. Lay 1 slice of bacon in fish and remainder on top. Pour cold water into pan sufficient to come up to the sides of fish but not the top. Sliced green onions may be added to the water. Heat on top of stove to boiling point. Remove and bake, covered, for 5 to 6 hours. Garnish with lemon quarters. Serves 6.
Note: Lemon juice may be added to water while cooking fish.
"This method makes a usually very bony fish into a boneless delight."

"Freeze fish in a milk carton filled with water; thaw in water."

Easy Baked Fish

1 pound fish fillets, any type
salt to taste
white pepper to taste

onion powder to taste
¼ cup mayonnaise
paprika

Preheat oven to 325. Line 8 x 10 inch dish with foil. Place fish in pan, sprinkle with seasonings. Use a pastry brush to sparingly coat tops and sides of fillets with mayonnaise. Top with generous sprinkling of paprika. Bake uncovered for about 20 minutes, until fish flakes when touched with a fork. Serves 4.
Note: No need to turn while baking. Any amount may be prepared by adjusting size of pan.

Baked Whole Fish

2½-3 pound whole fish, with or
*   without head*
2-3 lemon slices
2-3 onion slices
2-3 celery slices

salt and pepper to taste
onion salt to taste
4 tablespoons lemon juice
bacon strips
2-3 pats butter

Soak the fish in cold, salted water for 15 to 30 minutes; drain and dry slightly. Preheat oven to 400. Season cavity with lemon slices, celery, onion, salt, pepper and 2 tablespoons lemon juice. Close the fish and place bacon strips on top or around the fish. Sprinkle with salt, pepper, onion salt and remainder of lemon juice. Cover with pats of butter and bake until flesh is white and flakes apart with a fork (about 30 minutes for a 2½ pound fish or 40-45 minutes for a 3 pound fish). The fish may be broiled at the end to brown the bacon. Cut into 1½ inch wide sections and serve with lemon wedges. Serves 2-4, depending on the size of fish.

Note: Other vegetables such as potatoes and tomatoes may be cooked with the fish if desired.

"Top baked fish with butter, lemon juice and sliced toasted almonds."

Flounder Fillet In Herb Sauce

4 ribs celery, chopped fine
2 teaspoons onion, minced
3 tablespoons butter or margarine
2 teaspoons dill (or to taste)
½ teaspoon tarragon
1 cup sour cream

2½ cups condensed mushroom soup
1 teaspoon parsley
2 teaspoons Dijon mustard
salt and pepper to taste
16 ounces frozen fillet flounder,
*   thawed*

Preheat oven to 375. Sauté celery and onion in butter until tender. Add remaining ingredients, except fish, and mix well. Pour into a shallow 10 x 16 inch casserole. Lay the fish fillets in the sauce, spooning some over fish. Bake for 20-25 minutes. Serves 6.

"An easy recipe with an elegant taste."

Fish Fillets Thermidor

1 pound fresh or thawed fish fillets
1½ cups milk
1 teaspoon salt
¼ teaspoon pepper

3 tablespoons margarine, melted
3 tablespoons flour
¼ pound Cheddar cheese, grated
3 tablespoons lemon juice

Preheat oven to 350. Split fillets lengthwise and roll up, fastening with a toothpick if necessary. Place in shallow 10 x 16 baking dish. Pour milk over fish. Add salt and pepper; bake 30 minutes. When done, pour off milk and add slowly to melted margarine into which the flour has been added. Add cheese and stir until melted. Add lemon juice and pour sauce over fillets. Brown quickly under broiler. Serves 3-4, depending on the size of the fillets.

"Great dish for company!"

Fish in White Wine

3 pound fish
¾ cup white wine
½ cup water
1 onion, chopped
1 sprig parsley, chopped
1 sprig chervil, chopped

1 sprig thyme, chopped
2 bay leaves
salt
pepper
4 ounces margarine, in pats

Preheat oven to 350. Place fish in a 9 x 13 baking dish. Mix wine with water and pour over fish. Place onion, parsley and chervil under and over fish. Add bay leaves and thyme. Top with salt, pepper and margarine. Bake 25-30 minutes or until fish flakes with fork.

Note: Dried herbs may be substituted for fresh if needed.

Pan Fried Fish

6-12 small fish
(spot*, croaker, or trout)
salt

2 cups vegetable shortening
1-2 cups cornmeal

Clean fish and salt generously, inside and out. Melt shortening in a large, heavy frying pan. Shake fish individually in cornmeal that has been placed in a brown paper bag, and then put fish into HOT grease. Fry the fish on each side until golden brown, about 5 minutes on a side. Drain on paper towels. Serves 3-4.

Note: While cooking, medium heat should be used to maintain hot grease. If the grease is not hot enough, the fish will be greasy; if it is too hot, the fish will brown before being cooked through.

*The heads should be left on spot since there is a piece of "sweet meat" on the top of the heads.

Fish Roe

1 pint whole fish roe, or
  1 set shad roe
salt

3 tablespoons butter, melted
1 lemon, juiced
pepper

Preheat oven to 400. Parboil roe in salted water. Lift roe from water; drain well. Place in well-greased pie plate and pour melted butter over it. Pour lemon juice over roe and pepper it well. Run in hot oven for about 10 minutes. Serves two.

"Serve with scrambled eggs and fried potatoes. Garnish with lemon wedges."

James River Shad Roe

Prepare in any quantity. Salt and flour shad roe sets; sauté in ¼ cup bacon drippings until browned. Cover and cook 5-10 minutes until cooked through. Garnish with bacon strips and lemon.

Sautéed Shad Roe

2 sets shad roe	*2 teaspoons lemon juice*
1 quart salted water	*salt and pepper to taste*
4 sheets of waxed paper	*2 tablespoons bacon fat*

Soak shad roe in salt water for 15 minutes. Drain. Place each set of shad roe on a square of waxed paper. Season each with 1 tablespoon lemon, seasonings and 1 teaspoon bacon fat. Wrap sandwich style. Keep folded ends tucked underneath. Grease heavy skillet with remaining fat. Place wrapped roe in pan, edges tucked under; fry over medium heat 10-15 minutes on each side until roe browns (Browning can be seen through paper.) Unwrap and serve with lemon wedges. Serves 2.

Note: Allow one medium roe set per person.

"No popping!"

Clambake

24 inches aluminum foil (heavy-duty)	*1 baking potato, scrubbed and*
1 chicken piece, medium-size	*boiled 10 minutes*
1 lobster tail, fresh or frozen	*1 onion, peeled*
clams	*½ cup clam juice*
1 ear corn, silk removed	*salt and pepper to taste*

Wrap all ingredients together in foil, remembering to keep on the outer husks of corn. Seal foil with double fold. Wrap again in foil, reverse side up. Grill 4 inches from coals for 1 hour. Turn every 15 minutes. Serves 1 hearty eater!

"Great for the beach."

"In 1709 clams were valued for increasing vigor in men and making barren women fruitful."

Clam Fritters

1 pint clams, drained and minced *1 teaspoon baking soda*
1 egg, beaten *salt and pepper to taste*
flour, sifted *hot fat for frying*

Combine clams and egg; add enough flour to make the consistency of pancake batter. Add baking soda. Drop spoonfuls into a hot greased frying pan. Cook like pancakes. Serves 4.

"Oysters or crabmeat can be substituted for the clams for equally delicious fritters."

Spaghetti with White Clam Sauce

4-8 cloves of garlic *½ cup fresh parsley, chopped*
4 tablespoons butter or olive oil *¼ cup dry vermouth*
1 cup fresh mushrooms *1 pound spaghetti, cooked*
32 ounces canned minced clams, *Parmesan cheese*
  with juice

Fry the garlic in butter or oil (DO NOT substitute margarine or vegetable oil) for a few minutes; add the mushrooms, clams and clam juice. Just before serving, stir in parsley and wine. Toss boiled, drained spaghetti with butter and place on a platter. Pour the sauce over spaghetti and sprinkle generously with cheese. Serves 6.

"The secret is to use as many fresh ingredients as possible."

Crabmeat and Capers

1 pound crabmeat *2 heaping tablespoons capers, drained*
1 teaspoon onion, minced *½ lemon, juiced*
8 tablespoons mayonnaise *dash of Tabasco*
1 tablespoon butter, melted *salt and pepper to taste*
2 tablespoons sherry *cracker crumbs*

Preheat oven to 375. Toss ingredients, except crumbs, together and place in 2 quart greased casserole. Sprinkle cracker crumbs on top. Bake for 25-30 minutes. Serves 4.

Crabmeat Casserole

1 pound backfin crabmeat
1 cup mayonnaise
½ cup light cream

3 eggs, beaten lightly
salt and pepper to taste

Mix all ingredients lightly and bake in a 1½ quart casserole for 40 minutes at 350. Serves 4-6.
"For crab 'purists'—delicious and simple to fix. Serve with tossed salad."

Company Crab Casserole

1 pound crabmeat
1½ cups milk, scalded
1 cup soft bread crumbs
1 cup Cheddar cheese, grated
¼ cup butter, melted

1 tablespoon onion, grated
2 tablespoons green pepper, chopped
½ cup pimento, chopped
1½ teaspoons salt
3 eggs, beaten

Preheat oven to 375. Pour milk over bread crumbs to soften; add remaining ingredients except eggs. Stir in eggs. Pour mixture into a well-greased loaf pan or a 6 x 8 inch casserole. Set the dish in a container of hot water and bake for about 45 minutes or until an inserted knife comes out clean. Serves 6.
"This is very tasty."

Crab Newburg

1 pound fresh lump crabmeat
½ pound butter
3 tablespoons flour
½ teaspoon salt
1 teaspoon paprika

2 tablespoons onion, chopped
2 cups cream
3 egg yolks lightly beaten, with
* 2 tablespoons sherry*
6 slices toast, buttered

Melt butter in saucepan. Stir in flour, seasonings and chopped onion. Gradually stir in cream. Cook, stirring constantly until thickened and smooth. Add crabmeat and heat to serving temperature. Remove from heat. Stir in egg yolks. Serve on buttered toast. Serves 6.

Note: A great party dish . . . also excellent in a chafing dish and served in small patty shells or as an appetizer.

Virginia Crab Imperial

2 eggs, beaten
1/4 teaspoon dry mustard
dash of white pepper
2 pounds backfin crabmeat

4 tablespoons pimento, chopped
2 1/4 cups mayonnaise
1/2 cup Parmesan cheese

Preheat oven to 350. Beat the eggs with mustard and pepper. Add crabmeat, pimento and 2 cups mayonnaise. Spoon the mixture into a 2 quart casserole and spread 1/4 cup mayonnaise over the top. Sprinkle with cheese. Bake for about 20 minutes until brown and bubbly. Serves 8.

"Guests may prefer this to dessert!"

Hampton Roads Crab Imperial

1 pound crabmeat
1 egg
2 eggs, hard-boiled and chopped
2/3 cup pimento or green pepper
1 teaspoon dry mustard

1 teaspoon mustard
1/4 teaspoon curry powder
3 tablespoons mayonnaise
sprinkle of garlic salt
small handful bread crumbs

Preheat oven to 425. Mix all ingredients lightly and spoon into individual shells or 1 quart casserole. Sprinkle paprika and fine bread crumbs on top of each crab mixture. Bake for 15-20 minutes. Serves 4.
Note: 1/3 cup each of pimento and green pepper can be used.

"Everyone loves this!"

Crab Imperial
(Courtesy of White Marsh)

3 tablespoons flour
1/2 cup butter
1 cup milk
1 teaspoon mustard

1 teaspoon Worcestershire
2 tablespoons mayonnaise
1 pound crabmeat

Make a thick cream sauce using flour, butter and milk. Combine with the seasonings and mayonnaise. Flake the crabmeat into the sauce gently so that it does not break. This may be served in shells or in a casserole. This recipe should serve 4 but may be only sufficient for 3 hungry diners.

"A favorite of all seafood lovers!"

White Marsh

White Marsh was part of a land grant to Lewis Burwell in 1648. It was owned by the Burwells until 1798 when it was sold to Thomas Reede Rootes, from whom it descended to the Tabb family who owned White Marsh until 1905. Willie J. Burlee, the next owner, made extensive changes in the house. After 1912 it changed hands several times until it was purchased in 1947 by Mr. and Mrs. William Ingles. Remodeling was begun in 1965 and has restored the house to its original appearance. When and by whom White Marsh was built is not known, but it is assumed that the central part of the house was constructed between 1750 and 1800 with the wings to this lovely home in White Marsh being added later.

Puffing Crab

1 pound crabmeat
2 tablespoons butter
2 tablespoons flour
1 cup milk, hot
3 egg yolks

½ cup mayonnaise
salt and pepper to taste
dash of cayenne
3 egg whites
1 teaspoon paprika

Melt butter in saucepan and add flour; cook for 5 minutes. Gradually stir in milk and bring to a boil. Cool mixture. Beat in egg yolks, fold in mayonnaise and add crabmeat. Season to taste and add cayenne. Beat egg whites until stiff and fold in crab mixture. Place in greased 1½ quart soufflé dish or in 4 individual casseroles. Dust with paprika and bake at 400 until brown and puffed, about 25 minutes. Serves 4 generously.
"Elegant when served in individual dishes!"

Crabmeat Rolls

8 ounces Crescent dinner rolls
4 slices processed cheese
6½ ounces canned crabmeat
2 tablespoons mayonnaise

1 tablespoon green pepper, finely
chopped
¼ teaspoon salt

Unroll crescent rolls and separate into 8 triangles. Place ½ slice of cheese on each roll. Combine all other ingredients and spoon mixture onto rolls. Roll up and bake at 375 for 20 minutes or until rolls are brown. Serve with sauce.

Sauce:

1 cup sour cream
½ teaspoon curry powder

1 tablespoon butter
salt and pepper to taste

Melt butter and add other ingredients. Heat, but DO NOT BOIL. Serve over crab rolls. Serves 4.
"A delicious quick supper or luncheon dish!"

Sautéed Crab Quickie

Prepare in quantity desired. Melt a pat of butter in a skillet with lemon juice; add fresh crabmeat; toss and cook until lightly browned. Serve immediately.

Crab And Shrimp Casserole With Capers

1 pound crabmeat, regular or backfin	salt and pepper to taste
4 eggs	onion salt to taste
1½ cups mayonnaise	1 tablespoon Worcestershire
1 pound shrimp, cooked	3 tablespoons sherry or lemon juice
8 ounces mushrooms, canned or fresh	1 teaspoon lemon rind, grated
1 cup celery, diced	1 cup sharp cheese, grated
2 tablespoons capers	buttered bread crumbs

Preheat oven to 350. Beat eggs until frothy and blend in mayonnaise; add all other ingredients except bread crumbs. Pour into a 1½ quart greased casserole. Top with buttered crumbs and bake for 30-40 minutes, or for 25 minutes in individual casseroles. Serves 6-8.
"A treat for seafood lovers!"

Virginia Batter Crab Cakes

1 pound crabmeat	2 eggs, slightly beaten
1 heel bread	2 teaspoons mayonnaise
2 tablespoons butter, melted	2 teaspoons mustard

Break bread into the crabmeat and toss lightly. Mix the other ingredients and lightly fold them into the crab mixture with a fork. Shape into patties with a fork and spoon. Place on a floured platter and dust the tops with flour to hold them together. Brown quickly on each side in a small amount of hot fat. Cover and steam cook for 3 minutes. Drain on paper towels. Serves 6-8.
Note: Backfin crabmeat is best.
"Minced fresh parsley adds to the flavor. Garnish with lemon wedges."

Cheasapeake Bay Crab Cakes

1 pound fresh crabmeat, flaked	1 tablespoon mayonnaise
8 saltine crackers, crushed	½-1 teaspoon red pepper
1 egg	fresh parsley, chopped
1 tablespoon mustard	salt and pepper to taste

Mix together all ingredients. Shape into patties and sauté in hot butter until golden on both sides. Serves 4-6.

Creamy Deviled Crabs

Crab Mixture:

5 pounds claw crabmeat	1 tablespoon horseradish
5 ounces Worcestershire	4 tablespoons parsley flakes
5¼ ounces saltines, crumbled	4 tablespoons celery seed
salt and pepper to taste	4 tablespoons mustard
3 cups mayonnaise	

Mix above ingredients in a roasting pan and prepare sauce.

Sauce:

7 ounces margarine	2½ cups milk
5 tablespoons flour	

Put sauce ingredients in a saucepan and cook until sauce has thickened, stirring constantly. Add sauce to crab mixture until it is a good consistency (all of the cream sauce may not be needed). Fill individual shells with mixture and sprinkle with paprika. Bake in 350 oven until hot all the way through. Fills 36 shells.

"Freezes beautifully to have on hand whenever needed."

Fried Soft Shell Crabs

8 medium soft shell crabs, or	1 cup flour
12 small ones	fat for frying
salt and pepper to taste	

Soak crabs in cold salt water for 30 minutes. Drain. Season with salt and pepper. Dip crabs lightly in flour and pan fry in shallow hot fat. A combination of bacon drippings and oil adds to the taste of the crabs. Cook 4-5 minutes on each side depending on size of crabs. Drain well. Garnish with fresh parsley and lemon wedges.

Note: Soft crabs love to pop! Protect yourself by placing a lid crosswise over the pan while cooking. Do not completely seal pan with lid.

"These divine little creatures make the most luscious sandwiches in a bun with tartar sauce or lettuce, tomato and mayonnaise."

"For easy cleaning of soft-shell crabs, lift up the pointed ends and remove the spongy fingers; remove the face, apron and all spongy material underneath. Soak in cold salt water; dry thoroughly and cook as desired."

Tasty Deviled Crabs

2 cups fresh crabmeat
1 cup bread crumbs, soft and fine
1/2 cup milk, scalded and hot
1/3 cup butter, melted
2 eggs, well-beaten
1 tablespoon green pepper, minced
1/2 teaspoon dry mustard mixed
   with 1 teaspoon salt

1 tablespoon parsley, minced
1 tablespoon onion, minced
1/2 teaspoon paprika
1/2 teaspoon chili powder
2 teaspoons Worcestershire
buttered bread crumbs

Preheat oven to 375. Mix the soft bread crumbs and milk, and add other ingredients, saving crabmeat until last. Mix well and spoon mixture into individual crab shells or shallow 1 1/2 quart casserole. Spread with buttered crumbs and bake for 30 minutes or until very hot and well-browned. Serves 4.

"Before preparing all crab dishes, pick through crabmeat to remove all shell and cartilage. Nothing ruins an otherwise superb dish more than having your guests find foreign matter in their dinner."

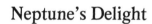

Neptune's Delight

1/2 cup butter
1/2 cup flour
1 quart milk, scalded
1/2 teaspoon salt
1/2 teaspoon dry mustard
1/2 cup sherry
2 teaspoons Worcestershire

1/2 pound lobster chunks, cooked
1/2 pound crabmeat
1/2 pound shrimp, cooked
1/2 cup Parmesan cheese
1/2 cup cracker meal
1/2 teaspoon paprika

Preheat oven to 400. Combine butter and flour in a saucepan; brown over low heat, stirring constantly. Add scalded milk and let come to a boil; whip with a beater until all lumps disappear. Add the spices and wine. Put the shellfish in a 2 quart casserole and cover with sauce. Sprinkle with cheese mixed with cracker meal and paprika. Brown lightly in oven for 15 minutes. Serves 6-8.

"Versatile as well as delicious—any combination of seafood may be used."

Artichoke-Lobster Newburg

30 ounces artichoke hearts
2½ cups condensed mushroom soup
5 tablespoons onion, chopped
6 tablespoons sherry
1 teaspoon salt

¼ teaspoon garlic salt
¼ teaspoon salt
4 cups lobster, cooked and cut
1 cup Cheddar cheese, grated
2 cups rice, cooked

Preheat oven to 400. Cook artichoke hearts and drain (omit if canned). Combine soup, onion, sherry and seasonings. Arrange hearts and lobster in a 2 quart casserole. Add soup mixture and top with cheese. Bake for 15 minutes. Serve with rice for 8 people.
"A different, delicious dish."

Lobster Newburg

3 egg yolks, well-beaten
2-3 ounces sherry
2 tablespoons butter
½ pint cream

2 cups lobster meat, cooked and
cut in chunks
salt and cayenne to taste
4 slices toast, buttered

In a small bowl add sherry to beaten egg yolks. Melt butter in medium saucepan and add cream; allow to boil gently for 30 seconds. Add lobster meat and again let reach a gentle boil. Add egg yolk mixture and season with salt and cayenne. Cook until thickened, stirring constantly. A *small* amount of flour may be added if more thickening is needed. Serve on buttered toast for 4 people.

Oyster Casserole

butter
8 ounces Ritz crackers, crushed
3 pints oysters, unwashed

salt and pepper to taste
5-10 ounces condensed
mushroom soup

Preheat oven to 400. Drain oysters and reserve liquor. Butter a 12 x 8 dish and spread a layer of cracker crumbs on the bottom. Then add a layer of uncooked oysters. Sprinkle oysters with butter, salt and pepper. Repeat. Dilute mushroom soup with a small amount of oyster liquor and pour it over the casserole, Top with a final layer of crumbs. Bake for 45 minutes or until bubbly. Serves eight.
"Great served as a buffet dish with sliced Smithfield or country ham!"

Mount Wharton

Typical of colonial homes on the Eastern Shore, Mount Wharton is a story and a half dwelling on the water. Though its entrance once faced the Bay, changes in transportation have caused the arched-ceiling back porch to become the main entrance. At one time this residence was the abode of John Wharton, notorious merchant and smuggler of the early 1800's. The brick-end structure is distinguished by five front dormer windows and two interior chimneys. This splendid home, restored and lived in by Mr. and Mrs. Fred Crebbin, III, is graced by period furniture, rare porcelains, Oriental rugs and magnificent portraits.

Scalloped Oysters
(Courtesy of Mount Wharton)

1½ pints large oysters
½ small lemon, juiced
6 tablespoons butter, melted

1 cup Uneeda crackers, crushed
½ cup milk

Drain oysters. Add lemon juice to melted butter. Butter shallow baking dish and put in a layer of oysters, half the crackers and half the lemon butter. Repeat to form a second layer. Add sufficient rich milk to moisten. Bake 30 minutes at 350.
Note: Do not add salt to unwashed seaside oysters.
"Delicious topped with a tablespoon of dry sherry after being removed from the oven."

Oysters Fried in Batter

1 cup flour	*½ cup beer*
½ teaspoon salt	*1 egg white*
1 tablespoon butter, melted	*oil*
1 egg, slightly beaten	*2 dozen oysters, shucked*

Sift ½ cup of flour and salt into a mixing bowl. Stir in the butter and egg. Pour the beer in gradually and mix only until the batter is fairly smooth—DON'T OVERMIX. Let the batter sit at room temperature for an hour. When ready to fry the oysters, beat the egg white until stiff peaks form. Fold the egg white into the batter gently until no streaks of white remain. Heat at least 3 inches of oil until it registers 375 on a deep-frying thermometer. Dip oysters in nest of flour; shake off any excess and dip in batter. Let excess batter drain off. Fry oysters 5 or 6 at a time for 3-4 minutes until they are puffed and golden brown. Drain on paper towels and keep warm in oven at 200 until all oysters have been fried. Serve at once. Serves 3.

Spicy Escalloped Oysters

1 quart oysters	*½ clove garlic, minced*
½ cup butter	*1 tablespoon lemon juice*
2 tablespoons flour	*1 teaspoon Worcestershire*
2 tablespoons onion, finely chopped	*salt and pepper to taste*
2 tablespoons green pepper,	*½ cup cracker meal*
finely chopped	

Preheat oven to 375. Heat oysters in their own juice. Melt butter in saucepan and add flour. Let brown slightly and then pour over oysters. Add all seasonings and cracker meal. Pour into a 1½ quart baking dish and sprinkle with additional cracker crumbs. Bake for 20 minutes. Serves 4-5.
"In the colonial days all seafood was plentiful and easily caught. Oysters were extremely popular."

Panned Oysters

Prepare in quantity desired. Melt a pat of butter in a skillet; add oysters and sauté until bodies puff and edges curl. Serve on toast points. Garnish with lemon quarters.
"Deliciously quick!"

Mr. McNamara's Oysters Rockefeller
(Courtesy of Mr. McNamara's Pier 1 Restaurant, Hampton, Virginia)

6 cups fresh whole spinach
1 small onion, minced
dash of garlic salt
salt and pepper to taste
6 strips thick cut bacon
32 large fresh oysters in shell

rock salt
1/4 cup butter, melted
1 1/2 ounces pale dry sherry
pimentos, chopped
1/2 lemon

Cook spinach in small amount of water with onion, garlic salt, salt and pepper until wilted. Fry bacon until very crisp and brown. Open oysters and leave on half shell, cutting them loose but not removing shell. Fill 4 sizzling platters with rock salt and place 8 oysters on half shell on each platter, directly on rock salt. Mix butter with sherry and brush equally on each oyster. Cover oysters with spinach and top with bacon, chopped medium fine, and pimentos. Place in 350 oven for 15 minutes; remove and place under broiler 1 minute. Serve on sizzling platters with lemon wedge. Serves 4.

"When buying oysters in the shell, make sure the oysters are alive, with the shells tightly closed. If the shell is slightly open, tap it; if the oyster is alive, the shell will close quickly."

Coquilles St. Jacques

1 pound mushrooms, sliced
1 lemon, juiced
5 tablespoons butter
1 pound fresh scallops, cut
1 cup dry white wine
1/4 teaspoon ground thyme

1 bay leaf
1/2 teaspoon salt
1/8 teaspoon pepper
3 tablespoons flour
1 cup light cream
3/4 cup soft bread crumbs, buttered

Preheat oven to 400. Sprinkle mushrooms with lemon juice and sauté in 2 tablespoons butter. Place scallops, wine and seasonings in a saucepan. Simmer, covered, for 10 minutes. Drain and reserve 1 cup of the broth. Make a white sauce with the remaining butter, flour, broth and cream. Add scallops and mushrooms. Spoon into buttered shells and top with bread crumbs. Bake for 10 minutes until browned.
"Also good in small patty shells served with cocktails."

Scallop Thermidor

1 pound scallops, cooked　　　　*dash of cayenne*
4 ounces canned mushrooms　　　*2 cups milk*
¼ cup margarine, melted　　　　*2 tablespoons parsley, chopped*
¼ cup flour　　　　　　　　　　*Parmesan cheese*
1 teaspoon salt　　　　　　　　*paprika*
½ teaspoon dry mustard

Preheat oven to 400. Cut large scallops in half. Fry mushrooms in margarine for 5 minutes. Blend in flour and seasonings. Add milk gradually and cook until thick, stirring constantly. Add scallops and parsley. Place in 6 well-greased individual shells. Sprinkle generously with cheese and paprika. Bake for 10-15 minutes. Serves 6.

Shrimp in Beer

1 quart beer　　　　　　　　　*1 teaspoon whole peppercorns*
4 tablespoons lemon juice　　　*1 teaspoon dried tarragon*
2 teaspoons salt　　　　　　　*2 pounds raw shrimp in shells*

Combine beer with seasonings in saucepan. Bring to a boil and simmer 10 minutes. Add shrimp and bring back to a boil. Lower heat and simmer 2-5 minutes, until shrimp turn pink. Drain, cool and shell shrimp.
"Serve with tankards of cold beer."

Jambalaya

3 onions, sliced　　　　　　　　　　*3½ cups canned tomatoes*
1 green pepper, chopped　　　　　　*½ teaspoon thyme*
1 clove garlic, minced　　　　　　　*¼ teaspoon basil*
¼ cup butter　　　　　　　　　　　*¼ teaspoon paprika*
2 cups shrimp, cooked and cleaned　　*¼ teaspoon Tabasco*
½ cup dry white wine　　　　　　　*1 cup rice, uncooked*

Sauté onions, green pepper and garlic in butter for 10 minutes. Add shrimp, wine, tomatoes and seasonings; mix well. Bring to a boil. Add rice gradually, stirring constantly. Reduce heat, cover and simmer for 25 minutes.
"Chopped ham may be used instead of shrimp—Either way, it's a great dish!"

Company Shrimp Casserole

½ cup celery, chopped
½ cup green pepper, chopped
2 tablespoons butter
2 cups rice, cooked
dash of red pepper

2-3 cups shrimp, cooked and cleaned
2½ cups condensed shrimp soup
¼ cup sliced almonds, toasted
dry sherry to taste
paprika

Preheat oven to 350. Sauté celery and pepper in butter until soft. Add to other ingredients in a 2 quart baking dish. Garnish with paprika. Bake for 20-30 minutes. Serves 4-6.

Second Helping Shrimp Casserole

2 pounds shrimp, cooked and cleaned
1 tablespoon lemon juice
3 tablespoons oil
¼ cup green pepper, diced
¼ cup onion, minced
2 tablespoons butter
¾ cup rice, uncooked
1 cup heavy cream

3 tablespoons sherry
1 teaspoon salt
⅛ teaspoon mace
dash of cayenne pepper
1 cup condensed tomato soup
½ teaspoon pepper
½ cup sliced almonds, lightly toasted
dash of paprika

Preheat oven to 350. Cover shrimp with lemon juice and oil; place in refrigerator until cold and crisp. Stir often so that all shrimp are marinated. Sauté pepper and onion in butter. Drain shrimp lightly and add with all remaining ingredients, except for half the almonds. Pour into a greased 1½-2 quart casserole. Sprinkle remainder of almonds and paprika on top. Cover and bake for 20-30 minutes. Serves 6-8.

"Almost everyone asks for a second helping!"

Shrimp Delight

¼ pound butter or margarine
1 medium green pepper, chopped
½ cup flour
1 quart milk, warmed
1 cup ripe or drained canned
  tomatoes

½ pound Velveeta cheese
4-6 eggs, hard-boiled
1½ pounds shrimp, cooked
½ pound mushrooms, sliced
  (optional)
salt and pepper to taste

In top of a double boiler melt butter and sauté pepper until soft. Add flour and milk slowly, stirring constantly. When mixture is thickened, add tomatoes and chunks of cheese. Stir until cheese is melted. Add shrimp, sliced eggs, mushrooms, salt and pepper. Spoon onto toast, waffles or patty shells. Serves 8.
"Chicken or crabmeat may be deliciously substituted for the shrimp!"

Shrimp in Zesty Tomato Sauce

2 large onions, sliced
oil
dash of garlic salt or juice
20 ounces canned whole tomatoes
salt and pepper to taste
1 teaspoon sugar

1-2 bay leaves
1-1 ½ pounds frozen, cooked medium
* shrimp (unthawed)*
¼ cup sherry (optional)
cooked bacon, chopped (optional)
Parmesan cheese (optional)

In a skillet, brown onions in oil; add the garlic and tomatoes, slightly drained. Chop tomatoes with a spoon. Add salt and pepper, sugar and bay leaves. Cook slowly on top of stove for 30 minutes. Put the shrimp, unthawed, in a 1½ quart casserole and cover with the tomato mixture. Top with remaining ingredients. Bake at 350 for 30-40 minutes. Can be served over cooked rice. Serves 4.
"Has a delightful flavor."

"Fresh celery leaves dropped into the water while boiling shrimp helps minimize the odor."

Shrimp Newburg

⅓ cup butter
2 tablespoons flour
2 cups light cream, warmed
4 egg yolks, slightly beaten
2 cups shrimp, cooked

¼ cup sherry
2 teaspoons lemon juice
salt to taste
1 tablespoon parsley flakes
4 patty shells

Melt butter and blend in flour. Stir in cream and cook slowly, stirring constantly, until mixture thickens. Stir small amount of the hot mixture into egg yolks and gradually return to hot mixture. Add shrimp and heat through. Add sherry, lemon juice, salt and parsley. Serves 4-5 in patty shells.
"A real gourmet delight!"

Meats

Unquestionably, the most famous of Virginia meats is the world renowned Smithfield ham. Even in the early stages of history, pork took its place beside the Virginia johnnycakes as a staple of diet; and, whatever else was served, ham, bacon or jowel also graced the table.

Hogs brought from England thrived on acorns, wild berries and roots in the Virginia woods. They soon became so abundant that one colonial writer stated "they swarmed like vermin upon the earth and were permitted to run as they listed and find their own support in the woods without any care of the owner." Because of their foraging, these hogs were lean and firm-fleshed, establishing a breed that persists to this day in Virginia known as "razorbacks" because of their thin, long legged, and sharp-snouted appearance.

Once the wilderness was tamed and peanuts were cultivated in vast tracts, the hogs were turned into the fields to root for remaining peanuts after the crop had been harvested. This custom is still practiced today. Peanut-fed pork is so delicious that a Swiss traveler journeying through Virginia in the early 1700's wrote that "all agreed that the Virginia pork was the best and the most delicate." As early as 1639, Virginia pork was so prestigious that pork and bacon were exported to New England; more than a century ago Queen Victoria ordered six Smithfield hams sent to England.

In addition to being a tasty dish, pork had the advantage of being preserved in more appetizing forms than any other type of meat. This was of importance because the threat of meat spoilage was constant, especially in the warm climate of Virginia. Home slaughtering was done in the fall and winter, and the meat was then smoked, potted, pickled, collared or dried under the supervision of the mistress of the house. Nothing was left to waste; lard was rendered, and sausage and meat puddings were made to be stored away. Dishes now un-

73

familiar to most city dwellers, such as pigs pettitoes, pigs feet and fricasseed pigs ears were also popular on the colonial menu and are still extremely popular in the Southside. You will not find a grocery store in the "country" that does not have them.

Cattle were also brought from England by the early settlers; in 1649 their number was reported to be 20,000 and by 1664 they had increased to 100,000. However, cattle were less plentiful than hogs because grazing lands were scarce in Virginia's wooded landscape. Often cattle were turned into forests to forage as best they could, and even though they were penned and fed with grain before butchering, they emerged lean and tough. Moreover, the size of full grown beef presented a problem in the limited pastures, and many cattle were slaughtered while young, giving rise to many veal dishes in the early cookbooks.

Due to its scarcity, one of the rarest treats a guest could be offered at any early colonial table was a haunch of mutton. Flocks had to be guarded from the wolves, and fodder was scanty. Mutton remained popular in the area until the late nineteenth century, when, for an unknown reason, mutton recipes were dropped from cookbooks.

Today, thanks to a greater variety of preservatives, refrigerated packing and fast shipment, Virginians enjoy an unlimited variety of meats. However, the favorite and stand-by remains the pride of the pork industry—Smithfield or Virginia country ham!

Rare Roast Beef

6-8 pound standing rib roast　　　　　*salt and pepper to taste*

Roast MUST be at room temperature. Preheat oven to 375. Rub roast with seasonings. Place on rack in roasting pan, rib side down. Roast 1 hour. Turn oven OFF. DO NOT OPEN OVEN. Roast must remain in oven for at least 3 hours and no more than 5. Before serving, turn oven ON to 375 and roast additional 30-45 minutes. DO NOT OPEN DOOR! At end of roasting time, remove roast and allow to cool 15 minutes before carving.

Note:　This process can be used on roasts up to 10 pounds. The final cooking time can be adjusted according to the degree of rareness desired. 30 minutes produces a rare roast. Opening the door ruins the process.

"Unbelievably tender; perfectly cooked."

Bordelaise Sauce

1 cup fresh mushrooms, sliced
1 tablespoon butter
3 tablespoons cornstarch
2 cups beef broth

3 tablespoons red wine
2 tablespoons lemon juice
dash of pepper

Sauté mushrooms in butter for 4 minutes. Stir in cornstarch. Blend in broth and cook until the mixture boils. Add wine, lemon juice and pepper. Simmer 15-20 minutes. Yields 2¼ cups.
"Superb with steak, roast beef or beef fondue!"

Fluffy Horseradish

1 cup sour cream
¼ cup horseradish, drained
1 tablespoon lemon juice

1 tablespoon sugar
1 tablespoon chives, minced

Mix ingredients; cover and chill several hours. Yields 1⅓ cups.
"Serve with rare roast beef."

Yorkshire Pudding

¼ teaspoon salt
1 cup flour
⅛ teaspoon baking powder

1 cup milk
2 eggs
¼ cup roast beef drippings

Preheat oven to 450. Mix salt, flour and baking powder; add milk gradually to form a smooth paste. Add eggs and beat with mixer for two minutes. Cover bottom of 8-inch square pan with drippings. Pour mixture in pan. Bake at 450 for 15 minutes. Reduce heat to 350 and bake 10 to 15 minutes longer. Cut in squares for serving.
"This is a traditional English 'must' to accompany roast beef."

Onion-Buttered Sirloin

½ cup butter
¼ cup parsley, snipped
¼ cup onion, minced

2 teaspoons Worcestershire
½ teaspoon dry mustard
½ teaspoon freshly ground pepper

Heat together until butter melts. Serve over broiled steak.

Chinese Beef

½ pound beef, thinly sliced
3 tablespoons salad oil
1 teaspoon salt
3 ribs celery, sliced on bias
1 large onion, thinly sliced
4 ounces canned sliced mushrooms
4 ounces canned water chestnuts,
  chopped

¼ pound snow peas, fresh or frozen
1 tablespoon cornstarch
5 tablespoons soy sauce
½ tablespoon sugar
½ cup water
1 cup rice, cooked

Brown beef in hot vegetable oil in skillet or wok. Add salt, celery, onions, mushrooms, water chestnuts and snow peas. Stir slowly a few minutes over high heat. Cover pan, turn heat down and simmer 3 minutes. Just before serving, stir in combination of cornstarch, soy sauce, sugar and water. Serve over rice. Serves 4.
Note: French style green beans may be substituted for snow peas.
"Freezes beautifully."

Fresh Beef Brisket

6 pounds fresh beef brisket
sliced onions
salt to taste
pepper to taste
garlic salt to taste

paprika
1 bay leaf
1 cup ketchup
flour
mushrooms (optional)

Preheat oven to 350. Place brisket on sheet of heavy-duty foil. Cover meat with onions and add rest of ingredients. Seal tightly and bake until tender, about 3 hours. Slice meat. Skim off fat from gravy and thicken with flour. Add mushrooms. Place sliced meat back into gravy. Reheat until bubbly. Serves 4-6.
Note: The cold meat is delicious in sandwiches.

Barbecue Sauce

1½ tablespoons bacon drippings
5 tablespoons onion, minced
¾ cup ketchup
6 tablespoons vinegar

3 tablespoons brown sugar
1½ teaspoons mustard
¾ teaspoon salt

Mix all ingredients in the blender. Baste spareribs, chops or chicken while baking. Yields 1½ cups.
"Keeps forever in refrigerator."

Barbecued Short Ribs

2 pounds short ribs
¼ cup onions, chopped
¼ cup celery, diced
2 tablespoons butter
½ cup water
2 tablespoons vinegar
1 tablespoon Worcestershire

1 lemon, juiced
2 tablespoons brown sugar
¼ cup chili sauce
½ cup ketchup
½ teaspoon salt
¼ teaspoon paprika
2-3 drops Tabasco

Preheat oven to 450. Trim excess fat from ribs. Place in shallow baking dish; cover loosely with foil and bake in oven for 15 minutes. Remove foil; drain and pour mixture of combined ingredients over ribs. Bake UNCOVERED at 350 for 1 hour. Baste as often as you like. Serve over noodles. Skim fat from top of sauce and use as gravy over noodles. Serves 4.

London Broil

1 tablespoon salad oil
1 teaspoon lemon juice
1 teaspoon salt
⅛ teaspoon pepper

½ teaspoon garlic powder
2 teaspoons parsley, chopped
2 pounds flank steak

Mix all ingredients except steak. Brush top of steak with half of mixture. Broil 4 inches from heat for 5 minutes. Turn, brush other side and broil 3-5 minutes longer. Slice thinly on diagonal and serve with mushroom sauce. Serves 4-5.

Mushroom Sauce:

3 ounces canned mushrooms,
    drained and minced
1 beef bouillon cube dissolved
    in ⅔ cup hot water
2 tablespoons butter

2 tablespoons flour
2 teaspoons Worcestershire
¼ cup sour cream
salt to taste
pepper to taste

Melt butter over low heat. Blend in flour, add bouillon and mix well. Cook until thick. Stir in mushrooms, Worcestershire and sour cream. Salt and pepper to taste. Serve hot.

Liver Jardiniere

2 pounds beef liver, sliced
3 tablespoons flour
1/2 pound bacon, fried and drained
1/2 cup bacon drippings
3 medium onions, thinly sliced
3 large green peppers, thinly sliced

2 teaspoons salt
1/4 teaspoon pepper
16 ounces canned whole tomatoes,
   drained
juice from tomatoes

Lightly coat liver with flour. Sauté liver in 1/4 cup bacon drippings, a few pieces at a time, until lightly browned. Remove from pan. Add remaining drippings, onions, green peppers, salt and pepper. Brown lightly. Add tomato juice; place liver on top; cover and cook over low heat 25 minutes, or until liver is tender. During last minutes of cooking, add tomatoes and bacon slices and heat. Serves 6-8.
"Unbelievably delicious! Serve with steamed rice."

Beef Burgundy

4 pounds chuck roast, cubed
1/4 cup vegetable oil
2 cups condensed onion soup
1 clove garlic, minced

2 cups Burgundy
6 ounces canned whole mushrooms,
   drained
4 cups rice, cooked

Preheat oven to 325. Brown beef in oil. Place in 3 quart casserole and add soup, garlic and wine. Cover tightly. Bake 2½-3 hours. Add mushrooms last 15 minutes. Serve over rice. Serves 8.
"Easy, yet delicious!"

California Marinade

1 cup salad oil
3/4 cup soy sauce
1/2 cup lemon juice
1/4 cup mustard

1/4 cup Worcestershire
1/4 cup onion, chopped
1-2 teaspoons cracked pepper
2 cloves garlic, minced

Mix and store in refrigerator until ready to use. Marinade for chicken, pork or beef.
Note: Marinade may be reused.

Fillet of Beef in Mushroom Sauce

6½ tablespoons butter
1½ tablespoons flour
2 cups beef broth
6 fillets of beef
1 pound fresh mushrooms

1 teaspoon salt
⅛ teaspoon pepper
½ cup madeira
2 teaspoons onion, chopped

Melt 1½ tablespoons butter in saucepan, blend in flour and cook until browned. Gradually add beef broth, stirring to the boiling point. Cook over low heat 30 minutes. Skim any fat and strain. Measure 1 cup. Melt the remaining 5 tablespoons of butter in a skillet. Brown fillets quickly. Remove. Sauté mushrooms in same pan for 5 minutes. Return fillets, add salt, pepper, madeira, onions and brown sauce. Cook over low heat for 5-10 minutes, depending on how well-done you like your steak. Serves 6.
"A fast and easy gourmet dish for company."

Beef Shish Kebab

Marinade Sauce:

½ cup Burgundy
1 clove garlic
½ cup salad oil
2 tablespoons ketchup
1 teaspoon sugar
1 teaspoon Worcestershire

½ teaspoon salt
½ teaspoon monosodium glutamate
1 tablespoon vinegar
½ teaspoon marjoram
½ teaspoon rosemary

Skewer Ingredients:

1 pound sirloin, cut in 1½ inch cubes
16 ounces canned whole white onions
3 green peppers, quartered

10-12 fresh large mushrooms
10-12 fresh cherry tomatoes

Mix marinade ingredients in a deep bowl. Marinate the meat cubes, pepper and mushrooms overnight in refrigerator or 3 hours at room temperature, covered. Fill skewers, alternating meat cubes with other ingredients. Broil over grill about 30 minutes. Brush with the remaining marinade while turning frequently. Serves 4.
Note: Fresh par-boiled onions may be used.

Round Steak Supreme

1 1/2 -2 pounds round steak
3/4 teaspoon salt
1/4 teaspoon pepper
3/4 teaspoon paprika
1/4 pound mushrooms, sliced
1 medium onion, sliced thin
2 ounces pimentos
1/2 cup bread crumbs

1/2 cup butter, melted
1 tablespoon boiling water
1 egg
12-15 stuffed green olives
1/4 cup flour
3-5 small onions
6-10 mushrooms
1-1 1/2 cups red wine.

Preheat oven to 350. Pound steak until thin. Rub in salt, pepper and paprika. Spread steak with sliced mushrooms. Cover with onions, pimentos and bread crumbs. Beat water and egg; dribble over crumbs. Top with a row of olives; roll meat and tie firmly. Flour outside of meat and brown in butter. Put in roaster with onions and mushrooms. Sprinkle with salt, pepper and paprika. Add red wine and bake for 2 hours. Serves 4.
"Deliciously different!"

Symphony Beef

2 tablespoons butter
1 pint sour cream
14 ounces canned artichoke hearts
1/2 cup dry vermouth

1 1/2 tablespoons Parmesan cheese
1/2 pound chipped beef
English muffins, buttered and
  toasted

Melt butter in skillet; add sour cream and stir until smooth. Slice artichoke hearts and add to sour cream. Add wine, cheese and chipped beef. Stir all together and keep warm. Serve over muffins. Serves 4.

Tournedos Brennan

1/2 cup canned sliced mushrooms
  (reserve liquid)
2 tablespoons butter
1 tablespoon flour
1/4 cup red wine
1/2 cup mushroom juice

1/2 teaspoon Worcestershire
1/4 teaspoon salt
dash of pepper
4 small fillets mignon
1 large ripe tomato, peeled

Drain mushrooms and reserve juice. Melt butter and sauté mushrooms. Add flour and cook slowly until slightly browned. Stir in wine, mushroom juice and seasonings. Cook until thickened. While sauce is cooking, grill fillets. Cut tomato in 4 slices and grill. Arrange slices on each fillet and pour mushroom sauce over all. Serves 4.

Note: Delmonico steaks may be used.

"Delightful sauce."

Lemon Barbecued Meat Loaves

1½ pounds ground chuck	*½ cup ketchup*
4 slices stale bread, cubed	*⅓ cup brown sugar*
¼ cup lemon juice	*1 teaspoon dry mustard*
¼ cup onion, minced	*¼ teaspoon allspice*
1 egg, slightly beaten	*¼ teaspoon ground cloves*
2 teaspoons seasoned salt	*6 thin lemon slices*

Preheat oven to 350. In bowl, combine ground chuck, bread, lemon juice, onion, egg and salt. Mix well and shape into 6 individual loaves. Place in a greased 9x13 baking dish. Bake 15 minutes. In small bowl, combine remaining ingredients except lemon slices. Cover loaves with sauce and top each with a lemon slice. Bake 30 minutes longer, basting occasionally with sauce from pan. Serves 6.

Stuffed Meat Loaf

2 eggs, beaten	*¼ teaspoon pepper*
¾ cup soft bread crumbs	*½ clove garlic*
½ cup tomato juice	*2 pounds ground beef*
2 tablespoons parsley	*6-9 ounces mozzarella cheese, shredded*
½ teaspoon oregano	*3 slices mozzarella cheese*
½ teaspoon salt	

Preheat oven to 350. Combine all ingredients except meat and cheese. Mix in ground beef, form 10x12 rectangle on waxed paper. Sprinkle cheese almost to edge. Beginning at short side, roll up meat, sealing edges and ends. Place seam side down in 9x13 baking dish. Bake 1¼ hours. Place cheese slices over top and return to oven to melt. Serves 8-10.

Note: Thin broiled ham slices may be used as stuffing under grated cheese.

Johnny Marzetti

6 medium onions, chopped
1 ½ pounds ground chuck
1 ½ teaspoons salt
¼ teaspoon garlic salt
⅛ teaspoon pepper
8 tablespoons butter

1 pound seashell macaroni, cooked
1 pound sharp cheese, grated
16 ounces tomato sauce
6 ounces canned chopped mushrooms,
   undrained
¼ cup Burgundy

Preheat oven to 325. Sauté onions, chuck and seasonings in 4 tablespoons butter for 15 minutes, stirring to prevent sticking. Toss macaroni with remaining butter. Place in two 2 quart casseroles. Add ⅔ grated cheese to meat mixture, cook and stir until melted. Add 8 ounces tomato sauce and mushrooms. Mix; divide and pour over macaroni. Top each with 4 ounces tomato sauce, sprinkle with remainder of cheese. Bake for 1¼ hours or until hot and bubbling. Drizzle wine on top and serve. Serves 8-10.
"Freezes well."

Noodles Romano

1 onion, chopped
1 clove garlic, minced
2 tablespoons salad oil
1 pound ground beef
8 ounces canned tomato sauce
6 ounces tomato paste
¼ cup water
1 bay leaf, crumbled
2 teaspoons salt

1 teaspoon oregano
8 ounces wide noodles, cooked and
   drained
2 eggs
10 ounces frozen spinach,
   thawed and drained
1 cup cottage cheese
¼ cup Romano cheese, grated
1 teaspoon basil

Preheat oven to 350. Brown onions and garlic lightly in 1 tablespoon oil. Add beef; cook until brown. Stir in tomato sauce, paste, water, bay leaf, 1 teaspoon salt and oregano; simmer 15 minutes. Beat 1 egg; add spinach, remaining oil, cheeses, remaining salt and basil; mix well. Beat remaining egg in bowl, pour over cooked noodles and mix well. Pour half tomato mixture into casserole. Top with half the noodles, spread with cheese-spinach mixture. Repeat noodle layer, top with rest of tomato mixture. Cover and bake for 50 minutes. Serves 6.

Lasagna

½ pound lasagna noodles
1½ pounds ground beef
1 medium onion, chopped
3 cloves garlic, minced
12 ounces tomato paste
1 cup hot water
2½ teaspoons salt
¼ teaspoon pepper
¼ teaspoon basil

2 teaspoons dry parsley
2 teaspoons Italian seasonings
2 eggs, beaten
16 ounces ricotta cheese
8 ounces mozzarella cheese
8 ounces Swiss cheese
8 ounces sharp cheese, grated
Parmesan cheese

Cook noodles for 15 minutes; drain. Brown beef; drain and add onion and garlic. Add tomato paste, water and seasonings. Simmer 5 minutes and reserve. Blend eggs with ricotta. In 2 quart baking dish place a layer of meat sauce, noodles and ricotta, Swiss and mozzarrella; repeat layers. Top with sharp cheese and Parmesan. Bake 30 minutes at 350. Serves 8.
Note: Cottage cheese may be substituted for ricotta.
"Great to prepare a day ahead!"

Spaghetti Sauce

1 pound ground chuck
1 green pepper, diced
2 medium onions, diced
½ teaspoon parsley
½ teaspoon oregano
¼ bay leaf

1 teaspoon salt
1 teaspoon sugar
½ clove garlic
pepper to taste
8 ounces tomato sauce
6 ounces tomato paste

Brown the ground chuck. Remove and drain. Sauté green pepper and onions in small amount of drippings. Return meat, add remaining ingredients. Cook over low heat 4-5 hours, stirring occasionally and adding water if the sauce becomes too thick. Remove garlic before serving. Serves 4.
Note: Recipe may be prepared in larger quantities.
"Freezes well."

Smithfield Ham

12 pounds or less Smithfield ham   6-7 cups water

Soak ham in cold water for eight hours or overnight. Preheat oven to 500. Wash ham and place in roaster with 6-7 cups water. Cover with tight-fitting lid. Close vents. Place in oven to bake for 20-25 minutes. Turn oven OFF. Leave ham in oven for 3 hours. DO NOT OPEN OVEN. At end of 3 hours, turn oven to 500. After the oven reaches this temperature bake for another 20-25 minutes. Turn oven OFF. Leave ham in oven for another 3 hours. DO NOT OPEN OVEN.

Note: If you are cooking ham in the evening, it may be left in the oven overnight.

Raisin Sauce For Ham

1 cup raisins
1 3/4 cups water
1/3 cup brown sugar, packed
1 1/4 tablespoons cornstarch
1/4 teaspoon cinnamon

1/4 teaspoon dry mustard
1/4 teaspoon ground cloves
1/4 teaspoon salt
1 tablespoon butter
1 tablespoon vinegar

Boil raisins and water 5 minutes. Mix dry ingredients. Add to raisin mixture. Cook 15 minutes. Stir in butter and vinegar. Yields 2 cups.

Hopping John

8 slices slab bacon,
*   cut into pieces*
2 small onions, chopped
5 cups canned black eyed peas,
*   including juice*

1 cup uncooked pork, cubed
2 1/2 cups water
1 cup rice, uncooked
1/8 teaspoon cayenne
salt to taste

Sauté bacon and onions until onions are tender. Remove from pan. Cook pork in the bacon drippings until lightly browned. Add other ingredients to pan and cook over medium heat about 25 minutes. Serves 6-8.

"Serve on New Year's Day for good luck all year!"

Pork Barbecue

2 pork shoulders
1 medium onion, minced and sautéed
1 cup vinegar
2-2½ cups ketchup
3 tablespoons Worcestershire

2 tablespoons mustard
2 tablespoons sugar
dash of salt
5-6 drops of Tabasco, or to taste

Preheat oven to 325. Bake shoulders in oven for 40 minutes per pound, or until very tender. Remove all fat. Slice meat. Add meat to above ingredients and simmer 30 minutes. Serves 8-10.
Note: Sauce can be used for other dishes.

Pork Chops in Sour Cream

4 loin pork chops, ½ inch thick
2 tablespoons flour
4 whole cloves
1 tablespoon butter
½ cup water

½ bay leaf
2 tablespoons vinegar
1 tablespoon sugar
½ cup sour cream
salt and pepper to taste

Preheat oven to 350. Coat chops with flour. Insert a clove in each chop. Heat butter in casserole and brown chops on both sides. Combine remaining ingredients and pour over chops. Cover casserole and bake for 1 hour. Serves 4.

Pork Tenderloin with Mustard Sauce

¼ cup soy sauce
¼ cup bourbon

2 tablespoons brown sugar
2½-3 pounds pork tenderloin

Mix ingredients and marinate pork several hours, turning occasionally. Preheat oven to 325. Remove from marinade and bake 1 hour, basting with marinade. Carve into thin slices and serve with sauce. Serves 8.

Sauce:

⅓ cup sour cream
⅓ cup mayonnaise

1 tablespoon dry mustard
2-3 green onions, chopped

Mix until smooth.
"Some prefer to use the marinade as the sauce."

Pungent Pork Roast

5 pounds pork loin
1 teaspoon seasoned salt
1/4 teaspoon seasoned pepper
3/4 cup dark brown sugar

1 teaspoon dry mustard
1/4 teaspoon ground ginger
2 tablespoons vinegar
1 teaspoon soy sauce

Preheat oven to 350. Sprinkle pork with salt and pepper; insert meat thermometer to center of meat. Bake in shallow roasting pan for 2½ hours, or until thermometer reads 175. Remove all fat from drippings in pan. Combine remaining ingredients as a glaze; spread all of it over pork. Roast pork about ½ hour or to 185 on thermometer, basting it occasionally with glaze from bottom of pan. Remove pork to heated platter. Remove fat from drippings; add ¼ cup water to drippings, bring to boil. Serve with pork. Serves 8-10.

Curried Fruit

3 cups peach halves, drained
3 cups pear halves, drained
3 cups apricots, drained
2 cups pineapple chunks, drained
1/4 cup butter

1 cup brown sugar
2 teaspoons curry powder
4 ounces Maraschino cherries
1 cup pecans, chopped

Preheat oven to 325. Drain fruit and pat dry between paper towels. Arrange fruits and nuts in 1½-2 quart baking dish. Melt butter, brown sugar and curry. Mix well and pour over fruit and nuts. Bake for 1 hour. Serves 8.
Note: Especially good with pork or Smithfield ham.

Sausage Casserole

1 pound hot sausage
2 medium onions, chopped
1 green pepper, chopped
16 ounces canned tomatoes

1 cup macaroni, uncooked
1 tablespoon sugar
1 cup sour cream
Parmesan cheese

Brown sausage and drain. Add onions and green pepper; sauté. Spoon off fat. Add remaining ingredients except sour cream. Cover and simmer for 20 minutes. Remove from heat and stir in sour cream. Place in serving dish and sprinkle with cheese. Serves 4.

Plum-Sauced Spareribs

1 tablespoon salt
2 tablespoons butter
1 medium onion, diced
17 ounces canned purple plums,
  with syrup (pitted)
6 ounces frozen lemonade
  concentrate, thawed

¼ cup chili sauce
¼ cup soy sauce
1 teaspoon Worcestershire
2 teaspoons mustard
1 teaspoon ground ginger
2 drops Tabasco
8-10 pounds spareribs

Prepare sauce the day before. In saucepan, melt butter and sauté onion until golden. In blender, purée plums with syrup; add to onion. Mix all other ingredients except ribs. Simmer uncovered 15 minutes. Cover and refrigerate. Cut ribs in serving portions; place in large kettle with salt and water to cover. Cover and simmer 1½ hours or until tender. Drain, place in large roaster. Preheat oven to 425. Pour sauce over ribs and bake 1 hour. Baste. Serves 10-12.

Note: The meat may be prepared the day before and refrigerated until baking time.

"Also great cooked on the grill!"

Roast Leg of Lamb

5-6 pounds leg of lamb
1½ teaspoons salt
¼ teaspoon pepper

3 tablespoons flour
¼ cup vinegar
1 teaspoon dry mustard

Preheat oven to 325. Wash leg of lamb, rub with salt and sprinkle with pepper and flour. Place uncovered, with fat side up, in shallow baking pan. Bake 30-35 minutes per pound. During the last hour of roasting, spread mixture of vinegar and mustard over meat. Serves 10.

Minted Lamb Sauce:

1 tablespoon sugar
1 tablespoon white wine vinegar
1 cup sour cream

2 tablespoons mint leaves,
  fresh or dried
drop of green food coloring (optional)

Combine sugar, vinegar and mint leaves. Put into blender with half of sour cream. Blend for 5 seconds. Add rest of sour cream and coloring; blend until thoroughly mixed. Chill several hours before serving.

Curried Lamb

(Courtesy of Hampton Manor)

3 tablespoons butter
1 cup celery, diced
2 tart apples, peeled and diced
½ cup onions, sliced
2 cups cooked lamb, diced

2 cups lamb broth, made from the
   bones
1½-2 teaspoons curry powder
2 tablespoons flour
1½ teaspoons salt

Melt butter in saucepan. Add celery, apples and onions and sauté until soft. Add lamb and lamb broth. Simmer 20-30 minutes. Blend curry powder with hot water and let stand 5 minutes. Blend flour and salt into the curry, adding cold water if necessary for a smooth paste. If lamb mixture is fairly dry, add about 1 cup of boiling water to the curry paste. Continue simmering 5 minutes, stirring frequently.

Hint: Serve on hot platter with border of fluffy boiled rice, garnish with parsley.

Curried Beef, Lamb or Veal

2 cups cold meat, cooked
3 tablespoons butter
½ medium onion, diced
1 clove garlic, diced
½ apple, diced

2 ribs celery, diced
2 tablespoons flour
2½ teaspoons curry powder
2 cups stock, gravy or tomato puree
boiled rice

Trim fat from meat. Sauté onion, garlic, apple and celery in butter. Add flour and curry powder. Cook for one minute, then add stock, gravy or purée. Stir until sauce boils. Add meat and simmer 10 minutes. Serve over rice with condiments. Serves 4-6.

Condiments:

chopped eggs
chopped peanuts
coconut
chopped sweet pickles
currant jelly

bacon bits
chow mein noodles
crushed pineapple
chutney

"Great for left-over meat!"

Hampton Manor

John Hampton DeJarnette built beautiful Hampton Manor in Caroline County during the golden age between the War of 1812 and the War Between the States. The plantation takes its name from Mary Hampton, who married Joseph DeJarnette, II, an officer in the militia during the Revolution. During the decade preceding World War II, this lovely home, built from Jeffersonian plans, was lived in by Salvador Dali, the surrealist painter.

89

Veal Bertrand

2 pounds veal round steak or cutlet
6 ounces canned whole mushrooms,
   drained
⅔ cup dry sherry

¼ cup parsley, snipped
dash of garlic powder
6 tablespoons butter
3 slices Swiss cheese

Cut veal into 6 portions; pound to ¼ inch thickness. Slash fat edges to prevent curling; place in shallow dish. Combine mushrooms, sherry, parsley and garlic powder. Pour over meat. Marinate 30 minutes at room temperature, turning several times. Drain meat, reserving marinade. In medium skillet, melt butter. Sauté half of the meat in butter for 3 minutes on each side. Remove; cook remaining meat. Return all meat to skillet, add marinade and bring to boiling. Reduce heat; place cheese on meat. Cover and cook over low heat until cheese melts, about 2 minutes. Serves 6.

"Egyptians thought mushrooms were the food of gods."

Veal Pojarski

(Courtesy of The Homestead, Hot Springs, Virginia)

1 pound lean veal, ground
½ cup butter, softened
2 ounces fresh bread crumbs

4 ounces half and half
salt and pepper

Preheat oven to 375. Mix well. Refrigerate for 10 minutes, then form into cutlets or patties. Pan sauté in butter and a little oil. Turn over; bake for 8 minutes. Serve with Sauce Stroganoff to 4-6.

Sauce Stroganoff:

¼ cup butter
1 whole onion, sliced
2 ounces tomato paste
1 tablespoon flour
pinch of thyme

¼ bay leaf
1 cup chicken or veal broth
¾ cup sour cream (room temperature)
¼ cup mushrooms, sautéed
salt and pepper to taste

Sauté onion in butter lightly. Add tomato paste and seasonings. Simmer on low heat for a few minutes. Add flour, mix well, and add boiling broth (more if too thick). Cook 30 minutes. Strain, then blend in sour cream and mushrooms.

Veal Scallopini Marsala

(Courtesy of Vic Zodda's Restaurant, Hampton, Virginia)

3 ounces fresh mushrooms   *flour*
3 ounces olive oil   *garlic powder*
salt and pepper to taste   *1½ ounces Marsala wine*
10 ounces veal, thinly sliced   *oregano*

Sauté mushrooms until almost tender in 1½ ounces of olive oil, and drain. Salt and pepper the veal slices and lightly dip in flour. Braise the veal slices in the remaining oil; add a pinch of garlic. When lightly browned, add mushrooms, wine and a dash of oregano. Simmer for 3-4 minutes in a covered saucepan. Serves 2.

Note: Sherry may be substituted for the Marsala.
"Garnish with lemon slices."

Veal Marsala

2 pounds veal round steak   *1 cup fresh mushrooms, sliced*
¼ pound ham, sliced very thin   *¼ cup Marsala or dry sherry*
2 tablespoons butter   *¼ teaspoon dried marjoram, crushed*
10¾ ounces condensed cream of   *1 tablespoon water*
   chicken soup   *2 teaspoons cornstarch*
8 ounces canned tomatoes,
   drained and chopped

Pound veal to ¼ inch thickness; cut into 18 rectangles, 3x1½ inches. Place a strip of ham on each piece of veal. Roll up jelly roll fashion. Secure with toothpick. Brown in butter. Push to one side and add blended soup, tomatoes, mushrooms, wine and marjoram. Cover and simmer for 30 minutes, stirring once or twice. Remove meat. Mix water and cornstarch, and blend into soup mixture. Cook, stirring constantly, until mixture bubbles. Cover meat with sauce and serve over rice. Serves 6.

Poultry and Game

It is little wonder that the Indians and early settlers, once they adjusted to the new wilderness, thrived in the river-laced woods of Virginia. Their food was all around them. They could combine their work and play in hunting and reap rich rewards. The lush forests were entangled with grape vines and Virginia creeper, providing a haven for deer, bear, rabbit, weasel, mink, fox, otter and muskrat. In the marshes wild geese, swans and ducks clustered in staggering numbers. Snipe, plover, woodcock, purlew, reed birds, sora and partridge were also plentiful, and wild turkeys — some of them weighing seventy pounds — abounded in the young colony.

The colonists copied the Indian methods for capturing the game, as well as devising new methods of their own. Robert Beverley writing in *The History and Present State of Virginia* in 1705 described one of the Indian methods of securing deer by stakes upon which they were impaled and tells of coon hunts by the 'light of the moon or stars," wolf traps and "pretty devices besides the gun, to take wild turkeys."

Succulent bear meat was the favorite of William Byrd II. He declared it had a "high relish and rested easily on the stomach," but "is not a very proper diet for saints . . . After eating it one is sure to dream of a woman or the devil or both."

Another native creature hunted by Indians and settlers alike was the opossum, which was usually found feeding on the abundant supply of persimmons and was described by Captain John Smith as having "an head like a swine, and a taile like a rat . . . and the bigness of a cat." In time opossum became a Virginia delicacy, as reflected in the words of early Negro field hands declaring "possums and 'simmons comes together, and bofe is good fruit."

The most coveted hunting of all was for the buffalo that chiefly frequented the Valley of Virginia but were mercilessly hunted there by the Indians. The last buffalo in Virginia was seen on the New River in 1797.

Another prized game dish imparted by the Indians to the colonists was that of the passenger pigeon, which at one time filled the trees and the skies. However, they became so popular with the new Americans that by 1914 they had become extinct.

While the men hunted, the women were back home devising and perfecting cooking methods to do justice to their mens' quarry. (The quarry itself wasn't *all that* important, by the way. Hunting was actually a kind of courting, for the hunters who excelled also had the special favors of the women!) To roast their meats to perfection, they had to concentrate on four things: the cleanliness of their equipment, the quality of their fire, the distance of their meat from the fire, and frequent basting. Much time and thought was given to the treatment of the game. It was very precious, even though plentiful, and each housewife had her own theories of bringing out the meat's distinctive flavor.

And so it was in early Virginia—that promised land of plenty—that "a stranger has no more to do but to inquire upon the Road, where any Gentlemen or good Houskeeper lives and there he may depend upon being received with hospitality," as noted by Robert Beverley. Perhaps we too in the 1970's could be as hospitable if *our* filet mignon and succulent goose were in our own backyards!

Colonial Batter Fried Chicken

2-2½ pound chicken, cut up
1 cup flour
2 teaspoons salt
½ teaspoon pepper
½ teaspoon baking soda
1 cup buttermilk
cooking oil to fill deep fryer

Preheat deep fat fryer to 350. Shake each piece of chicken separately in a paper bag containing flour, salt and pepper. Add soda to buttermilk. Dip chicken in mixture and then back into flour mixture. Cook in deep fat 20-25 minutes. Drain on absorbent paper. Serves 4-6.

Hint: Always soak chicken in salt water before flouring to fry. Water seals in juices and keeps out grease.

Oven Fried Chicken

1 frying chicken, cut up or 6 breasts	*½ teaspoon pepper*
1 cup flour	*½ teaspoon paprika*
2 teaspoons salt	*½ cup margarine*

Preheat oven to 400. Shake chicken in bag of flour and seasonings. Line 9x13 glass baking dish with foil; add margarine and place dish in oven until margarine sizzles. Place chicken in dish, skin side down. Bake for 30 minutes; turn and bake another 30 minutes. Do not cover. Serves 4-6.

Chicken and Broccoli Casserole

4½-5 pounds chicken, cut up	*1 cup milk*
5 cups water	*2 cups chicken broth*
1 teaspoon salt	*1 cup mayonnaise*
2-3 peppercorns	*1 teaspoon lemon juice*
1 rib celery, cut in half	*½ teaspoon curry powder or mace*
1 carrot	*1 bunch of fresh broccoli* or
1 onion	*20 ounces frozen broccoli*
½ cup flour	*1-2 cups buttered crumbs*

Combine chicken, water, salt, peppercorns, celery, carrot and onion. Simmer in large kettle until chicken is tender. Remove chicken. Strain broth. Cube meat. Preheat oven to 350. Make sauce as follows. Blend flour and milk until smooth. Add broth and cook until thickened. Remove from heat. Add mayonnaise, lemon juice and curry powder. Cook broccoli until tender. Drain and break into pieces. Place in greased 9x12 baking dish. Top with chicken, then sauce and crumbs. Bake about 45 minutes until crumbs are brown. Serves 6.

Chinese Chicken

2 cups cooked chicken, cubed	*10¾ ounces condensed cream of*
1 cup celery, diced	*chicken soup*
1 cup rice, cooked	*4 ounces water chestnuts,*
¾ cup mayonnaise	*drained and slivered*
1 cup fresh mushrooms, sliced	*½ cup butter*
1 teaspoon onion, chopped	*½ cup slivered almonds*
1 teaspoon lemon juice	*1 cup corn flakes*
1 teaspoon salt	

Preheat oven to 350. Mix all ingredients together except butter, almonds and corn flakes. Put in 2 quart casserole. Melt butter. Add almonds and corn flakes. Sprinkle on top of casserole. Bake 35 minutes. Serves 6-8.
"Great party dish!"

Company Chicken

8 ounces crumb-type stuffing mix	*½ cup self-rising flour*
½ cup celery, chopped	*¼ teaspoon salt*
½ cup onion, chopped	*pepper to taste*
3-4 cups cooked chicken,	*4 cups chicken broth*
cut in pieces	*6 eggs, beaten*
½ cup margarine	

Preheat oven to 325. Prepare stuffing mix with onion and celery. Spread in 9x13 inch dish. Top with chicken. Melt margarine. Blend flour, salt and pepper. Add broth and cook until thick. Stir small amount of hot mixture in eggs. Blend with rest of mixture. Pour over chicken. Bake for 40-45 minutes until knife comes out clean. Let stand 5 minutes to set. Cut in squares. Serves 12.
Note: If frozen, warm at 200 with foil on top for approximately 30 minutes.

Sauce:

10¾ ounces condensed cream of	*1 cup sour cream*
mushroom soup	*¼ cup pimento, chopped*
½ cup milk	

Heat ingredients in saucepan. DO NOT BOIL. Put in side bowl to pour over each square at serving.

Hot Chicken Salad

2 cups cooked chicken	*½ cup sliced almonds*
10½ ounces condensed cream of	*⅔ cup mayonnaise*
chicken soup	*2 teaspoons onion, minced*
¾ cup celery, diced	*½ lemon, juiced*
3 hard-boiled eggs, chopped	*10-15 potato chips*

Preheat oven to 350. Mix ingredients. Spoon into 8x12 baking dish. Top with crumbled potato chips. Bake for 20 minutes. Serves 6-8.
Note: For variation, substitute bread crumbs or cornflakes for potato chips; add ½ cup shredded Cheddar cheese or Swiss cheese with potato chips.

Chicken Casserole Supreme

4 ounces chipped beef
6-8 chicken breast halves, boned
6-8 slices bacon (optional)
dash of pepper

4 ounces canned button mushrooms
10½ ounces condensed cream of
  mushroom soup
1 cup sour cream

Preheat oven to 275. Shred chipped beef into the bottom of a 10x12 shallow greased casserole. Wrap a slice of bacon around each half of chicken breast. Place the breasts on top of the beef. Sprinkle with pepper. Blend the soup with the sour cream and pour over the chicken breasts. Cover and bake for 3 hours. Serves 6-8.

Hint: No salt is needed because the chipped beef makes the casserole salty enough.

"This is great to serve for a dinner party because it can be prepared ahead of time!"

Chicken and Wild Rice Casserole

2 3-pound fryers
1 cup water
1 cup dry sherry
½ teaspoon curry

½ cup celery, sliced
1½ teaspoons salt
1 medium onion, sliced

Place ingredients in deep kettle. Simmer 1 hour. Take chicken out and refrigerate. Strain broth. Cut cooled chicken in small pieces.

12 ounces long grain and wild
  rice mix
chicken broth plus enough water
  for cooking rice
1 cup sour cream

10½ ounces condensed cream of
  mushroom soup
1 pound fresh mushrooms, sliced and
  sautéed in ¼ cup margarine or
    1 pound canned mushrooms, sliced

Cook rice in broth and water. Combine rice, chicken, sour cream, soup and mushrooms. Place in 9x13 baking dish. Refrigerate. When ready to use, bake 1 hour at 350. Serves 8-10.

Hint: This casserole is best made a day ahead. It also freezes well.

Bar-B-Q Sauce

1 cup ketchup
1/2 cup dry sherry
1/3 cup water
2 tablespoons lemon juice
1 small onion, grated

1 tablespoon Worcestershire
2 tablespoons margarine, melted
1 tablespoon plus 1 teaspoon
* brown sugar*

Preheat oven to 325. Combine ingredients in skillet and simmer 10-15 minutes. Pour over chicken. Bake 1 hour and 25 minutes *or* bake 1 hour and put on grill for 25 minutes. Yields 2 1/3 cups.
Note: This sauce can be frozen.

Chick-In-The-Garden

2 chicken breasts
1 medium tomato, skinned
1 medium onion, peeled
3 fresh mushrooms
2 green pepper rings
2 tablespoons uncooked rice

1 teaspoon Worcestershire
3/4 teaspoon salt and dash pepper
dash garlic salt (optional)
dash paprika
butter

Prepare charcoal. Place all vegetables just off the center of a doubled yard of foil with chicken breasts. Sprinkle with rest of ingredients, and dot with butter. Seal foil tightly. Cook over glowing coals about 1 3/4 hours, turning every 20 minutes. Serves 1.
"A complete meal in one—prepare one for each guest!"

Island Broiled Chicken

1 cup oil
1/3 cup lemon juice
3 tablespoons soy sauce
1 teaspoon oregano
1 clove garlic, minced

1 teaspoon Accent
1/2 teaspoon salt
1/4 teaspoon pepper
1 chicken, split lengthwise

Combine all ingredients except chicken. Chill chicken in sauce at least 4-5 hours. Broil skin side down 7 inches from heat for 20 minutes or until lightly browned. Brush occasionally with sauce. Turn and continue broiling about 20 minutes or until tender, basting with sauce. Serves 4.

Chicken à la Vanderbilt
(Courtesy of Castle Hill)

1 Bermuda onion, finely sliced	*8 slices cooked chicken breast*
½ cup butter	*1 cup cream*
1 cup mushrooms, sliced	*1 tablespoon paprika*
8 thin slices cooked ham	*Parmesan cheese*

Cook onion in butter for 5 minutes. Add mushrooms and sauté. Spread onion and mushrooms in a 9x13 baking dish. Add ham. Top each piece with a slice of chicken and enough cream to cover. Sprinkle Parmesan and paprika on top. Place in the oven until brown on top, about 15 minutes at 350. Serves 6-8.
Note: It may not be necessary to use all of the cream.

Country Captain

1 fryer, cut in pieces or	*paprika*
6-8 chicken breasts	*butter*
flour	

Roll chicken in flour and paprika. Brown chicken in butter and place in a roaster or a 3½ quart casserole. Prepare sauce as follows:

1 large onion, chopped	*1 tablespoon Worcestershire*
1 clove garlic, chopped	*1 teaspoon curry powder*
1 large green pepper, chopped	*1 teaspoon thyme*
½ cup butter	*1 teaspoon salt*
1 cup tomatoes, quartered	*1 teaspoon pepper*
½-1 cup parsley, chopped	*4 ounces canned mushrooms*
2 teaspoons vinegar	*1 cup currants*
2 teaspoons dry mustard or	*2½ ounces slivered almonds, toasted*
2 tablespoons mustard	

Preheat oven to 300. Fry onion, garlic and green pepper in butter. Add tomatoes, parsley and all other ingredients except the currants, mushrooms and almonds. Cook slowly until well-blended. Add mushrooms and pour sauce over chicken. Cook slowly 1 hour. Add currants over top 15 minutes before serving. Sprinkle toasted almonds and serve with rice. Serves 6.

Castle Hill

Castle Hill is a National Historic Landmark near Charlottesville. It was here that Jack Jouett broke his famous ride. Castle Hill is actually two houses. The first, built in 1764 by Dr. Thomas Walker, a prominent Virginia citizen and guardian of Thomas Jefferson, is a story-and-a-half frame structure. The dormer windows provide a view of Walnut Mountain and remnants of the plantation complex. In 1824 Dr. Walker's grand-daughter, Judith Page Walker and her husband, Senator William Cabell Rives, Minister to France, built the brick addition which connects the original structure through a central hallway. No house in Virginia more beautifully captures the spirit of her continually renewing pride, graciousness and historic traditions than Castle Hill, lovingly restored and maintained.

99

Chicken Curry And Chutney

12 chicken breasts
salt
3 tablespoons butter
paprika
1¼ cups orange juice
¼ cup chutney

½ teaspoon cinnamon
dash of thyme
½ cup raisins
½ cup blanched split almonds
½ teaspoon curry powder

Preheat oven to 425. Arrange chicken in greased 9x13 shallow baking dish. Lightly salt chicken, if desired. Spread with butter which has been melted and mixed with paprika. Bake for 15 minutes or until golden brown. Meanwhile, prepare the sauce in a pan by combining the other ingredients and simmer 10 minutes. Pour sauce over browned chicken. Reduce heat to 350. Bake covered for 1 hour or until tender. Serve with rice and the following curry accompaniments.

1 cup green onion, sliced
1 cup crisp bacon, crumbled

1 cup coconut chips
1 cup parsley, chopped

Serves 8-10.
Note: Cover tightly, so it will steam and not dry out.

Divine Chicken Curry

12 chicken breasts
salt and pepper
¼ cup butter
3 10½ ounce cans condensed
    cream of chicken soup
¾ cup mayonnaise

½ cup chicken broth
1 teaspoon curry powder
1½ cups sharp Cheddar cheese, grated
1 tablespoon lemon juice
slivered almonds, lightly toasted
4 ounces canned mushrooms, sliced

Preheat oven to 375. In greased 3½ quart casserole, place skinned chicken breasts. Sprinkle with salt and pepper and dot with butter. Add 1 inch of water, cover with foil and bake for 1 hour. Remove, pour off broth and save ½ cup. Lower oven temperature to 350. Mix soup, mayonnaise, broth, curry, cheese and lemon juice in a pan. Place the chicken in a 9x13 pan. On top of the chicken spread the drained mushrooms and almonds. Then cover with the sauce. Cover with foil. At this point it may be refrigerated and baked 1 or 2 days later. Bake covered for 30-45 minutes. Serves 12.
"Great for a buffet or seated dinner since chicken falls off the bone! Non-curry diners will love this dish!"

Chicken Dijon

4 chicken breasts, split, skinned
   and boned
3 tablespoons margarine
2 tablespoons flour

1 cup chicken broth
1/2 cup light cream
2 tablespoons Dijon mustard
tomato wedges and parsley

In large skillet, cook chicken in margarine about 20 minutes. Remove chicken. Stir flour into drippings. Add chicken broth and cream. Stir and cook until thick. Stir in mustard. Add chicken. Heat 10 minutes. Garnish with tomato wedges and parsley. Serves 4.

Hint: Brown chicken and make sauce ahead. Then heat together when ready to serve.

Chicken Parisienne

12 small chicken breasts,
   skinned and boned
16 ounces currant jelly
1 tablespoon cornstarch
1 cup water

1/4 cup fresh lemon juice
2 tablespoons Worcestershire
2 teaspoons ground allspice
3 teaspoons salt
1 teaspoon pepper

Preheat oven to 450. Place chicken breasts in uncovered roasting pan, large enough so that they do not overlap. Mix all other ingredients in a saucepan and bring to a boil. Simmer 5 minutes. Pour sauce over the chicken breasts and bake for 15 minutes. Reduce heat to 350 and bake 30 minutes, basting frequently. Serve with wild rice. Serves 8.

Note: If sauce becomes too thick during the baking period, add water.

Wine Marinade For Chicken

1/2 cup Burgundy
1/2 cup chili sauce
1/4 cup salad oil
3 tablespoons wine vinegar
salt and pepper

1 clove garlic, sliced
2 tablespoons onion, chopped
1 teaspoon Worcestershire
2 bay leaves

Combine ingredients and marinate chicken 6 hours to 3 days. This is enough to marinate a whole chicken.

Roast Chicken in Brandy
(Courtesy of Shirley Plantation)

1 large roasting chicken,
  cut in serving pieces
salt to taste
white pepper to taste

3 cups dry white wine
½ cup butter
1 cup brandy

Salt and pepper chicken. Marinate in wine overnight. Preheat oven to 375. Sauté chicken in butter until golden brown. Place in a roaster with the butter and the marinade. Cover and bake 50 minutes. Add more wine if necessary while baking. Lower heat to 350. Roast until tender. When serving, place cut-up fowl on warm platter and pour brandy over it. Ignite and bring to the table flaming. Use leftover juices in the pan to quench the flames. *"Magnificent!"*

Sherried Chicken

4 tablespoons butter
1 cup fresh mushrooms, sliced
¼ cup green onions, sliced
4 chicken breasts
1 teaspoon salt
⅛ teaspoon pepper

⅛ teaspoon garlic powder
½ teaspoon paprika
¼ teaspoon crushed rosemary
¾ cup dry sherry
¼ cup water
½ teaspoon cornstarch

Melt ½ of the butter and add the mushrooms and onions. Sauté and set aside. Melt the rest of the butter. Brown the breasts and sprinkle with condiments. Add sherry. Cover and simmer until tender, about 40 minutes. Blend the water and cornstarch and add to chicken. Cook, stirring constantly, until thick. Add the mushrooms and onions. Serves 4.

Sherry Chicken

6 chicken breasts
½ cup butter
2 10¾ ounce cans condensed
  cream of mushroom soup

1 cup sour cream
½ cup sherry
4 ounces canned button mushrooms
  (optional)

Preheat oven to 325. Brown chicken in butter. Make sauce of soup, sour cream and sherry. Add mushrooms, if desired. Put chicken in a 1½ quart casserole and pour over sauce. Bake covered, 1 hour. Serves 4-6.

Shirley

Shirley Plantation, named for Cecilly Sherley, wife of Lord De La Warr, first Royal Governor of Virginia, was occupied as early as 1613. The first mansion built at Shirley by Colonel Edward Hill, I, was torn down in the nineteenth century and rebuilt at Upper Shirley. It has passed from the Hill family to the Carter family through marriage. The present mansion was remodeled in the early 1770's by Charles Carter whose descendants continue to own and love this grand home with its four handsomely built dependencies. The four story brick house displays the traditional carved pineapple, the eighteenth century symbol of hospitality. This James River mansion is noted for its "flying" walnut staircase which has no visible support. Shirley contains many antiques, priceless portraits and family silver to be appreciated by plantation visitors.

Herbed Chicken Rosé

4 large pieces of frying chicken or
chicken breasts
¼ teaspoon garlic salt
¼ teaspoon paprika
1 tablespoon flour
2-3 tablespoons shortening,
half butter

¼ teaspoon dried rosemary
¼ teaspoon dried basil
½ cup rosé wine
½ teaspoon cornstarch mixed with
1 tablespoon water
½ cup sour cream or yogurt

Dredge chicken with garlic salt, paprika and flour, mixed. Brown chicken on both sides in hot shortening. Sprinkle with herbs. Add wine and cover. Cook slowly until tender, about 25 minutes. Remove chicken to serving bowl. Skim any excess fat from pan liquid. Thicken gravy with cornstarch mixture. Stir in sour cream or yogurt. Pour over chicken. Serve hot. Serves 4.
"This is excellent served with rice and mushrooms as a side dish!"

Chicken Veronique

6 tablespoons butter
2 chicken breasts, halved
12 medium mushrooms
2 tablespoons flour
1 cup light cream

¼ cup dry white wine
½ cup country ham, diced
salt and pepper
¾ cup white seedless grapes, drained,
if canned

Preheat oven to 350. Melt butter and brown chicken. Place in 1½ quart casserole. Melt more butter in skillet. Sauté mushrooms and sprinkle over chicken. Reduce heat and stir flour into remaining butter. Cook 1 minute. Add cream and wine, stirring constantly. Cook until sauce is thick. Add ham, salt and pepper. Pour sauce over chicken, cover and bake 40 minutes. Uncover casserole, scatter grapes on top and bake 10 minutes more. Serves 4.

Note: This dish may be made ahead, refrigerated and reheated, but grapes should not be added and cooked until 10 minutes before serving. Garnish tray with additional white grapes, if desired.

Rock Cornish Hens

4 hens
salt and pepper
2 cups seasoned croutons
1/2 cup wheat germ
1/2 cup celery and leaves, finely
  chopped

1/2 cup chicken broth
6 tablespoons butter, melted
1 teaspoon sugar
crab apple slices

Preheat oven to 425. Salt and pepper cavity of each hen. Mix dressing with remaining ingredients except crab apples. Stuff hens and tie legs together with tail. Brush hens with butter. Roast 1 hour in open pan, basting occasionally. The last 15 minutes of roasting, cut strings and brush with sauce. Garnish with crab apple slices. Serves 4.

Sauce:

10 ounces red currant jelly
1/2 cup golden raisins
1/4 cup butter

2 teaspoons lemon juice
1/4 teaspoon allspice

Mix ingredients in saucepan. Cook for 10 minutes, stirring occasionally until well-blended. Use to baste hens. Serve remaining sauce.

Rock Cornish Game Hens with Orange Sauce

4 ounces wild rice
1 small onion, minced
2 ounces fresh mushrooms, chopped

1 egg
3 tablespoons Burgundy
4 hens

Preheat oven to 350. Cook rice. Mix with onion, mushrooms, egg and wine. Season to taste. Stuff hens and bake for 45 minutes. After hens are cooked, spoon on orange sauce. Remove hens to warm plate and serve with extra sauce. Serves 4.

Orange Sauce:

6 ounces concentrated frozen
  orange juice
6 ounces water
1/4 cup cognac or sherry

1 tablespoon sugar
1/2 teaspoon salt
1 orange, peeled and thinly sliced
1 tablespoon cornstarch

Mix all ingredients except cornstarch and simmer on stove for 10 minutes. Add cornstarch moistened with water to thicken.

Wild Rice Dressing

1 cup celery, chopped
1 cup mushrooms, sliced
¹/₂ cup parsley, chopped
6 tablespoons butter

6 ounces wild rice, cooked
2 ounces pimento
8 ounces stuffing mix
1 cup boiling water

Preheat oven to 350, if planning to bake. Sauté celery, mushrooms and parsley in butter. Mix all ingredients together. Stuff a fowl or bake in a greased 9x12 dish for 15 minutes or until warmed through. Serves 8.

Oyster Stuffing

1 cup butter or margarine
2 cups onion, finely chopped
2 cups celery, thinly sliced
3 loaves bread
4 teaspoons parsley, chopped

2 teaspoons salt
1 teaspoon pepper
4 teaspoons sage or to taste
1 quart oysters, drained

Melt butter in large pan. Add onion and simmer until soft. Add celery and simmer 5 minutes. Cut crusts from bread. Pull bread into crumbs. Add to onion-celery mixture and toss thoroughly. Add parsley, salt and pepper. Season with sage and add oysters. Mix well. Yields stuffing for a 20-25 pound turkey.

Hint: For variety, use 2-3 tins smoked oysters and add an 8 ounce can of mushrooms.

Turkey Stuffing Cakes

16 slices bread, cubed
1 teaspoon sage
1 teaspoon salt
¹/₂ teaspoon thyme

1 cup onion, chopped
2 cups celery, chopped
¹/₂ cup margarine
¹/₃ - ¹/₂ cup turkey stock

Preheat oven to 400. Mix bread and seasonings. Sauté onion and celery in butter. Add to bread, mixing well. Moisten with stock. Form into cakes. Put on greased sheet. Bake for 10-15 minutes until lightly browned. This makes about 9 cakes. Serves 6-9.

Hint: This recipe can be doubled. Extra cakes can be frozen on trays in freezer. When frozen, cakes can be wrapped individually or in desired number. Defrost cakes before baking. Fresh stuffing every time!

Cornbread Dressing

2 cups cornbread, crumbled
2 yeast rolls, crumbled
2 cups turkey broth, seasoned
1/2 cup buttermilk
2 medium onions, quartered

1/4 teaspoon baking soda
4 eggs, beaten
1/2 cup turkey fat or butter
1 tablespoon celery seed

Preheat oven to 350. Crumble bread and rolls into a bowl. Pour warm broth over and let sit until all bread is softened. Blend milk, onions and soda in blender. Add to crumbs. Stir in eggs, fat and celery seed. Pour into well-greased 9x12 pan and bake until brown, about 1 hour. Serve hot with giblet gravy. Serves 8-10.

Dove or Pheasant Breast Casserole

18 dove breasts or *4 pheasant breasts,*
  or a combination
10 1/2 ounces condensed cream of
  mushroom soup
1 medium onion, sautéed

1/4 - 1/2 cup sherry or dry wine
pinch of oregano
pinch of rosemary
salt and pepper to taste

Preheat oven to 350. Place game in large roaster. Mix remaining ingredients and pour over game. Cover and bake for 1 hour, turning occasionally. Bake uncovered another 20 minutes. Serves 6-8.
Note: For variation, add 1 cup sour cream the last 20 minutes of cooking.

Wild Duck or Coot

4-6 ducks, split in half lengthwise
4 tablespoons butter
3 tablespoons flour
1/2 cup white wine or sherry

2 cups chicken stock or
2 chicken bouillon cubes dissolved
  in 2 cups boiling water
salt and pepper to taste

Preheat oven to 350. Brown ducks in butter in a frying pan. Place in a 2 1/2 quart casserole. Add flour to remaining butter in pan. Stir in stock, wine and seasonings. Blend well and pour over duck. Cover and cook for 1 hour. Serves 4-6.
Note: Coot, which is not a duck but a mud hen, is best cooked in a pressure cooker. After splitting coot and browning, cook with 1 cup water for 20 minutes in pressure cooker. Prepare gravy as above and put coot in it. Cover pan and cook 10-15 minutes.
"This game is delicious served with wild rice."

107

Pheasant Smithfield
(Courtesy of The Williamsburg Inn)

1 young pheasant
½ cup cooked wild rice
1 slice Smithfield ham

Cointreau
2 ounces Perigoudine Sauce

Bone pheasant breast and stuff with wild rice. Shape breast and hold with piece of foil around the bottom. Secure legs with toothpick. Roast in 350 oven for 1 hour. Serve on slice of ham. Sprinkle Cointreau over pheasant, and mask with Perigoudine Sauce (a basic Madeira sauce with chopped truffles). Serves 1.

Hot Turkey Soufflé

6 slices white bread
2 cups cooked turkey, diced
½ cup green pepper, chopped
½ cup celery, chopped
½ cup mayonnaise
¾ teaspoon salt

dash of pepper
2 eggs, beaten
1½ cups milk
10½ ounces condensed cream of
*   mushroom soup*
½ cup sharp cheese, grated

Cube 2 slices of bread. Place in bottom of 8x8 dish. Combine turkey, vegetables, mayonnaise and seasonings. Spoon over bread. Trim the crusts from the remaining slices of bread and arrange on top of the turkey mixture. Combine the eggs and milk, pouring over all. Cover and chill 1 hour or overnight. When ready to cook, preheat oven to 325. Spoon soup over all. Bake for 1 hour. Sprinkle the cheese on top the last few minutes. Serves 5-6.

Quail, the Hunter's Delight

4-8 quail
4 tablespoons butter
3 tablespoons flour

2 cups chicken stock
½ cup sherry
salt and pepper to taste

Preheat oven to 350. Wash and truss quail. Brown in butter in a frying pan. Put quail in a 1½ quart casserole. Add flour to remaining butter in pan. Slowly stir in stock and sherry, blending well. Add salt and pepper. Pour over quail. Cover and bake for 1 hour. Serves 2-4.
"Sauce is also delicious over rice!"

Wild Rabbit Stew

1 rabbit, cut-up	*1/4 cup white vinegar*
1/2 cup margarine	*1/4 cup green olives, sliced*
2 garlic cloves, minced	*10 drops Tabasco*
1 medium onion, sliced	*salt and pepper to taste*
1/2 cup oil	*5 medium potatoes, peeled and sliced*
8 ounces tomato juice	*1 cup sherry*

Brown rabbit in margarine in a dutch oven or a heavy skillet that can be covered. Add all ingredients except potatoes and sherry. Cover and simmer for 1 hour. Add the potatoes and sherry. Simmer another 30 minutes. Serves 4.
"Children will love this!"

Venison Stroganoff

2 pounds venison, cubed	*3 beef bouillon cubes*
1/2 cup butter	*8 ounces tomato paste*
salt and pepper	*1 pint sour cream*
onion or garlic salt	*4 ounces canned mushrooms*
Worcestershire	*cooked rice, seasoned to taste*
3 cups water	

Brown venison in butter in heavy skillet. Add seasonings and Worcestershire to taste. Add water and bouillon cubes. Simmer covered 3-4 hours until meat is tender. About 20 minutes before serving, stir in sour cream. Heat thoroughly, but DO NOT BOIL. Serve over rice. Serves 8.

Hint: This keeps well in a chafing dish and can be doubled or tripled for a large crowd.

Venison Roast

4-6 pound venison roast	*Season-all*
garlic salt	*1/2 pound salt pork, cut into*
pepper	*thin strips, or bacon*

Preheat oven to 200. Mix equal amounts of seasonings and rub well into the surface of the roast. In a lattice-work pattern, put salt pork on roast. Cover loosely with foil. Bake for 1 hour per pound. Serves 8-10.

Egg and Cheese Dishes

Before emerging as a fairly commonplace meat substitute, eggs and cheeses were looked upon superstitiously as rare and wonderful objects in past civilizations. The ancient Romans looked upon the egg not only as food but as a device for determining the sex of an unborn child. Moreover, because of its scarcity, the egg was considered a special delicacy.

Numerous centuries ago, the Chinese developed a method of stretching their scanty supply of eggs by preserving them in caustic lime, which prevented them from spoiling but shrank the inside to a dark, jellylike substance. Only two centuries ago, our own colonial housewives altered this preserving procedure by packing the eggs in lime water. Other methods of carrying surplus eggs from plentiful to meager laying periods in colonial times included packing the eggs in salt or greasing them with mutton suet and then packing them in bran, small end down.

Cheese, a more recent newcomer thought to date to 9000 BC, has always been held in high esteem and was attributed to the god Aristaeus, guardian of farmers and shepherds, by the ancient Greeks. This "divine gift" was used by the Greeks to feed Olympic athletes and to reward children.

The legendary origin of cheese is given to an Arab who crossed the desert with his supply of milk in a pouch made from a sheep's stomach. After many hours of travel he paused to quench his thirst and found only a thin watery liquid afloat a heavy white solid substance; driven by his great hunger and thirst, the Arab tasted the white curd and found it delicious.

What seemed miraculous to that weary sojourner was simply the basic formula for producing cheese—in this case a reaction produced jointly by the heat of the sun and the enzymes of the sheep's stomach. Several centuries and continents removed, colonial housewives produced their own cheeses with homemade rennet which had been made from a calf's stomach that had been cleaned and either dried and salted or preserved in brandy or wine.

Until about 1850, all American cheeses were made at home, basically by draining or pressing the curd to remove the whey, then breaking the curd into fine particles, salting it, wrapping it in a cloth, and placing it in the cheese press. Once the cheese had been pressed, it was greased and turned daily until it became firm.

Both egg and cheese dishes have been popular fare in American menus. Omelettes and scrambled eggs were so common in the seventeenth century that early cookbooks omitted basic recipes and carried only their more interesting variations. Bonny-clabber, a jellylike milk substance served with cream and nutmeg, was another favorite early Virginia dish.

Virginia tradition has kept alive the use of eggs and cheese dishes through the years as a means of "frugal but elegant" eating. Today luncheons, brunches and breakfast parties featuring delicious and satisfying dairy dishes have become an extremely popular means of informal entertaining.

Hearty Breakfast

1 egg, beaten
1 cup milk
2 tablespoons shortening, melted

1 cup pancake mix
1 cup pork sausage links,
cooked and sliced

Preheat oven to 450. Combine egg, milk, shortening and pancake mix; beat until smooth. Pour into a greased 8x12 pan and top with sausage slices. Bake 20 minutes. Cut in squares and serve hot with butter and syrup. Serves 4-6.

Brunch Dish

For a quick brunch dish that will serve as many as you wish—line a shallow 8x13 glass dish with ham or Canadian bacon. Top with a layer of Swiss cheese. Break eggs over all. Drizzle cream over the egg whites until the yolks peek through. Bake in a 450 oven for 10 minutes. Sprinkle with Parmesan cheese. Bake for 10 minutes more. Cut in squares to serve.

Brunch Egg Casserole

2 cups plain croutons
4 ounces Cheddar cheese, grated
4 eggs, beaten
2 cups milk
1/2 teaspoon salt

1/2 teaspoon mustard
1/8 teaspoon onion powder
dash of pepper
4 slices bacon, crumbled

Preheat oven to 325. Put croutons and cheese in bottom of a greased 10x6x1¾ inch casserole dish. Combine eggs, milk, salt, pepper, mustard and onion powder; mix until blended. Pour over croutons and sprinkle with crumbled bacon. Bake 1 hour or until eggs are set. Serves 6.
"A Virginia Hostess might add bacon curls for a touch of elegance!"

Brunch Eggs

1/4 cup butter
1/3 cup flour
4 ounces Cheddar cheese, grated
10¾ ounces condensed cream of
mushroom soup
1/2 cup milk

1 tablespoon onion, chopped
1 tablespoon dry mustard
dash Tabasco
salt and pepper to taste
1½ hard boiled eggs per person

Stir butter, flour and cheese over medium heat until melted. Add soup, milk, seasonings and heat through. Slice eggs and carefully add to sauce. Serves 6-8.
Note: If doubled, do not double milk.
"Delicious served over toast."

Note: Fool-Proof Hard-Boiled Eggs.   Use heavy pan with tight-fitting lid.

To Cook: Place desired number of eggs in cool water. Bring to boil; cover IMMEDIATELY and remove from heat. Let stand 25 minutes. Rinse in cold water and peel immediately!

To Peel: Rattle eggs briskly in metal pan to THOROUGHLY crack shells. Shells will fall off!

"Perfectly peeled eggs with completely yellow yolks!"

Curried Eggs

8 eggs, hard-boiled
1/3 cup mayonnaise
1/4 - 1/2 teaspoon salt
1/2 teaspoon paprika
1/2 teaspoon curry powder
1/4 teaspoon dry mustard
2 tablespoons butter

2 tablespoons flour
10 3/4 ounces condensed cream of
  mushroom soup
1 soup can milk
1/2 cup Cheddar cheese, shredded
1 cup soft bread crumbs
1 tablespoon butter

Preheat oven to 350. Halve the eggs, remove and mash yolks. Mix with mayonnaise, salt, paprika, curry powder and mustard. Refill the eggs and place in a 10x6 inch baking dish. Melt 2 tablespoons butter, add flour, soup and milk. Stir and cook until bubbly, add cheese and stir until melted. Cover eggs with sauce. Mix crumbs with 1 tablespoon butter and sprinkle around edge of casserole. Bake 20 minutes or until hot. Serves 6-8.

Ham and Egg Pudding
(Courtesy of Smithfield Foods, Smithfield, Virginia)

1/4 cup butter, melted
1 pound sliced ham
white pepper
6 eggs, well-beaten

2 cups milk
2 cups flour, sifted
1 teaspoon salt

Preheat oven to 425. Spread butter evenly in a 9x13 pan. Line bottom of pan with ham slices and sprinkle with pepper. Beat eggs until light. Beat in milk. Add flour and salt, beat until smooth. Pour mixture evenly over ham. Bake for 40-45 minutes or until brown and crusty. Cut into squares and serve. Can be topped with your favorite brown gravy, if desired. Serves 8.

Shad Roe 'N' Eggs

Chop roe into small pieces and heat quickly in a small amount of butter or margarine or bacon drippings. Stir and brown on all sides. Stir into eggs or use to fill an omelet.
Note: Delicious way to use cold leftover shad roe.

Eggs Fromage
(Courtesy of Farmer's Delight)

6 eggs, well beaten	*½ cup American cheese, grated*
8 teaspoons cream	*2-3 shakes Worcestershire*
3 ounces deviled ham	*salt and pepper to taste*

Add cream, ham, cheese and seasonings to eggs. Mix well. Cook over boiling water, stirring until soft scrambled. Serve on thin triangles of buttered toast. *"Marvelous breakfast for company or a delightful supper!"*

Swiss Oven Omelet

8-10 slices bacon, cooked	*2 teaspoons salt*
(reserve fat)	*¼ teaspoon pepper*
½ cup onion, chopped	*8 ounces sliced Swiss cheese,*
8 eggs	*cut in strips*
1 cup milk	

Preheat oven to 350. Cook onion in bacon fat. Combine eggs, milk, salt, pepper and beat until mixed. Add onion. Pour into greased 1½ quart casserole and add strips of cheese. They will sink down into eggs. Top with bacon slices or crumbled bacon. Bake for 40 minutes until puffed high. Serve at once. Serves 8.

"Add a shake of curry powder and crumbled bacon bits to the yolk mixture of deviled eggs."

Cheese Fondue

¾ pound Swiss cheese, cut in	*dash of pepper*
thin strips	*dash of nutmeg*
1 tablespoon flour	*3 tablespoons dry sherry*
1¼ cups sauterne	*French bread, cut in*
1 clove garlic, halved	*one inch cubes*

Toss cheese with flour. Pour sauterne into saucepan rubbed with garlic. Add cheese strips gradually, stirring mixture constantly. When mixture is smooth and thick, add seasonings, and sherry. Pour into fondue pot or chafing dish. Dip bread cubes in fondue, using wooden skewers or forks. Serves 6.

Farmer's Delight

Farmer's Delight was called the oldest brick house in Loudon County by *Hardesty's Encyclopedia* of 1883. Colonel Joseph Lane acquired an earlier stone house, made additions and named it Farmer's Delight in 1791. He was buried there in 1803. Located in Middleburg, the farm was originally a part of Goose Creek tract taken by Robert Carter for Lord Fairfax in 1727. Later it was acquired by the Reverend Charles Green. This magnificent home is presently owned and loved by former Ambassador and Mrs. George McGhee.

Cheese Custard With Asparagus

2 cups milk
8 ounces Swiss cheese, diced
½ teaspoon salt
½ teaspoon Worcestershire
dash cayenne or white pepper

2 tablespoons butter or margarine
4 eggs
10 ounces frozen asparagus,
  cooked and drained

Preheat oven to 325. Scald milk. Reduce heat to low and add cheese, salt, Worcestershire, pepper and butter. Stir until cheese melts. Remove from heat and cool. Beat eggs in a medium-sized bowl. Add cheese mixture gradually, beating constantly. Pour mixture into a well-buttered 4 cup ring mold. Place mold in a baking pan; add enough boiling water to come as high as the mixture is in the mold. Cover the mold loosely with foil. Bake 40-50 minutes or until a knife comes out clean. Loosen custard carefully. Unmold on a plate. Arrange asparagus in the center of the ring. Serves 6.

"Wonderful for a brunch or good as a family supper with sausages!"

"Never cook cheese or eggs at high temperatures: cheese becomes tough, eggs become rubbery."

Garlic Cheese Grits

2 cups grits
1½ quarts water
2 6-ounce rolls garlic cheese,
  cut up
½ cup milk

4 eggs, beaten
½ cup margarine
salt and pepper to taste
Parmesan cheese, grated
paprika

Preheat oven to 300. Cook grits in water. Add cheese, milk, eggs, margarine, salt and pepper. Pour into a buttered 4 quart casserole. Sprinkle with Parmesan cheese and paprika. Bake for 30-45 minutes. Serves 10.

Note: For a change add ½ cup sharp Cheddar cheese in place of Parmesan; or add 1 cup sour cream to existing recipe. Can be easily halved or frozen.

"This is delicious with roast beef, steak or lamb."

Creamy Macaroni and Cheese

7 ounces elbow macaroni
2 cups cottage cheese
1 cup sour cream
1 egg, slightly beaten

¾ teaspoon salt
dash of pepper
8 ounces sharp Cheddar cheese, grated
paprika

Preheat oven to 350. Cook macaroni and drain well. Combine cottage cheese, sour cream, egg, salt and pepper. Add cheese and mix will. Stir in cooked macaroni. Pour into greased 4 quart baking dish. Sprinkle with paprika. Bake for 45 minutes. Serves 8-10.
Note: This can be halved easily.
"A delicious variation of an old favorite."

Cheese Pudding

6 slices bread
4 eggs
1¾ cups milk
1 teaspoon dry mustard

1¼ teaspoons salt
¼ teaspoon pepper
2 cups sharp cheese, grated

Butter slices of bread and cut into cubes. Place in a buttered 2 quart casserole, alternating with layers of cheese. Beat together eggs, milk, salt, pepper and mustard. Pour on top and chill one hour or longer. Preheat oven to 350. Bake 45-60 minutes or until set. Serves 6.
Note: This may chill in refrigerator overnight.

Virginia Rabbit
"The Virginia hostess used rabbit as a name for rarebit."

¼ cup margarine
½ cup flour
2 cups milk, hot
1 pound sharp Cheddar cheese, grated

2 teaspoons Worcestershire
1½ teaspoons Tabasco
2 teaspoons mustard with horseradish
1 cup beer

Melt margarine in top of double boiler, add flour and stir until smooth. Blend in milk and then cheese by handfuls. Stir until melted. Add remaining ingredients in order. Serve over toast. Serves 6-8.

Cheese Rarebit
(Courtesy of Monroe House)

1-1½ pounds sharp Cheddar cheese	¼ teaspoon sugar
½ cup butter or margarine	¼ teaspoon Ac'cent
6 tablespoons flour	2 tablespoons Worcestershire
1 teaspoon dry mustard	2 13-ounce cans evaporated milk
½ teaspoon salt	2 13-ounce cans hot water
¼ teaspoon onion salt	

Cut cheese into small pieces. Make a double boiler of a 3 quart saucepan and larger pan filled with simmering water. Blend butter, flour and seasonings in top of double boiler until smooth. Remove mixture from hot water and stir in Worcestershire. Blend in evaporated milk. Return mixture over hot water and add water. Add cheese, stirring constantly, until cheese is melted. Serve over toasted buns, biscuits or other type of bread. Makes 9 cups and serves 16.

Cheese Souffle

3 tablespoons margarine, melted	1 cup milk
2 tablespoons cornstarch	1 cup sharp cheese, grated
½ teaspoon salt	4 eggs, separated
¼ teaspoon onion salt	

Preheat oven to 350. Blend margarine, cornstarch, salt and pepper. Remove from heat and add milk slowly. Cook until thickened. Add cheese and well-beaten egg yolks. Fold in stiffly beaten egg whites and pour into a greased 2 quart casserole. Set casserole into pan of hot water and bake 1 hour and 15 minutes. Serves 4.

Crab Custard Casserole

6 slices bread, cubed	½ cup butter, melted
½ pound Old English cheese, cubed	2 cups milk
1 pound crab meat	3 eggs

Place bread cubes, cheese and crab into a buttered 2 quart casserole. Pour butter over mixture. Beat together milk and eggs. Add salt and pepper to taste. Pour over mixture. Refrigerate at least 3 hours. Bake 1 hour at 350. Serves 6.

Note: This casserole may be made a day ahead and set in refrigerator until ready to bake.

118

Monroe House

The house in which James Monroe lived when he practiced law in Fredericksburg is an excellent example of an eighteenth century townhouse. Its wide edge-pine floors, handsome moldings, panelings, and original handmade pegged mantels have attracted many visitors. The Monroe house has been lovingly restored by its present owners, Mr. and Mrs. L. Dexter Hubbard. Colonial iron box locks with small brass knobs have been placed on all the doors. Originally two floors, this comfortable house acquired a third floor and was stuccoed before the War Between the States.

Cheese Shrimp Casserole

6 slices white bread
1/2 pound Old English cheese
  slices
1 1/2 pounds shrimp, cooked
1/4 cup butter, melted

1/2 teaspoon dry mustard
salt to taste
3 eggs, beaten
1 pint half and half

Break bread and cheese into bite-sized pieces. Arrange shrimp, bread and cheese in layers in a greased 2 quart casserole. Pour butter over this mixture. Add mustard and salt to beaten eggs; add half and half to eggs; mix. Pour over ingredients in casserole and let stand overnight in refrigerator. Bake 1 hour at 350. Serves 4.

Green Pepper Frittata

3 tablespoons vegetable oil
3 green peppers, sliced
1 onion, sliced
dash of salt
1/8 teaspoon garlic powder

dash of oregano
dash of pepper
6 eggs
1 tablespoon light cream
1/4 cup Parmesan cheese

Sauté green peppers and onion in oil until slightly wilted. Sprinkle with seasonings; add eggs. Stir gently, ONE TIME ONLY. When eggs begin to set, top with cheese and cover for 2-3 minutes. Invert on a serving platter. Surround with broiled tomatoes. Cut into wedges and serve. Serves 4.

Note: To broil tomatoes—top drained canned tomato quarters with butter, garlic salt and Parmesan cheese. Broil lightly until golden brown.

"A delicious brunch or supper dish."

Crab Meat Quiche

3 eggs
1 cup light cream
3/4 teaspoon salt

1 1/4 cup Gruyère cheese, grated
1/2 pound crab meat
8 inch pie shell, unbaked

Preheat oven to 375. Beat eggs, cream and salt together. Combine cheese and crab meat and spread evenly on bottom of crust. Pour in cream mixture. Bake on lowest rack of oven 35-40 minutes, or until puffed and brown. Serves 4-6.

Quiche Honfleur

1 large onion, sliced
2 tablespoons butter
1-1½ pounds shrimp, cooked
2 tablespoons pimento, chopped
¼ cup bread crumbs
9 inch pastry shell, unbaked

5 eggs
1 cup heavy cream
dash of salt, nutmeg, cayenne
1 cup Gruyère cheese, grated
¾ cup sour cream

Preheat oven to 350. Sauté onion in butter. Add shrimp and pimento. Coat bottom of pastry shell with crumbs. Put shrimp mixture in pastry shell. Mix eggs, cream, nutmeg, salt and cayenne. Pour over the shrimp and cook for 30 minutes. When pie is cooked, combine cheese and sour cream, put on top, and run under broiler. Serves 6-8.

Quiche Lorraine

8 slices bacon, diced
½ cup green onions, chopped
6 eggs, beaten
1 teaspoon onion salt

1 cup Swiss cheese, grated
2 cups light cream or milk
9 inch pie shell, unbaked

Preheat oven to 375. Cook bacon until golden; sauté onion in fat. Drain fat. Combine eggs, onion salt and cheese. Stir into cooled onions and crumbled bacon. Add cream and blend well; pour into pie shell. Bake 30-35 minutes or until golden brown. Serves 6.

Mini Quiches

1 package Butterflake dinner rolls
4 ounces canned shrimp, drained
1 egg, beaten
½ cup light cream

½ teaspoon salt
dash of pepper
1⅓ ounces Gruyère or Swiss cheese

Preheat oven to 375. Grease 2 dozen 1¾ inch muffin tins. Separate each roll in half and press into pan. Place one shrimp in each. Combine other ingredients, except cheese, and spoon into each tin. Slice cheese into 24 triangles and place on each quiche. Bake for 20 minutes.

Note: After cooking, wrap in foil and freeze. To serve from freezer, bake for 10-12 minutes.

121

Vegetables

Unlike their English ancestors, the colonial Virginians had a real appreciation of vegetables and used them generously in the preparation of meals. From the Indians they developed a taste for roasted corn, succotash, pumpkins, squash, wild onions and tuckahoe roots. As a matter of fact, the Indian method of roasting green ears of corn in the husk before an open fire was so popular among the colonists that when Thomas Jefferson represented the infant government as American minister to France, he cultivated Indian corn in his Paris garden in order not to become homesick for his local favorite.

Although the very first settlers relied on daily feasts from native wild vegetables, as soon as the 1620's Virginians were boasting that their plantations were growing not only native vegetables but every kind of vegetable that was known in England—and superior to boot! And indeed, the new varieties of beans and peas, including blackeyed peas, in addition to other native and English legumes, gave the colonists a greater variety of vegetables than any other people at that time. Moreover, they found that by planting crops successively they could have many of their favorite vegetables on their tables from early spring until late fall.

At the end of the first century in the New World, one native inhabitant reported of the Virginians: "They live in so happy a climate, and have so fertile a soil, that no body is poor enough to beg, or want food, though they have abundance of people that are lazy enough to deserve it."

Although the very early cookbooks ignored vegetables except as garnishes or when included among various ingredients of other dishes, cookbooks at the end of the eighteenth century began featuring them as individual items—sometimes sprucing them up in French, Spanish, Dutch or German dress. However, many were simply "boiled with bacon in the Virginia style." Root vegetables

122

were usually boiled, drained and seasoned with a sauce or brown gravy—or else they were mashed or chopped, seasoned and then reheated. One of the local favorites, described as "tasty and delicious," was cabbage or another leafy green vegetable boiled with pork or beef.

So enamoured of vegetables were our forefathers that during the years of his presidency, Thomas Jefferson—revered patriot, statesman and gourmet— kept a careful record of the seasonable vegetables on the Washington market, and no less than 37 kinds were listed. Surprisingly, such delicacies as artichokes, mushrooms, broccoli and endive (items readily available at most American grocery stores only within the last decade) appeared frequently on the Presidential table in 1800!

Artichokes Au Gratin

20 ounces frozen artichokes,
  cooked and drained
1/2 cup Swiss cheese, grated
2 tablespoons flour
2 tablespoons butter

1/2 cup half and half
1 chicken bouillon cube dissolved in
  1/2 cup boiling water
1 tablespoon dry sherry
salt and pepper to taste

Preheat oven to 350. Place artichokes in well-greased 1½ quart baking dish, flat side up. Make white sauce from flour, butter, cream and bouillon. Blend in Swiss cheese, sherry, salt and pepper to taste. Pour over artichokes. Sprinkle remaining cheese over top. Bake for 10 minutes or until bubbly. Serves 8.

Asparagus Parmigiano

20 ounces frozen asparagus
3/4 cup sour cream
1/2 cup Parmesan cheese
2 teaspoons lemon juice

1 teaspoon salt
1/2 cup sliced almonds, toasted
dash of paprika

Cook asparagus and drain. Combine sour cream, cheese, lemon juice and salt in a saucepan. Heat slowly, but do not boil. Arrange asparagus on a platter. Top with cream sauce. Sprinkle paprika and almonds as a garnish. Serves 8.

Asparagus And Mushrooms

2 pounds fresh asparagus
6 ounces mushrooms, drained
2 tablespoons butter
3 cups white sauce

1 teaspoon chives or green onion tops
2 tablespoons pimento, finely chopped
3 hard boiled eggs, sliced
bread crumbs, buttered

Preheat oven to 350. Cut asparagus in pieces. Cook until tender and place in greased 1½-2 quart baking dish. Sauté mushrooms in butter. Combine all ingredients except crumbs and pour over asparagus. Sprinkle with crumbs. Bake for 20 minutes. Serves 8.

"A small pinch of baking soda will preserve the color of fresh vegetables."

Asparagus Vinaigrette

1-1½ pounds fresh asparagus
2 hard boiled eggs, chopped
¾ cup olive oil
¼ cup vinegar
2 tablespoons Dijon mustard
1 tablespoon chopped chives

2 tablespoons shallots or spring
    onions, minced
2 tablespoons fresh parsley, chopped
1 teaspoon fresh tarragon, chopped
    (or ½ teaspoon dried tarragon)

Cook and chill asparagus. Combine other ingredients to make sauce. Pour sauce over asparagus and serve. Serves 4-6.

"All green vegetables should be slightly crisp after cooking. Over-cooking removes sweetness and beauty."

Green Beans Julienne

1 pound fresh green beans
½ cup ham
3 tomatoes, peeled, seeded, and
    chopped

1 small clove garlic, minced and
    crushed
3-4 tablespoons butter
salt and pepper

Cook green beans; drain well. Cut ham into julienne strips. Add all ingredients to green beans. Simmer together for a few minutes until the tomatoes are somewhat reduced. Serves 4.

"Truly a gourmet treat."

Green Beans en Sauce

2 pounds canned French-style
  green beans
1/2 cup mayonnaise
1/4 cup salad oil

1 hard-boiled egg, mashed
1/4 teaspoon Worcestershire
1/4 teaspoon mustard
1/4 onion, grated

Drain beans slightly; heat to boiling. Make a sauce from other ingredients. Serve by using a heaping teaspoon of sauce over each serving of beans. Serves 8-10.

Broccoli and Celery Casserole

10 ounces frozen chopped broccoli
2 cups celery, chopped in 1/2 inch
  pieces
1/4 cup butter
1/4 cup flour

2 cups milk
1/2 teaspoon salt
1/4 teaspoon pepper
1 cup Cheddar cheese, shredded

Preheat oven to 350. Cook broccoli and drain. Cook celery in boiling, salted water until crisply tender, about 5-6 minutes. Combine the two vegetables in a buttered 1 1/2-2 quart shallow baking dish. Melt butter in saucepan, add flour and blend. Add milk, stirring constantly and cook until smooth and thickened. Add salt and pepper, pour over vegetables. Cover with cheese. Bake for 15-20 minutes or until heated through. Serves 6.
Note: Can be prepared ahead.

Broccoli and Cheese Bake

20 ounces frozen chopped broccoli
2 eggs
2 tablespoons flour

8 ounces Cheddar cheese, grated
3/4 cup cottage cheese
2 tablespoons margarine

Preheat oven to 350. Cook and drain broccoli. Beat eggs and add flour, grated cheese, cottage cheese and broccoli. Melt margarine in 1 1/2 quart casserole and add mixture. Bake for 25-30 minutes. Serves 8.
Note: Spinach may be substituted for broccoli.

Broccoli Pierre

20 ounces broccoli spears, thawed
¼ cup onion, grated
10½ ounces condensed cream of
    mushroom soup

1 cup sour cream
⅓ cup Parmesan cheese
¼ cup herb seasoned bread crumbs

Preheat oven to 350. Place UNCOOKED broccoli in a 1½ quart casserole. Mix onion, soup, sour cream and Parmesan cheese. Spread over broccoli. Top with bread crumbs. Bake for 35 minutes or until broccoli is just tender. Serves 6-8.

Broccoli with Sour Cream

20 ounces frozen broccoli
½ cup mayonnaise
½ cup sour cream

1 lemon, juiced
butter
bread crumbs

Preheat oven to 275. Cook broccoli and drain. Arrange in 1½ quart baking dish. Mix mayonnaise, sour cream and lemon juice together and cover broccoli. Cover with buttered bread crumbs. Bake for 20 minutes. Serves 6.

Hollandaise Sauce

2 egg yolks
⅓ cup cream
½ teaspoon salt

1 lemon, juiced
¼ cup butter

Place all ingredients, except butter, into a double boiler. Stir until mixture begins to thicken. Remove from heat; stir in butter. Serve on broccoli or spinach soufflé. This will not curdle and may be kept in the refrigerator. Yields ¾ cup.

Cabbage Oriental

1 pound cabbage, coarsely chopped
4 ribs celery, coarsely chopped
1 green pepper, coarsely chopped
1 large onion, cut in rings

2 tablespoons oil
3 tablespoons soy sauce
¼ teaspoon paprika

Sauté cabbage, celery, pepper and onion in oil over low heat for 10 minutes. Add soy sauce and paprika. Stir and serve. Serves 4.

Carrot Casserole

6 medium carrots
2 medium onions, chopped
4 tablespoons butter
10¾ ounces condensed cream of
    mushroom soup

salt and pepper to taste
⅓ cup bread crumbs
⅓ cup American cheese, grated

Preheat oven to 350. Wash and peel carrots. Boil in salted water until tender. Sauté onions in butter until golden. Place carrots in greased 1 quart baking dish and mash. Add onions and soup. Blend well, adding salt and pepper. Sprinkle with bread crumbs and cheese. Bake until bubbly—25 minutes. Serves 4.

Carrot Soufflé

2 pounds medium carrots
3 eggs, separated
3½ tablespoons sugar
2 teaspoons salt

2½ tablespoons unsalted butter,
    melted
1⅓ teaspoons cornstarch
¾ cup milk
¾ cup light cream

Preheat oven to 350. Cover the carrots with water and cook until tender. Let cool slightly, peel and put through food chopper or sieve. Beat eggs, yolks and whites separately, until light. Add to the carrot mixture. Add the sugar, salt and melted butter. Mix cornstarch with milk to make a paste, add cream and mix well. Fold into carrot mixture. Place in a buttered 2 quart soufflé dish and set in pan of hot water. Bake for 45 minutes or until light brown. Serves 10.

Copper Pennies

5 cups carrots, sliced and cooked
1 medium onion, chopped
1 green pepper, chopped
10¾ ounces condensed tomato soup
½ cup oil
1 cup sugar

¾ cup vinegar
1 teaspoon salt
1 teaspoon dry mustard
½ teaspoon pepper
1 teaspoon Worcestershire

Mix first 3 ingredients. Blend all other ingredients into a sauce. Pour sauce over vegetables. Place in covered jars. Refrigerate overnight. Will keep in refrigerator for 2 weeks. Yields 3 pints.
"An interesting relish. Very different."

Curried Cauliflower

1 large head cauliflower
½ teaspoon salt
10½ ounces condensed cream of
  chicken soup
1 cup Cheddar cheese, shredded

⅓ cup mayonnaise
1 teaspoon curry powder
¼ cup dried bread crumbs
2 tablespoons butter, melted

Preheat oven to 350. Break cauliflower into flowerets. Cook 10-15 minutes in boiling water; drain. Stir soup, cheese, mayonnaise, and curry powder in a 2 quart casserole. Add cauliflower and mix well. Toss bread crumbs in butter and sprinkle on top. Bake until hot and bubbly. To freeze, prepare all but bread crumbs. Thaw in refrigerator all day. Preheat oven to 350 and bake uncovered 40 minutes. Serves 8-10.
"A good party dish—the curry does not overwhelm the casserole!"

Cauliflower With Shrimp Sauce

1 medium head cauliflower
10¾ ounces condensed shrimp soup
½ cup sour cream

¼ cup slivered almonds
salt and pepper
paprika

Preheat oven to 350. Break cauliflower into flowerets and cook in small amount of boiling salted water (covered) for 10-15 minutes. Drain. Heat soup. Add sour cream and almonds to soup to make sauce. Place cauliflower in 2 quart baking dish and cover with sauce. Season with salt, pepper and paprika. Bake until bubbly. Serves 4-6.
Note: A slice of lemon or a teaspoon of vinegar added to water for boiling cauliflower will prevent discoloring.
"Mark Twain once labeled a cauliflower as a cabbage with a college education."

Celery Casserole

3-4 cups celery, cut in
  1 inch lengths
4 ounces water chestnuts,
  drained and sliced
6 ounces mushrooms,
  drained and chopped

2 ounces pimento, chopped
10¾ ounces condensed cream
  of chicken soup
bread crumbs
3 tablespoons margarine

128

Preheat oven to 350. Cook celery covered in a small amount of water for 10 minutes or until tender. Combine ingredients and place in 1½ quart baking dish. Top with crumbs and dot with margarine. Bake for 25 minutes. Serves 8. *"Good accompaniment for fowl."*

Creamed Corn

2 slices bacon	*3 tablespoons flour*
6 ears white or yellow corn	*water*
2 tablespoons sugar	*salt and pepper to taste*

Fry bacon and remove from skillet. Cut corn from cob and add the sugar to the corn. Scrape the cob to get all the milk. Add corn to skillet which contains drippings. Mix the flour with approximately ½ cup water to make a thin paste. Fill the cup with water to make 1 cup; add to corn and stir while it thickens and cooks. Cook 10-15 minutes. Serve with fresh butter beans. Serves 4-6.

"Don't add salt to water when cooking corn, it toughens it! Add salt when serving."

Eggplant Casserole

1 medium eggplant	*1 cup Cheddar cheese, coarsely grated*
½ cup onion, chopped	*½ cup croutons, chopped*
¼ cup green pepper, chopped	*8 saltine crackers*
3-4 tablespoons butter	*2-3 tablespoons butter*
½ teaspoon salt	*1 cup ripe olives (optional)*
⅛ teaspoon pepper	

Preheat oven to 350. Peel eggplant and cut in 1 inch cubes; boil in ¾ cup water and ¼ teaspoon salt until tender. DO NOT OVERCOOK. Sauté onions and green pepper in butter over low heat until tender. Stir in remaining salt, pepper, cheese and croutons. Remove from heat immediately. Add drained eggplant. Put mixture in buttered 1-1½ quart baking dish. Sauté crumbled crackers in butter, coating well. Place on top of casserole. Bake until bubbling hot, about 25 minutes. Serves 6.

Stuffed Eggplant

(Courtesy of Merrifield Farms)

1 medium eggplant	*2 eggs*
1 tablespoon shortening	*salt and pepper to taste*
1 small onion, chopped	*1 cup cracker crumbs*
1½ cups canned tomatoes	*Holland Rusk crumbs*
2 ribs celery, chopped	*1 tablespoon butter*

Scoop out eggplant. Soak pulp in salted water 2 hours. Drain and boil in fresh water until tender. Put through ricer. Melt shortening in 1½ quart saucepan. Add eggplant and onion. Cook about 5 minutes. Add tomatoes, celery, eggs, salt, pepper and cracker crumbs. Cook until dry. Stuff eggplant. Cover with Holland Rusk crumbs. Dot with butter and bake at 350 until brown.

"Serve one hot vegetable dish with a cold summer dinner."

Italian Eggplant

2 medium eggplants	*½ teaspoon celery salt*
salt	*1 bay leaf*
1 cup flour	*1 teaspoon dried basil, crumbled*
1 cup olive oil	*1 teaspoon salt*
1 tablespoon butter or margarine	*dash of pepper*
2 cloves garlic, minced	*½ teaspoon sugar*
2 cans (1 lb, 12 oz each) tomatoes,	*½ cup dried bread crumbs*
coarsely chopped	*½ cup Parmesan cheese, grated*

Peel eggplant, cut in 1 inch cubes. Sprinkle with salt and let stand at room temperature for 30 minutes. Drain, dry with paper towels; sprinkle with flour. Toss to coat eggplant lightly. Heat oil in large skillet, add eggplant. Sauté 3-4 minutes. (Divide eggplant and oil; do half at a time if necessary.) Melt butter in skillet over medium heat. Sauté garlic 1 minute. Add tomatoes, celery salt, bay leaf, basil, salt, pepper and sugar. Bring to boiling. Reduce heat; simmer uncovered 10-12 minutes. Preheat oven to 400. Place eggplant in buttered 2-2½ quart baking dish. Pour tomato mixture over eggplant. Sprinkle with combined crumbs and cheese. Bake 25 minutes. Serves 8.

Merrifield Farms

Dating to approximately 1740, Merrifield was built on land granted from the King of England to the Poague family. The original house burned and another home was later built by Robert Poague. The home was restored in 1928 and the land served for some time as a horse farm. The farm was purchased by Mr. and Mrs. Edward Monroe Bonfoey in 1948. A wing was added to the structure, and the family completely refurbished this lovely house in Staunton.

131

Mushroom Soufflé

2 pounds fresh mushrooms, chopped
 and sautéed in ½ cup butter
2 tablespoons butter
2 tablespoons flour

½ cup light cream
3 eggs, separated
salt and white pepper

Preheat oven to 350. Sauté mushrooms 5 minutes; drain and reserve juice. Make a roux of 2 tablespoons of butter, flour, mushroom juice and cream. Cool sauce and add mushrooms. Beat egg yolks and add to mushroom mixture. Add salt and pepper to taste. Beat egg whites until stiff and fold into mushroom mixture. Place in buttered 1 quart casserole or soufflé dish and set in a pan of water. Bake for 30 minutes or until set. Serve immediately. Serves 4-6.

"To prevent a rubbery taste in white sauces, always bubble flour and butter at least one minute before adding milk. Always stir with a wooden spoon."

Williamsburg Style Creamed Onions

15½ ounces canned medium white
 onions
10¾ ounces condensed cream of
 celery soup

chopped peanuts
buttered bread crumbs

Heat thoroughly onions and soup. Garnish lavishly with chopped peanuts and bread crumbs. Serves 4.
"This is a simple variation of a popular old Williamsburg vegetable dish."

Peas And Celery

2 tablespoons butter
½ cup celery, bias-cut
3 ounces canned mushrooms
2 tablespoons pimento, chopped
2 tablespoons onion, finely chopped

½ teaspoon salt
¼ teaspoon savory (optional)
dash of pepper
10 ounces frozen peas, cooked

Melt butter in skillet. Add remaining ingredients except peas. Cook uncovered, stirring frequently, until celery is crisply done, about 5-7 minutes. Add peas and heat thoroughly. Serves 4.
"Thomas Jefferson prided himself on the many varieties of fine peas grown in his garden."

Company Peas

⅓ cup onion, chopped
2 tablespoons butter or margarine
10 ounces frozen peas, cooked
* and drained*
1 teaspoon sugar

3 ounces canned broiled mushrooms,
* sliced and drained*
dash of thyme
½ teaspoon salt
dash of pepper

Cook onions in butter until tender but not brown; stir in remaining ingredients. Season with salt and pepper. Cover and cook over low heat until warm. Serves 4.

Potatoes Au Gratin

4 baking potatoes
2 tablespoons butter or margarine
1½ teaspoons salt
½ teaspoon Worcestershire
dash black pepper

½ cup sharp Cheddar cheese, shredded
2 tablespoons parsley, chopped
¼ cup onion, chopped
½ cup half and half

Preheat oven to 350. Peel potatoes and cut length-wise in ¼ inch slices. Place potatoes on large sheet of heavy-duty foil. Dot with butter, sprinkle with remaining ingredients, except cream. Turn edge of foil up to form a container. Pour cream over potatoes. Fold foil carefully and seal. Bake for 1 hour or until tender. Serves 6.

Note: Small packets may be cooked on a grill for approximately 45 minutes.
         Turn several times.

"Easy and delicious."

Creamy Stuffed Potatoes

6 medium baking potatoes
2½ ounces Parmesan cheese, grated
½ cup butter, softened
1 tablespoon onion, grated

¼ cup evaporated milk
1 cup bread crumbs
4 teaspoons chopped chives

Preheat oven to 400. Bake potatoes until soft. Cut in half lengthwise. Scoop out potatoes in mixing bowl. Add remaining ingredients. Beat until mixed. Refill potato skins or foil potato holders. Reheat under broiler. Serves 6 or 12.

Note: Can be completely prepared and frozen. To serve, thaw in 350 oven
         for 30-40 minutes.

Baked Potato Dressing

½ cup butter, softened
1 cup American cheese, shredded

½ cup sour cream
2 tablespoons green onions, chopped

Mix ingredients with electric mixer. May be made ahead of time and stored in the refrigerator. If kept in the refrigerator allow to reach room temperature before serving. Serve on baked potatoes. Serves 6.
Note: Also delicious topping for green vegetables.
"Makes a baked potato a company special."

Stuffed Baked Potatoes

6 potatoes
1½ cups sour cream
6 tablespoons butter
2 tablespoons chives

1 egg (optional)
salt and pepper
10 slices bacon, cooked and
*   crumbled*

Bake potatoes. Cut in half and scoop out potatoes. Mash with other ingredients except bacon. Restuff potatoes. Add bacon. Heat on baking sheet in oven for several minutes. Serves 12.
Note: Prepare ahead of time and chill or wrap in foil to freeze. Bake at 400 to serve.

Curried Rice Indienne

2 tablespoons butter, divided
1 teaspoon curry powder
1 cup rice
2 cups chicken broth
⅔ cup seedless raisins
⅓ cup green onion, chopped
⅓ cup green pepper, chopped

⅓ cup celery, chopped
½ teaspoon seasoned salt
1 tablespoon chutney
2 tablespoons pimento, chopped
2 tablespoons pine nuts (optional)
1 tablespoon vinegar
1 tablespoon brown sugar

Combine 1 tablespoon butter with curry powder and rice. Cook, stirring over low heat 5 minutes. Add chicken broth and heat to boiling. Stir; cover tightly, and cook over low heat about 15 minutes or until liquid is absorbed. Meanwhile, sauté raisins, onions, green pepper and celery in remaining butter until soft. Add remaining ingredients, and toss lightly together. Pile hot rice on serving platter and spoon raisin mixture over top. Serves 4-6.

Gourmet Rice

1 cup rice
2 cups water
3 chicken bouillon cubes
1 teaspoon salt
1/2 cup green onion, chopped

1/2 green pepper, chopped
1/4 cup butter or margarine
3 tablespoons pimento, chopped
1/2 cup ripe olives, sliced

Cook first 4 ingredients until liquid is absorbed, about 25 minutes. Sauté onions and pepper in butter until tender, but not browned. Add to rice along with pimento and olives. Serves 4-6.

Browned Rice With Peas

1 cup rice
2 1/2 cups boiling water
1/2 cup butter
1/4 cup onions, chopped
1/4 cup sliced mushrooms, drained

10 ounces frozen peas, thawed
8 ounces canned water chestnuts,
   drained and diced
3 tablespoons soy sauce

Preheat oven to 350. In dry skillet, brown rice, stirring often. Turn into a 1 1/2 quart casserole; add water and stir with fork to separate grains. Cover and bake for 30 minutes or until rice is tender. Meanwhile in skillet, over low heat, melt butter, add onion and mushrooms and sauté. Remove from heat; add peas, chestnuts and soy sauce. Add to rice and blend gently. Bake uncovered for 15 minutes. Serves 8.

Hint: Add 1 tablespoon oil, butter or margarine to rice before boiling to make grains separate and rice will never stick to pan.

Spinach Casserole

3 eggs
2 tablespoons flour
10 ounces chopped spinach

2 tablespoons margarine
4 ounces cottage cheese
6 ounces Cheddar cheese, grated

Preheat oven to 350. Beat eggs and flour until smooth. Cook and drain spinach. Add all ingredients to egg mixture and stir. Melt margarine in 10 inch square pan. Pour mixture in; bake 30 minutes. Let set after baking for about 10 minutes. Serves 6.

Note: May be made a day ahead and cooked at serving time. Broccoli may be substituted for spinach.

Spinach And Mushroom Casserole

2 pounds fresh spinach or	2 teaspoons salt
20 ounces frozen spinach	1/4 teaspoon white pepper
3 tablespoons butter	1/4 teaspoon nutmeg
3 tablespoons onion, grated	2 cups light cream
1 pound mushrooms, chopped	4 tablespoons Swiss cheese, grated
3 tablespoons flour	

Preheat oven to 325. Wash fresh spinach, drain well and chop coarsely, or drain frozen spinach very well after thawing. Melt butter in saucepan, sauté onion and mushrooms for 5 minutes. Blend in flour, salt, pepper and nutmeg. Add cream gradually, stirring steadily to boiling point; cook over low heat 5 minutes. Arrange successive layers of spinach and sauce in a buttered 1½ quart casserole ending with sauce. Sprinkle with cheese. Place in a shallow pan of hot water. Bake for 45 minutes. Serves 4-6.
"Attractive and flavorful."

"When substituting canned mushrooms for fresh sautéed ones, the contents of one six ounce can is equivalent to one pound of fresh cooked mushrooms."

Spinach Stuffed Onions

3 ounces cream cheese, softened	1/4 teaspoon salt
1 egg	dash of pepper
1/2 cup soft bread crumbs	16 ounces chopped spinach,
1/4 cup Parmesan cheese, grated	cooked and well-drained
1/4 cup milk	1 large onion

Preheat oven to 350. Beat together cream cheese and egg until light. Add crumbs, cheese, milk, salt and pepper; mix well. Stir in spinach. Peel onion and cut in half crosswise. Separate layers and form shells. Place in shallow 1½ quart baking dish. Fill base of shells with smaller onion pieces, if necessary. Spoon spinach mixture in onion shells. Cover with foil and bake for 35-40 minutes or until onion shells are tender and filling is set. Serves 4-6.

Note: Use 2 onions for more uniform cases. Remove the odor from hands by rubbing with salt, lemon or celery salt.

Spinach Soufflé

1/4 cup onion, chopped
1 tablespoon butter
3 eggs, separated
white sauce

1 cup chopped spinach,
  cooked and drained
1/2 cup Parmesan cheese, grated

Preheat oven to 350. Sauté onion in butter. Beat egg yolks until thick and lemon-colored. Stir into hot white sauce along with spinach and cheese. Fold in egg whites beaten until stiff, not dry, peaks are formed; turn into greased 1½ quart casserole. Set in pan of hot water and bake about 50 minutes. Serve at once. Serves 6.

White Sauce:

2 tablespoons butter
2 tablespoons flour
1 cup milk or light cream

1/2 teaspoon salt
1/8 teaspoon pepper

Melt butter, stir in flour and heat until bubbly. Gradually add milk or cream, stirring constantly; cook 1-2 minutes. Season with salt and pepper. Makes about 1 cup sauce.

Baked Stuffed Squash

4 large squash (summer yellow or
  zucchini)
Mixed Vegetable Stuffing

salt
pepper

Preheat oven to 350. Scrub squash. Cut in half lengthwise. Drop halves in slightly salted boiling water. Boil 5 minutes, drain. With teaspoon scrape out seeds and pulp. Sprinkle with salt and pepper. Fill with stuffing. Bake 20 minutes in a buttered baking dish. Serves 8.

Mixed Vegetable Stuffing:

10 ounces frozen mixed vegetables
1 clove garlic, crushed
1/2 teaspoon salt
1/2 teaspoon pepper

1 cup fresh tomatoes, chopped
  and peeled
2 cups herb-seasoned bread stuffing
1/2 cup sharp cheese, grated

Cook vegetables, adding garlic, salt and pepper. Drain. Add tomatoes and stuffing. Mix well. Spoon into squash. Sprinkle with cheese. Yields 4 cups.
"A real show stopper! Absolutely delicious!"

137

Zucchini Squash Casserole
(Courtesy of Berkeley)

10 zucchini squash	*½ teaspoon salt*
½ cup butter	*¼ cup chives*
¾ cup Cheddar cheese	*½ teaspoon paprika*
¼ cup Gruyère cheese	*1 cup crumbs*
1 cup sour cream	*Parmesan cheese*

Preheat oven to 350. Slice zucchini in hunks. Cook for a few minutes in boiling salted water. Drain thoroughly. Make a sauce from the butter, Cheddar cheese, Gruyere, sour cream, salt, chives and paprika. Put squash in a 3 quart casserole dish. Pour sauce over the top. Sprinkle crumbs on this. Dot with butter. Grate Parmesan cheese over the crumbs. Bake until heated through. Serves 8.

Garden Vegetable Casserole

3 yellow squash, sliced	*2 small onions, sliced thinly*
3 tomatoes, peeled and quartered	*⅓ cup instant rice*
1 green pepper, cut in strips	*butter, salt and pepper*

Preheat oven to 350. Alternate layers of vegetable mixture, pats of butter, salt and pepper and rice. Bake in covered 2 quart casserole for 1 hour. Serves 4-6.
Note: This is better with fresh vegetables.

Zucchini Casserole

1 cup red onion rings	*4 tomatoes, peeled and*
1 cup green pepper rings	*cut in wedges*
¼ cup butter	*salt and pepper*
2 cups zucchini, cut in	*Parmesan cheese*
1 inch slices	

Preheat oven to 375. Sauté onion and green pepper in butter. When vegetables wilt, add zucchini and sauté about 5 minutes longer. Add tomatoes and cook until soft (about 5 minutes). Season with salt and pepper. Turn vegetables into a 1 quart baking dish and sprinkle with Parmesan cheese. Just before serving time, bake until topping browns and vegetables are hot. Serves 6.
"A lovely summer dish."

Berkeley

Most historic of all the beautiful James River plantations, Berkeley was the site of the first official Thanksgiving in 1619. The Georgian mansion, which is reputed to be the oldest three-story brick house in Virginia, was built in 1726 by Benjamin Harrison, whose family later produced two Presidents of the United States. Its heritage is enhanced by the fact that it served as a headquarters for General McClellan at one point during the War Between the States; and in 1862, "Taps" was composed there. A beautifully restored example of Virginia's "Golden Age", Berkeley is superbly furnished and graced by handsome, terraced boxwood gardens.

Summer Squash

3 cups summer squash,
    scrubbed and diced
1/4 cup sour cream
1 tablespoon butter
1 tablespoon sharp cheese, grated

1/2 teaspoon salt
1/8 teaspoon paprika
egg yolk, beaten
1 tablespoon chives, chopped
bread crumbs

Preheat oven to 375. Simmer squash in small amount of water until squash is tender. Drain. In saucepan, place next five ingredients. Stir over low heat until cheese melts. Remove from heat and add egg yolk and chives. Add squash and place mixture in 1 quart baking dish. Top with bread crumbs. Heat for 15 minutes or until heated thoroughly. Serves 6.

Hint: Squash stored in a cool dry place (60°F) may be held several months.

Yellow Squash Casserole

2 1/2 pounds yellow squash
1 large carrot, grated
2 teaspoons pimento
1 cup cream of chicken soup

1/2 pint sour cream
salt and pepper
1/2 cup margarine
8 ounces crumb-type herb stuffing mix

Preheat oven to 375. Boil, drain, cool squash. Mix in carrot, pimento, soup and sour cream. Add pinch of salt and pepper. Melt margarine and mix with stuffing. Place half of mixture in bottom of 2 quart casserole. Add squash mixture. Top with rest of stuffing. Bake for 30 minutes. May be frozen. Serves 8.

"Astoundingly delicious! Great for those who profess no love of squash!"

Bourbon Sweet Potatoes

4 pounds sweet potatoes
1/2 cup butter, softened
1/2 cup bourbon
1/3 cup orange juice

1/4 cup light brown sugar, packed
1 teaspoon salt
1/2 teaspoon apple pie spice
1/3 cup pecans, chopped

Preheat oven to 350. Scrub potatoes and cook in salted boiling water in large saucepan until tender. Peel and mash potatoes; add remaining ingredients except pecans. Beat until well mixed. Place in greased 9x12 baking dish. Sprinkle with pecans. Bake for 45 minutes. Serves 8.

"Great holiday dish—smells yummy."

Sweet Potato Soufflé

6 cups sweet potatoes, cooked
   and mashed
1 cup brown sugar
1/4 cup butter

1/8 teaspoon nutmeg
pinch of salt
3 eggs
1/2 teaspoon vanilla

Preheat oven to 400. Combine all ingredients in large bowl and mix well. Pour into lightly buttered 2 quart casserole. Bake until light brown. Serves 8.

Note: May be placed in an orange half and baked in same manner with marshmallows on top.

"Sweet potatoes stored at cool room temperature may be held several months."

Sweet Potato Pudding

1 can (1 lb, 13 oz) sweet potatoes,
   drained and finely mashed
1/2 cup margarine, melted
1 cup sugar
1/2 cup milk

1 egg, beaten
3/4 teaspoon cinnamon
1/4 teaspoon cloves
1/4 teaspoon nutmeg

Preheat oven to 350. Stir all ingredients together except nutmeg, mixing thoroughly. Pour into buttered 2½ quart casserole; sprinkle with nutmeg. Bake 45 minutes. Serves 6.

Note: This can be a vegetable or a dessert topped with meringue.

Candied Yams

2 large sweet potatoes
1 cup sugar
1 teaspoon cinnamon
1 teaspoon nutmeg

1 teaspoon ginger
1/2 cup water
1 teaspoon lemon juice
1/4 cup butter, sliced

Boil sweet potatoes until tender and remove skins. Mix sugar, cinnamon, nutmeg and ginger; add water. Quarter the potatoes and put them in a heavy skillet. Pour sugar mixture plus lemon juice over potatoes and top with butter. Cook over low heat, turning several times. Cook 20-30 minutes. May freeze. Serves 3-4.

"Easy, economical and good!"

141

Baked Tomatoes

6 tomatoes
½ cup fresh bread crumbs
2 tablespoons butter, melted
several sprigs parsley, chopped

1 teaspoon basil
salt to taste
sesame seeds

Preheat oven to 350. Core tomatoes and slice horizontally. In a bowl, mix together the next 5 ingredients. Spread the mixture on top of the tomato halves and sprinkle with a generous coating of sesame seeds. Bake for 15 minutes. Serves 6-12.

"Peel and freeze summer tomatoes to use in winter soups and stews."

Tomatoes Stuffed With Broccoli

10-12 small tomatoes
salt to taste
2 tablespoons onion, grated
4 tablespoons butter

10 ounces chopped broccoli, cooked
    and drained
¼ cup sharp cheese, grated
10-12 slices sharp cheese

Preheat oven to 350. Slice tomatoes in half, remove stems and arrange in baking dish, cut side up. Salt generously. Sauté onion in butter. Mix broccoli, onion and grated cheese. Mound broccoli on top of tomatoes. Top with a slice of sharp cheese. Bake for 20 minutes, but watch carefully. Serves 10-12.

Rice Stuffed Tomatoes

6 large, firm ripe tomatoes
¼ cup onion, minced
2 tablespoons butter
½ cup milk
2 cups sharp cheese, grated

2 cups rice, cooked
1 teaspoon salt
¼ teaspoon marjoram
½ teaspoon oregano
¼ cup bread crumbs, buttered

Preheat oven to 350. Cut a slice from top of each tomato and scoop out center. Invert and drain 15 minutes. Cook onions in butter until soft; add milk and heat thoroughly. Remove from heat. Add cheese, rice and seasonings. Toss lightly until cheese is melted. Fill tomatoes with cheese-rice mixture. Sprinkle top with crumbs. Place in rectangular baking pan that has ½ inch of water in bottom. Bake 30 minutes. Serves 6.
Note: Goes well with tossed green salad and hot muffins.

The Gracious Virginia Hostess Would:

. . . sprinkle canned asparagus with Parmesan cheese; top with butter and broil golden brown to serve immediately.

. . . brush tomato halves with butter; sprinkle with salt, pepper, curry powder or basil; wrap in foil and bake at the edge of a hot grill about 10 minutes for a luscious outdoor vegetable.

. . . combine petite green peas, canned broiled mushrooms, cracked pepper, crumbled bacon and butter pats to heat in a 325 oven for a great buffet dish.

. . . place unpared, cooked new potatoes in a silver bowl; cover with cooked green peas; top with gobs of sour cream and cracked pepper to serve with lamb. A spring-time delight!

. . . sauté fresh cut corn in butter and sugar; add a small amount of cream or canned milk and simmer 3-5 minutes before serving.

. . . prepare sautéed squash and onions with bacon drippings and sugar and top with fresh cut corn during the last 5 minutes of cooking.

. . . peel fresh tomatoes by plunging them into boiling water for a minute; remove immediately and peel. Chill until ready to use.

. . . add a little dried red pepper when boiling cabbage for extra flavor and heartiness.

. . . sprinkle freshly ground nutmeg or chopped fresh mint over buttered peas for a delightful change of taste.

. . . top pineapple rings with a sprinkling of brown sugar, curry and butter to broil until well-browned for quick and easy curried pineapple.

. . . mix hot, buttered rice with raisins and curry for a pleasant accompaniment for lamb, veal or chicken.

. . . combine cooked broccoli, cauliflower and brussel sprouts in a large casserole; top with white sauce and cover with sharp cheese to bake until bubbly for a buffet supper.

. . . add onion and thyme to her favorite scalloped potato recipe and bake with pork chops on top.

. . . reheat baked potatoes by dipping in HOT water and baking again in a moderate oven.

. . . toss cut okra in corn meal, salt and pepper to fry in hot oil for a crunchy dish.

Salads

Nature's bounty from spring to fall generously bestowed an incredible variety of salad "pickins" upon the colonists. From thick carpets of wild flowers and weeds, they were provided with herbs, violets, primroses, marigolds, greens and onions; and from the farm came an assortment of vegetables and fruits. By 1620 the colonists were cultivating such salad materials as lettuce, cabbage, radishes, parsley, thyme, savory and hysop. Somewhat over a century later, in response to the great popularity of salads, Thomas Jefferson grew nineteen varieties of lettuce for salads in his garden at Monticello.

During winter months the average colonial housewife learned how to tastily convert salads from lettuce to cabbage and to substitute celery seed or vinegar for fresh celery.

Usage and knowledge of salads in the colonial menu was so commonplace that few recipes or references to them are mentioned in old cookbooks. Apparently, then as now, the list of salad materials was vast and limited only to the imagination of the cook.

More versatile than any other dish, the salad may take many forms—raw, cooked, frozen, congealed or molded. Moreover, it may be used as a first course, as the main course or as a dessert, depending on the ingredients. The most glamorous and sophisticated of the salad varieties is the molded or congealed salad, of which aspics are considered the jewel. Varieties of aspic are limitless; an aspic may be clear and simple as in tomato aspic, it may be laced with meats and/or chopped vegetables, or it may be filled with fruits.

To enhance the great diversity of flavor or flair with which a salad is blessed, the dressing is of utmost importance and is an art with which the cook bestows her own particular magic to the dish. During colonial times oil and vinegar dressings were the most commonly used, and Thomas Jefferson tried diligently, but unsuccessfully, to introduce the African benne seed into the young colony as a source of salad oil to replace the olive oil imported from Italy.

Today's homemaker has in addition to oil and vinegar dressings a sweeping assortment of bases to choose from, such as roquefort and blue cheese, marinades, sour cream and yogurt dressings, and numerous other "bonus" dressings.

Even though salads have been an important part of the meal for hundreds of years, they have only recently received their just due as a vital nutrient in our daily diet. Modern dietitians now voice the thought that "a salad a day keeps the doctor away." And, as a matter of fact, salads—especially the raw varieties—do contain mineral salts and vitamins essential to growth and physical well-being.

Orange Apricot Salad

6 ounces orange gelatin	3 cups canned crushed pineapple,
2 cups hot water	drain and reserve 1 cup juice
3 cups canned apricots, drain	1 cup combined reserved juices
and reserve 1 cup juice	(save remainder for topping)
	¾ cup miniature marshmallows

Dissolve gelatin in water. Add fruit juice and chill until it begins to congeal. Fold in fruits and marshmallows. Chill until firm and add topping.

Topping:

½ cup sugar	2 tablespoons butter
3 tablespoons flour	⅔ cup Cheddar cheese, grated
1 egg, slightly beaten	½ cup heavy cream, whipped
1 cup fruit juice	

Cook sugar, flour, egg and juice until thickened. Add butter and cheese. Cool. Fold in cream. Spread over gelatin mixture. Chill. Serves 12.

Molded Sherried Cherries

1 pound canned dark, sweet cherries,
pitted
½ cup currant jelly
¾ cup sherry

3 ounces cherry gelatin
¼ cup lemon juice
¼ cup pecans, chopped

Drain cherries, reserving ¾ cup syrup. Combine syrup, jelly and sherry. Bring just to boil. Remove from heat. Add gelatin. Dissolve completely. Add cherries and lemon juice. Chill until partially set. Add nuts. Chill in 3 cup ring mold overnight. Serves 6.

Frozen Cranberry Salad

6 ounces cream cheese, softened
2 tablespoons mayonnaise
2 tablespoons sugar
20 ounces canned crushed
pineapple, drained

1 pound whole cranberry sauce
½ cup nuts, chopped
1 pint whipping cream, whipped

Blend cheese and mayonnaise with sugar. Add fruit, nuts and cream. Pour into an 8½x4½ inch loaf pan. Freeze for 6 hours or overnight. Let stand at room temperature for 15 minutes before removing from pan. Slice and serve on lettuce. Serves 8-10.

"Cranes were a favorite meat of New England colonists. While hunting them, they noticed they fed on berries which the colonists named "Crane-berries." The term was gradually changed to cranberries."

Frosty Cranberry Tiptops

1 pound whole cranberry sauce
3 tablespoons lemon juice
1 cup heavy cream, whipped
3 ounces whipped cream cheese

¼ cup mayonnaise
¼ cup confectioners' sugar, sifted
1 cup nuts, chopped
6-8 large paper cups

Crush cranberries with fork. Add lemon juice and pour into paper cups. Combine cream, cheese, mayonnaise, sugar and nuts. Spread over cranberries and freeze. Remove cups to serve. Nestle in a bed of greens. Serves 6-8.

Governor's Mansion Cranberry Salad
(Courtesy of Mrs. Mills Godwin)

2 cups cranberries, ground
1 orange, ground with berries
2 cups sugar
6 ounces lemon gelatin

2 cups hot water
1 cup ice cubes
1 cup celery, diced
1 cup pecans, chopped

Combine ground berries and orange with sugar and let stand. Dissolve gelatin in water. Cool and then add all other ingredients. Pour into individual molds and chill. Serve with or without dressing. Serves at least 12.
Note: For variation add diced tart apples or crushed pineapple.
"Navel oranges are the best to use."

Frozen Fruit Salad

1 pound canned white cherries,
   pitted
1 pound canned pineapple chunks
2 grapefruits, sectioned
3 oranges, sectioned

1/2 cup heavy cream, whipped
1/2 cup mayonnaise
2 tablespoons boiled dressing
2 tablespoons sugar
1 lemon, juiced

Drain fruits and combine. Prepare dressing of remaining ingredients. Mix fruit with one half of the dressing. Reserve the rest to use as a topping for the salad. Place fruit mixture in 2 quart container and freeze. To serve, unmold on greens and pour rest of dressing over the top. Serves 12.
Note: Marzetti's dressing may be substituted for boiled dressing.

Boiled Dressing:

1/2 teaspoon dry mustard
3 tablespoons sugar
1 1/2 tablespoons flour
2 egg yolks

2/3 cup milk
1 cup cider vinegar
1 1/2 tablespoons salt
3 tablespoons butter

Mix mustard, sugar, flour, yolks and milk together. Stir in vinegar. Add salt and butter. Cook in double boiler, over hot water, until thickened. Stir constantly. Yields 1 cup.
Note: Use this dressing over slaw, in Waldorf salad, chicken salad, or potato salad to give it a special tang. It keeps well in the refrigerator.

147

Heavenly Cheese Mold

20 ounces crushed pineapple
6 ounces lemon gelatin
2 cups boiling water

1 cup mayonnaise
1 cup sharp Cheddar cheese, grated

Drain pineapple and reserve ¾ cup juice. Dissolve gelatin in water. Add juice. Gradually add mayonnaise. Mix well and chill until slightly thickened. Fold in pineapple and cheese. Pour into 1½ quart mold. Chill. Unmold on bed of lettuce. Serves 8.

Lemon-Lime Delight

3 ounces lime gelatin
3 ounces lemon gelatin
2 cups boiling water
20 ounces crushed pineapple
1-2 tablespoons horseradish

1 pound creamed cottage cheese
1 cup evaporated milk
1 tablespoon onion juice
1 cup mayonnaise
½ cup walnuts, chopped

Dissolve gelatins in boiling water. Chill. When partially set, add all other ingredients. Pour into 2½ quart mold. Chill until firm. Serves 16.
"For variation and color, add 1 grated carrot."

Orange Sherbet Salad

11 ounces mandarin oranges
1 cup crushed pineapple
3 ounces orange gelatin

3 ounces lemon gelatin
1 pint orange sherbet

Drain juices from fruit and add water to make 1½ cups liquid. Boil and add to gelatins to dissolve. Stir in orange sherbet. Pour into 6 cup mold. Chill until partially set, and fold in fruit. Chill until firm. Garnish with mint leaves and mayonnaise, and serve with chicken or pork. Serves 8-10.

Peach and Melon Salad

1 small cantelope, diced
2 cups peaches, peeled and sliced
¼ cup orange juice

¼ cup sliced almonds, toasted
2 tablespoons lemon juice
¼ cup sugar

Toss fruit with juices, almonds and sugar. Cover and chill at least 3 hours. Serves 6.

Strawberry Mold

6 ounces strawberry gelatin
1½ cups hot water
1 cup crushed pineapple

10 ounces frozen strawberries, thawed
8 ounces sour cream

Grease 6 cup mold lightly with mayonnaise. Dissolve gelatin in water. Add fruit. Fill half of mold with gelatin mixture. Chill until firm. Spread with sour cream and add remaining strawberry mixture. Chill. Serves 8.
Note: For variation, add sliced bananas.

Celery Seed Dressing

½ cup sugar
1 teaspoon dry mustard
1 teaspoon salt
½ small onion, grated

⅓ cup cider vinegar
1 tablespoon celery seed
1 cup salad oil

Beat until smooth. Do not use blender. Yields 1½ cups. Keeps several weeks.
"Good on fruit or avocado salads."

Fruit Salad Dressing

¼ cup pineapple juice
¼ cup orange juice
1 tablespoon lemon juice
3 tablespoons cold water

1 tablespoon cornstarch
1 egg, lightly beaten
¼ cup sugar
½ cup heavy cream, whipped

Combine juices, water and cornstarch in top of double boiler. Cook over boiling water 10 minutes, stirring constantly. Combine egg and sugar and add to cooked mixture. Cool. Fold in cream. Yields 1½ -2 cups.
Note: Prepare and use the same day.
"This dressing is excellent on fresh fruit."

Minted Mayonnaise

¾ cup mayonnaise
6 tablespoons white dinner mints,
    crushed
1½ teaspoons lemon juice

1 tablespoon cream
dash of salt
1 drop green food coloring

Combine all ingredients. Chill. Serve on any type of fresh or molded fruit salad.
Yields 1 cup.

Poppy Seed Dressing

1½ cups sugar
1 teaspoon dry mustard
1 teaspoon salt
⅔ cup white vinegar

2 tablespoons onion juice
2 cups vegetable oil
3 tablespoons poppy seeds

Mix all ingredients except oil and seeds. Add oil slowly. Add seeds and beat
well. Chill. Keep for several weeks. Yields 1 quart.
"Use with fruit salad—especially grapefruit!"

Caesar Salad

1 clove garlic
1 egg yolk, hard-boiled
1 inch square Roquefort cheese
4 anchovies
½ lemon, juiced
½ teaspoon salt

½ teaspoon pepper
¼ cup vinegar
¼ cup olive oil
1 large head romaine lettuce
½ cup croutons

Rub large salad bowl with a split garlic clove. Discard. In a small bowl, mash
the egg yolk, cheese and anchovies until pasty. Add all ingredients except lettuce and croutons. Blend until smooth. Toss with lettuce and croutons. Serves 4.

Crouton Salad

1 cup Hellmann's mayonnaise
1 tablespoon lemon juice
2 tablespoons Parmesan cheese
1 clove garlic, crushed

1 tablespoon butter
1 cup croutons
2 heads lettuce

Make dressing of mayonnaise, lemon juice, cheese and garlic. Chill. Toss croutons in butter over low heat until golden brown. Drain. Place torn lettuce in bowl; add dressing and croutons. Toss. Sprinkle with additional cheese. Serves 8.
"This is a great winter salad!"

Croutons

Stir cubed bread (preferably ends) in a bowl with melted butter. Spread on a cookie sheet, sprinkle with garlic salt, place on low oven rack; broil until brown. Cut oven off and let sit for several hours. Store in plastic containers.
"These are good even to nibble with a before-dinner drink!"

Dig Deep Salad

1 head lettuce, shredded
2 medium red onions, sliced
1-2 green peppers, sliced
3-4 ribs celery, chopped
8 ounces water chestnuts, sliced
10 ounces frozen green peas,
    uncooked

2 cups Hellmann's mayonnaise
Romano cheese
3 eggs, hard-boiled
4 strips bacon, crumbled
1-2 tomatoes, sliced

Layer first six ingredients in a serving bowl in order, beginning with lettuce. Spread mayonnaise over the top layer. Sprinkle with cheese. DO NOT STIR. Cover and refrigerate for 24 hours. 45 minutes before serving, remove from refrigerator. Garnish with sliced eggs, bacon and tomatoes. Serves 12-14.
Note: Amounts may be varied according to size bowl used.
"Be creative with this fantastic salad that is prepared 24 hours before your guests arrive! Strips of meat or cheese would make it a light supper or luncheon dish."

151

Green Salad with Hot Bacon Dressing

2 heads Boston lettuce
12 radishes, thinly sliced
10 slices bacon
2 teaspoons sugar
½ cup red wine vinegar

½ teaspoon horseradish
¼ teaspoon pepper
12 scallions, including tops,
   chopped
1 egg yolk, boiled and grated

Early in day, wash, dry, tear and crisp lettuce. Prior to serving, add radishes and allow to remain in refrigerator. Prepare dressing. Fry bacon until crisp, drain and crumble. Add sugar, vinegar, horseradish and pepper to the bacon fat in the skillet. Mix, add scallions and heat until bubbling. Pour immediately over lettuce. Toss. Top with bacon and egg yolk. Serves 8.
"Must be served immediately!"

Lettuce Salad with Sesame Seed Dressing

½ cup sesame seeds
1 tablespoon butter
¼ cup Parmesan cheese
1 cup sour cream
½ cup mayonnaise
1 tablespoon tarragon vinegar
1 tablespoon sugar

1 teaspoon salt
dash of white pepper
1 clove garlic, minced
¼ cup green pepper, chopped
¼ cup cucumber, diced
2 tablespoons onion, minced
2 heads iceberg lettuce

Sauté sesame seeds in butter until light brown. Remove from heat, cool and add cheese; reserve. Blend sour cream, mayonnaise and vinegar with all remaining ingredients except lettuce. Sprinkle torn lettuce with three-fourths of seed mixture. Toss with dressing, rest of seeds and extra cheese. Serves 8.
Note: Sesame seeds and dressing can be prepared ahead of time.

Tossed Spinach Salad

1 pound spinach
1 medium red onion, thinly sliced
2 tablespoons Parmesan cheese

2 eggs, boiled and chopped
6 slices bacon, cooked and chopped
1 cup garlic croutons

Wash spinach well, dry thoroughly, tear into small pieces and chill in plastic bags for several hours.

Dressing:

1/2 cup salad oil
1/4 cup wine vinegar

1/4 cup lemon juice
salt and pepper to taste

Prepare the dressing. Oil spinach lightly with dressing half an hour before serving. When serving, place spinach in bowl; toss with onions, cheese, eggs, bacon and dressing. Place croutons on top and serve immediately. Serves 8-10.

Spinach Salad Supreme

1 pound fresh spinach
6 strips bacon
1 teaspoon prepared mustard
1/2 teaspoon sugar
1 small onion, grated

1 tablespoon bacon drippings
1 cup mayonnaise
1/4 cup salad oil
1/4 cup vinegar
1/4 cup Parmesan cheese

Wash spinach 3 times. Dry, tear and chill for several hours. Fry bacon, reserving drippings. Make dressing by beating all other ingredients together. When serving, toss spinach with dressing, top with bacon and additional cheese.
Note: Dressing keeps well.
"All of the dressing may not be necessary for one salad."

Blue Cheese Dressing

1 pint sour cream
2 tablespoons vinegar
2-3 tablespoons mayonnaise
1 teaspoon salt
1/2 teaspoon garlic salt

1/2 teaspoon celery salt
1/2 teaspoon pepper
1/2 teaspoon paprika
4-8 ounces blue cheese

Mix all ingredients except cheese. Fold in cheese gently. Chill. Serves 8. Keeps several weeks.

Buttermilk Blue Cheese Dressing

1 cup mayonnaise
1/2 cup buttermilk
1 clove garlic, crushed

2 tablespoons lemon juice
2 tablespoons fresh parsley, minced
1/2 pound blue cheese

Mix in blender and age for 24 hours. Store in tight jar. Yields 1 pint.

Easy Blender Caesar Dressing

2 egg yolks
1 tin anchovies, diced
½ cup oil
¼ cup vinegar
1 clove garlic
½ teaspoon dry mustard

½ teaspoon salt
¼ teaspoon pepper, freshly ground
salad greens
garlic croutons
Parmesan cheese

Blend all ingredients except greens, croutons and cheese. Toss greens with dressing; top with croutons and cheese.
Note: If desired, oil from anchovies may be used for oil ingredient.
"Keeps for weeks!"

Dixie Salad Dressing

⅓ cup ketchup
⅓ cup sugar
¼ cup vinegar

½ cup vegetable oil
1 teaspoon onion, grated
1 teaspoon paprika

Mix well and chill. Serve over grapefruit, avocado, canned artichokes or green salad.
Note: Use malt vinegar in place of regular vinegar for a delicious variation of French dressing.

Green Goddess Salad Dressing
(Courtesy of Exchange)

1 clove garlic, grated
3 tablespoons anchovy, finely
   chopped or
   1 tablespoon anchovy paste
3 tablespoons olives or green onions,
   finely chopped
1 tablespoon lemon juice

3 tablespoons tarragon wine
   vinegar
½ cup sour cream
1 cup mayonnaise
⅓ cup parsley, finely chopped
salt and coarse black pepper to taste

Combine ingredients in the order given and chill thoroughly. Makes about a pint. Can be kept for 2 weeks. It is better after standing at least overnight.
Hint: A great addition to salads or broccoli!

Exchange

One of Tidewater Virginia's oldest homes, Exchange, was built in Gloucester around 1720. The gabled brick ends of the house, the number of its original dependencies, the rolling lawns, the remaining great trees and the strategic location on the North River are distinguishing characteristics of this once great plantation. It has been owned by only six families — the Andersons, Tabbs, Buckners, Dabneys, Gleysteens and presently the McKelvys.

Garlic Cheese Dressing

8 ounces sour cream
1 cup buttermilk
1/2 package blue cheese dressing mix

1/2 package garlic dressing mix
1/4 cup Italian dressing or
   salad oil

Combine and beat with mixer. Do not use blender. Serve over mixed greens, tomatoes or cucumbers. Yields 14 ounces.
Note: Keeps one week.

Sour Cream Casa Grande Dressing

2 green onions
1 cup sour cream
2 tablespoons mayonnaise

2-3 tablespoons lemon juice, fresh
1/2 cup blue cheese
salt and pepper to taste

Chop onions, including tops, very fine. Combine all ingredients and allow to ripen several hours. Serve on wedges of lettuce. Yields 1½ cups.

Roquefort Cheese Dressing

2 cups mayonnaise
1/2 cup parsley, chopped
2 cloves garlic, minced
1/2 cup onion, chopped
1 cup sour cream

2½ ounces Roquefort cheese
2 tablespoons vinegar
2 tablespoons water
2 tablespoons lemon juice

Mix well and refrigerate. Yields 1 quart.

Williamsburg Dressing

10¾ ounces condensed tomato soup
1/2 cup sugar
1½ cups salad oil
1 tablespoon Worcestershire
¾ cup vinegar

1 teaspoon dry mustard
1 teaspoon salt
1 teaspoon pepper
1 tablespoon ketchup
1 clove garlic, peeled

Mix all ingredients except garlic. Place in quart jar. Add garlic and allow to remain for 24 hours. Remove.
Note: One teaspoon of grated onion or ¼ cup sugar may be added to make a type of Persian dressing.

Chicken Cranberry Layers

1 tablespoon gelatin
1/4 cup cold water
1 pound whole cranberry sauce

9 ounces crushed pineapple
1/2 cup nuts, broken
1 tablespoon lemon juice

Soften gelatin in water. Dissolve over hot water. Add remaining ingredients. Chill until firm in 10x16 inch dish. While chilling, prepare chicken layer.

1 tablespoon gelatin
1/2 cup cold water
1 cup mayonnaise
3 tablespoons lemon juice

3/4 teaspoon salt
2 cups chicken, cooked and diced
1/2 cup celery, diced
2 tablespoons parsley, chopped

Soften gelatin in cold water. Dissolve over hot water. Blend in mayonnaise, lemon juice and salt. Add remaining ingredients. Spread over cranberry layer and chill until firm. When serving, cut into squares and garnish. Serves 8-10.

Chicken Salad Deluxe

2 1/2 cups chicken breast, cubed
1 cup celery, finely sliced
1 cup white grapes, sliced
1/2 cup sliced almonds, toasted

1 teaspoon salt
4-6 ounces mayonnaise
4 ounces heavy cream, whipped

Combine all ingredients and toss gently. Garnish with bunches of grapes and toasted almonds for a divine dish for entertaining at a buffet. Serves 6.
Note: All of the mayonnaise and cream may not be necessary. Do not drown the salad!

Chicken and Wild Rice Salad

2 cups cooked chicken, diced
6 ounces wild rice and long
   grain mixture
1/4 cup green pepper, chopped
2 tablespoons pimento, chopped

1/2 cup mayonnaise
2 tablespoons Russian dressing
1 tablespoon lemon juice
1/4 teaspoon salt
2 avocados

Cook rice, cool. Add chicken, green pepper and pimento. Combine mayonnaise, salad dressing, lemon juice and salt. Add to rice mixture and toss gently. Chill. Garnish with avocado slices. Serves 4.

157

Paella Salad

6 ounces yellow rice
2 tablespoons tarragon vinegar
1/3 cup vegetable oil
1/8 teaspoon salt
1/8 teaspoon dry mustard
1/4 teaspoon Accent
2 1/2 cups chicken, cooked and
    diced

1 tomato, peeled and chopped
1 green pepper, chopped
1/2 cup green beans, cooked
1/4 cup onion, minced
1/3 cup celery, chopped fine
1 tablespoon pimento, chopped
1 teaspoon salt

Cook rice according to package directions. Mix hot rice with vinegar, oil, 1/8 teaspoon salt, mustard and Accent. Cool at room temperature. Add remaining ingredients. Toss lightly and chill 2-3 hours. Place on lettuce. Serves 6.

Peaches 'n' Chicken Salad

1/2 cup sour cream
1/2 cup mayonnaise
1/2 teaspoon rosemary
dash of salt
dash of sugar
dash of pepper

2 cups chicken, cooked and cubed
1 cup sliced peaches, drained and
    diced
1/2 cup croutons
4 green pepper rings
peach slices

Combine all ingredients except croutons, green peppers and peach slices. Toss and chill. Just before serving fold in croutons. Spoon onto pepper rings. Garnish with peach slices. Serves 4.

Crab Louis

1 head iceberg lettuce, shredded
1 pound fresh crabmeat
1 large lemon, juiced

3/4 cup mayonnaise
3-4 tablespoons chili sauce

Make a bed of lettuce in a large salad bowl. Top lettuce with crabmeat. Cover with lemon juice. Beat mayonnaise, add chili sauce and blend well. Pour over crabmeat. Mix lettuce, crab and dressing thoroughly. Serves 4.

Crab Orientale

2 teaspoons Dijon mustard
3 tablespoons soy sauce
3 tablespoons vinegar
1/2 teaspoon Tabasco
1 cup olive oil
3 cups rice, cooked
8 ounces fresh mushrooms, sliced

1 cup water chestnuts, sliced
1 cup green pepper, chopped
3 pimentos, minced
2 cups crabmeat
1/4 cup parsley, chopped
1/2 cup chives, chopped

Make sauce of mustard, soy sauce, vinegar, Tabasco and oil in a large wooden bowl. Mix in other ingredients, chill and serve on lettuce. Garnish with tomato slices. Serves 12.
"Delightful summer luncheon dish."

Crabmeat Mousse

2 tablespoons gelatin
1/2 cup cold water
10 3/4 ounces condensed tomato soup
9 ounces cream cheese, softened
1 cup mayonnaise
1 tablespoon lemon juice

1 cup celery, chopped
2 tablespoons green pepper, chopped
2 tablespoons green onions, chopped
1/4 cup stuffed olives, chopped
13 ounces canned crabmeat

Add gelatin to cold water and soak 5 minutes. Heat soup to boiling, remove from heat, add gelatin and stir until dissolved. Cream the cheese well and gradually stir in the hot soup mixture. Stir until smooth. When almost cool, fold in mayonnaise and all other ingredients. Pour into mold and chill. Unmold on a bed of greens. Serves 10.

Crab Salad

1 pound crabmeat
1/2 cup mayonnaise
1/4 cup celery, chopped
2 tablespoons onion, chopped

2 tablespoons green pepper, chopped
2 tablespoons dill pickle, chopped
1 teaspoon Worcestershire
dash of Tabasco

Mix well and chill at least 3 hours. Serves 4.

159

Lobster Salad
(Courtesy of Brompton)

1 cup cold cooked rice
1 cup cold cooked green peas
1 cucumber, chopped
2-4 ounces pimentos, chopped
4 tomatoes, diced

French dressing
salt to taste
1-2 pounds lobster meat (or king
  crab, shrimp, or combination)
1/2-3/4 cup mayonnaise

Marinate all vegetables and rice in good French dressing several hours. Salt to taste. Just before serving, add lobster and enough mayonnaise to bind the salad. Serves 10-12.
"A marvelous summer meal!"

Curried Shrimp Salad

2 cups medium shrimp, cooked
1 cup celery, sliced
1 tablespoon onion, minced
1 1/2 tablespoons fresh lemon juice

1 teaspoon curry powder
1/2 cup mayonnaise
salt and pepper to taste
lettuce cups

Mix all ingredients. Chill well. Serve on lettuce. Best if made a day ahead using fresh steamed shrimp. Serves 6.

Shrimp and Macaroni Salad

1 cup elbow macaroni
1/2 cup sour cream
1/3 cup French dressing
3/4 teaspoon salt
1/4 teaspoon garlic salt
1/8 teaspoon seafood seasoning
dash of pepper

1/4 cup pimento, diced
16 ounces canned green peas, drained
2 cups shrimp, cooked and chilled
1/3 cup celery, chopped
1/4 cup onion, chopped
1 pound crabmeat (optional)

Cook and rinse macaroni. Mix sour cream, French dressing, salt, garlic salt, seasoning and pepper. Fold in remaining ingredients and chill. Serves 10.
Note: If crabmeat is added, salad will serve 14.

Brompton

The official residence of the President of Mary Washington College, Brompton overlooks the city of Fredericksburg from Marye's Heights. A location of two battles in the War Between the States, it is considered one of the loveliest homes on an American campus. No dates concerning Brompton are certain, but it seems quite likely that the original part of the structure was built in the eighteenth century and additions were made in stages until about 1840. Restoration of the mansion emphasized its three periods—Georgian, Federal, and Greek Revival. Today Brompton is the center of many of the College's social events and receptions for the community.

Shrimp Salad

1 pound shrimp, cooked and cleaned
1/2 cup celery, sliced
1/4 cup stuffed olives, sliced
1 teaspoon onion, minced
1/3 cup mayonnaise

1/4 cup French dressing
salt to taste
lemon to taste
1/2 cup walnuts, chopped
   (optional)

Combine all ingredients, chill and serve on greens with assorted garnishes. Serves 4.

Shrimp Rice Salad

6 large tomatoes
2 cups shrimp, cooked and cut
1 1/2 cups cooked rice
1/3 cup celery, chopped
1/4 cup ripe olives, pitted
1 tablespoon parsley, snipped
1/4 cup salad oil

2 tablespoons red wine vinegar
1 small clove garlic, minced
1/4 teaspoon dry mustard
1/4 teaspoon paprika
1/2 teaspoon salt
pepper to taste

Cut tomatoes into 6 wedges. Do not cut through base. Spread apart and scoop out pulp. Dice and drain pulp. Chill shells. Combine pulp, shrimp, rice, celery, olives and parsley. Blend remaining ingredients and toss with shrimp mixture. Add salt and pepper to taste. Chill. Just before serving, stuff shells and garnish with watercress and additional shrimp. Serves 6.

Vegamato Shrimp Salad

2 cups V-8 juice
3 ounces lemon gelatin
1/2 teaspoon salt
dash of Tabasco

1 tablespoon lemon juice
1/2 cup celery, chopped
1/2 cup cucumber, chopped
2 cups shrimp, cooked and chopped

Heat V-8 and dissolve gelatin in it. Add salt, Tabasco and lemon juice. Chill until partially set. Add rest of ingredients and pour into an oiled 6 cup mold. Chill until firm. Unmold on lettuce and serve with mayonnaise. Serves 6.

Asparagus Molded Salad

10¾ ounces condensed
  asparagus soup
3 ounces lime gelatin
8 ounces cream cheese, softened
½ cup cold water

½ cup mayonnaise
¾ cup celery, chopped
1 tablespoon onion, grated
½ cup green pepper, chopped
½ cup pecans, chopped

Heat soup to boiling. Remove from heat; add gelatin. Stir until dissolved and add cheese, mixing until melted. Add water and mayonnaise; heat until blended. Add remaining ingredients. Pour into 1½ quart mold. Chill. Garnish with asparagus spears. Serves 6-8.
Note: Best made a day ahead.

Green Bean Salad from "The Ordinary"

(Courtesy of Historic Michie Tavern Museum, Charlottesville, Virginia)

2 pounds canned cut green beans
¼ teaspoon sugar
¾ cup vinegar
¼ cup vegetable oil

1¼ tablespoons garlic salt
¼ tablespoon pepper
¾ tablespoon oregano

Rinse green beans in cold water; drain. Combine sugar, vinegar and oil, and pour over beans. Add garlic salt, pepper and oregano. Toss generously. Chill overnight. Serves 6-8.

Green Vegetable Marinade

½ cup sugar
¼-½ cup olive oil
¾ cup tarragon vinegar
8 ounces canned petite peas,
  drained
1 small onion, diced

1 pound canned French-style green
  beans, drained
1 cup celery, chopped
1 cup green pepper, chopped
1 teaspoon salt

Dissolve sugar in hot oil and vinegar. Pour over vegetables. Toss lightly and chill. Serves 10-12.
Note: At serving time you may leave in bowl or drain and serve on a bed of lettuce garnished with tomatoes.

Molded Beet Aspic

3 ounces lemon gelatin
1 ¼ cups hot water
¾ cup beet liquid
¼ teaspoon salt
2-3 tablespoons vinegar
4 drops Tabasco

1 teaspoon horseradish
1 teaspoon Worcestershire
1-1 ½ teaspoons onion, grated
1 ½ cups beets, diced
½ cup celery, diced

Dissolve gelatin in water. Mix in all ingredients except beets and celery. Chill until partially set. Add vegetables and chill until firm. Serves 6.
"Anyone who likes beets will be fond of this."

Broccoli and Egg Aspic

1 ½ tablespoons gelatin
¼ cup water
10 ¾ ounces beef consomme
10 ounces broccoli spears, frozen
4 eggs, hard-boiled

¾ cup mayonnaise
salt and pepper to taste
Tabasco to taste
vinegar to taste
lemon juice to taste

Soften gelatin in water. Heat consomme and dissolve gelatin. Cool. Oil 4 cup salad mold, and garnish bottom with broccoli flowerets, cut from broccoli spears, and 2 sliced eggs. Pour cooled gelatin mixture over eggs and flowerets just to cover. Allow to set partially. Chop remainder of broccoli and sieve 2 eggs. Combine with rest of gelatin mixture. Add mayonnaise and other ingredients. Mix and pour over chilled portion. Chill until firm. Serves 8.
"Great-looking ladies' fare."

Broccoli Vinaigrette

4 tablespoons red wine vinegar
4 tablespoons salad oil
¼ teaspoon salt
dash of pepper
2 teaspoons parsley, minced
2 teaspoons pickle, minced

2 teaspoons green pepper, minced
2 teaspoons chives, minced
1 teaspoon capers, minced
10 ounces frozen broccoli spears,
   cooked and chilled

Combine all ingredients except broccoli. Shake and pour over broccoli.
"Excellent to prepare ahead; a favorite with broccoli lovers!"

Layered Cole Slaw

1 large cabbage
1 large onion
1 green pepper
1 cup sugar
¾ cup oil

1 cup vinegar
1 teaspoon dry mustard
1 teaspoon celery seed
1 tablespoon salt

Shred in order listed. DO NOT STIR. Pour sugar over this. DO NOT STIR. Combine remainder of ingredients and bring to boiling point. Pour over cabbage while hot. DO NOT STIR. Refrigerate at least overnight. Serves 10.
"This delicious slaw keeps 2-3 days."

Cucumber Molded Salad

3 ounces lime gelatin
¾ cup hot water
6 ounces cream cheese, softened
1 cup Miracle Whip
1 teaspoon horseradish
¼ teaspoon salt

1 lemon, juiced
¾ cup unpared cucumber, grated,
  drained
¼ cup green onions with tops,
  sliced fine

Dissolve gelatin in hot water. Add cheese, Miracle Whip, horseradish and salt. Beat until smooth with mixer. Add lemon juice. Chill until partially set. Stir in cucumber and onion. Pour into 4 cup mold, lightly greased with mayonnaise. Serves 4-6.
"Marvelous summer salad to accompany barbecued chicken. Men love it!"

Cucumbers and Sour Cream

2 cucumbers, peeled and thinly
  sliced
1 small onion, thinly sliced
½ cup white vinegar

salt and pepper to taste
2 tablespoons sugar
8 ounces sour cream

Place cucumbers and onions in shallow dish. Cover with vinegar, salt, pepper and sugar. Chill overnight. Next day, drain well and mix with sour cream. Chill.
"Tasty side dish for cookouts."

German Potato Salad

12 medium potatoes
2 teaspoons salt
pepper to taste
2 onions, chopped
12 slices bacon

2 tablespoons flour
1 cup water
1 cup vinegar
2 tablespoons sugar

Cook potatoes in skins. When tender, drain, peel and cube. Season with salt, pepper and onion. Set aside. Dice bacon and fry until crisp. Reserve 3 tablespoons drippings, pour off rest. Stir flour into reserved drippings, stirring constantly for 1-2 minutes. Add water, vinegar and sugar. Cook until mixture bubbles. Pour over potatoes and toss gently. Serve immediately. Serves 10.

Sauerkraut Salad

27 ounces canned sauerkraut
1 cup celery, chopped
1 cup green pepper, chopped
1/4 cup onion, chopped

1/2 cup salad oil
1 cup sugar
1/4 cup cider vinegar
1/2 teaspoon salt

Drain sauerkraut. DO NOT RINSE! Mix vegetables. Prepare dressing of the remaining ingredients. Pour over vegetables, cover and chill for several hours. Serves 8-10.
"Especially good with hot dogs."

Tomato Aspic

5 tablespoons gelatin
1 1/2 cups water
1 cup sugar
2 teaspoons salt
4 cups tomato juice
1 cup vinegar

2 teaspoons Worcestershire
4 tablespoons onion, minced
2 cups cabbage, shredded
2 cups celery, chopped
1 cup carrots, shredded

Dissolve gelatin in water. Add sugar, salt, boiling tomato juice, vinegar and Worcestershire. Mix well and add vegetables. Pour into 3 quart mold and chill. Serves 18-24.
"Great to serve with seafood."

Tomato Aspic for Four

1 tablespoon gelatin
2 teaspoons sugar
14 ounces V-8 juice
¼ teaspoon salt
½ teaspoon Worcestershire
2 tablespoons lemon juice

¼ cup stuffed olives, diced
⅓ cup celery, diced
4 ounces whipped cream cheese
  with chives
1 tablespoon mayonnaise
lettuce leaves

Mix gelatin and sugar in small saucepan. Slowly add half of V-8 juice, stirring well. Cook over medium heat, stirring constantly, until gelatin dissolves. Remove from heat, and stir in rest of V-8 juice, salt, Worcestershire, lemon juice, olives and celery. Fill four custard cups and chill until firm. Make dressing of cream cheese and mayonnaise. Chill. To serve, remove aspic from cups, place on lettuce and cover with dressing. Serves 4.

Tomato Aspic with Stuffed Artichokes

48 ounces tomato juice
3 bay leaves
3-4 celery tops
¼ small onion
3¼ tablespoons gelatin, softened
1 small onion, grated
1 tablespoon Worcestershire
3-4 shakes of Tabasco

1½ lemons, juiced
1 teaspoon horseradish
3 tablespoons cider vinegar
14 ounces canned artichokes, drained
3 ounces cream cheese, softened
1-2 teaspoons mayonnaise
½ teaspoon horseradish
½ cup chopped pecans

Heat one cup of tomato juice with the bay leaves, celery tops and the piece of onion. Simmer 5 minutes and strain. Dissolve gelatin in heated tomato juice. Add onion, Worcestershire, Tabasco, lemon juice, horseradish and vinegar. Pour enough of mixture into a 2 quart mold to cover bottom 1 inch deep. Chill until almost set and place stuffed artichokes into the partially congealed aspic. Chill to firm. Add rest of mixture to cover. Serves 12.

To stuff artichokes—mix cream cheese, mayonnaise, horseradish and pecans into a paste. Push finger into center of artichoke to make space for filling. Stuff and close.
"Absolutely elegant for a dinner party. Each guest finds an artichoke concealed in his salad."

Fire and Ice Tomatoes

6 large tomatoes, peeled and
   quartered
1 green pepper, sliced in strips
1 red onion, sliced in strips
1 large cucumber, peeled and sliced
¾ cup vinegar
1½ teaspoons celery salt

½ teaspoon salt
4½ teaspoons sugar
⅛ teaspoon pepper
⅛ teaspoon red pepper
¼ cup cold water
1½ teaspoons mustard seed

Place all vegetables, except cucumbers, in bowl. Prepare dressing by combining all other ingredients in saucepan and boiling for 1 minute. While hot pour over vegetables in bowl. Let stand until cool. Just before serving, add cucumber. Serves 6.

Note: 1½ teaspoons prepared mustard may be substituted for the mustard seed, red pepper and water.

"In the eighteenth century, tomatoes were called 'love apples.' They were considered poisonous and thus not a part of the diet."

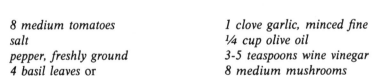

Marinated Tomatoes and Mushrooms

8 medium tomatoes
salt
pepper, freshly ground
4 basil leaves or
   ½ teaspoon dried basil, crumbled

1 clove garlic, minced fine
¼ cup olive oil
3-5 teaspoons wine vinegar
8 medium mushrooms
black olives

Peel and slice tomatoes. Sprinkle with salt, pepper and basil. Add garlic to oil. Drizzle half of the oil over tomatoes. Sprinkle sparingly with 1-2 teaspoons vinegar. Rinse mushrooms. Do not remove stems. Slice lengthwise. Arrange over tomatoes. Season with salt, pepper, and remainder of oil. Sprinkle with remainder of vinegar. Cover with plastic wrap and chill well. Garnish with black olives. Serves 10.

"Guaranteed to bring raves from men and women at any summer party!"

The Gracious Virginia Hostess Would:

. . . combine fresh spinach, mandarin oranges, sliced red onions and creamy French dressing for a delightful taste treat.

. . . toss lettuce, fresh cauliflower, olives, onions and blue cheese with oil and vinegar for a spicy salad.

. . . add thinly sliced, unpared, raw zucchini or broccoli stems and capers to a green salad and dress with Italian dressing.

. . . mix a cup each of mayonnaise and sour cream with gobs of lemon-pepper seasoning to make a superb dressing for lettuce, tomatoes, grated cheese, chopped egg and croutons. A meal in itself!

. . . stuff canned pears with a mixture of cream cheese, pear juice and pecans, and serve on lettuce.

. . . always wash, dry and chill lettuce ahead of time for extra crunchy salads. Never cut lettuce; always tear gently!

. . . combine crabmeat, celery, mayonnaise, salt, pepper and grapefruit sections for an English treat.

. . . add lemon juice and nutmeg to her homemade chicken salad.

. . . make a luncheon treat of cooked peas, diced Cheddar cheese, minced onion, mayonnaise, lemon, salt and pepper.

. . . make a salad of lettuce, tomatoes, avocados and sliced hard-boiled eggs tossed with Miracle Whip, salt and cracked pepper for a summer delight!

. . . always have a shaker of Parmesan cheese to shake on top of most any salad for looks and good taste.

. . . make her own croutons from stale French bread sautéed in garlic butter, dried in a slow oven and stored in a glass jar.

. . . serve cold asparagus on a bed of lettuce topped with mayonnaise and lemon juice and garnished with pimento strips.

. . . entertain casually in the summer with an extensive chef's salad bar and allow guests to concoct their own.

. . . frost grapes with slightly beaten egg white, sprinkle with sugar, and let dry on rack to use as a salad garnish.

. . . serve fruit salads from melon bowls or pineapple boats.

Breads

For centuries bread has been called the staff of life, and so it was in early Virginia. The grain upon which Southern cooking rests is corn, a New World grain which was grown by the Indians and called maize. No matter what the Indian dialect, the word for corn translated to mean "Our Life," and the plant was considered by some prehistoric people to be sacred.

Immediately the settlers adapted corn meal to suit their needs, and since then the frequent use of corn meal in breads along with hominy (grits), rice and other cereals in the Southern diet has helped to offset any dietary deficiencies associated with general use of pastry flours.

Numerous breads can be produced from corn meal. The corn pone (from the Indian word appone) of the settlers was baked Indian-fashion before the fire; ashcake, baked on the hearth and slightly dried, was covered with ashes and left until well done; and hoecake was simply baked on the blade of a hoe, inserted into the fireplace. These breads became the "constant bread" of the slaves and poorer people.

Another popular by-product of corn meal is a bread known as "hush puppies," made by putting corn bread batter into deep fat. This was first used to quiet the barking puppies, hence the name. Corn dodgers, eaten daily by George Washington, were pone-shaped corn sticks so hard that if thrown when first baked, they had best be dodged! Cracklin' bread, made with the crisp pieces of pork remaining after lard had been made, is another variation of the pone.

During the latter seventeenth and eighteenth centuries many excellent breads such as batter bread, egg bread and corn bread were developed. One of the most outstanding of these originating from Indian porridge is spoon bread, which is still a favorite in Southern households.

In the latter part of the eighteenth century wheat flour became the leading product of Virginia, and by the nineteenth century flour-milling had become such a large-scale industry in the state that Richmond was known as the flour capital of the nation. From wheat flour, the Virginia cook created a variety of products. A favorite of these was salt rising bread, created when homemade yeasts were unreliable and difficult to prepare and keep. Likewise, no breakfast or tea table in olden Virginia was complete without beaten biscuit. French rolls, buns, rusks, muffins and the incomparable Sally Lunn are also part of the fine heritage of Virginia cookery.

Before a Harvard professor invented baking powder in the 1850's, lightness in bread was gained only by beating air into the dough along with eggs or by adding yeast, spirits or an American product known as pearlash. Today, with reliable baking powder, dependable yeasts and accurate modern ovens, breadmaking is no longer the difficult task it once was. The contemporary homemaker can now place home baked bread on the table every week with only a little effort. And nothing smells so delectable as bread rising or tastes so good as bread homemade.

Country Biscuits

2 cups flour
4 teaspoons baking powder
1 teaspoon salt
1 teaspoon sugar

½ cup shortening
1 egg in measuring cup with milk
  to equal ⅔ cup liquid

Preheat oven to 450. Combine dry ingredients. Add shortening and cut in until well blended and the mixture resembles meal. Add egg and milk. Stir into flour mixture until there are no dry particles. Turn out onto floured counter and work gently for a moment until dough looks smooth. DO NOT OVER HANDLE. Roll out ½ inch thick. Cut; bake 8-10 minutes or until barely brown. Yields approximately 1 dozen.

Note: These may be frozen and also may be cut as cocktail biscuits for ham.

Batter Bread
(Courtesy of Westover)

1½ cups cornmeal
1 teaspoon salt
3 teaspoons baking powder
1 teaspoon sugar

2 cups boiling water
3 eggs
4 tablespoons shortening
2 cups hot, not boiling, milk

Preheat oven to 375. Put 1½ quart well-greased baking dish in oven while mixing batter. Sift dry ingredients in mixing bowl. Add water to make soft mush. Add eggs, shortening and milk to make thin batter. Pour batter into greased dish. Bake approximately 40 minutes or until crust is golden brown.
"An old Virginia favorite!"

James River Corn Bread

1 tablespoon oil
2 eggs
2 cups buttermilk

1 teaspoon baking soda
2 cups white water-ground cornmeal
1 teaspoon salt

Preheat oven to 450. Generously grease 9 inch square pan with oil. Heat in hot oven while mixing batter. Beat eggs, buttermilk and soda. Add cornmeal; beat well. Add salt. Pour into hot pan, bake 20-25 minutes.
Note: These can be made in 12 muffins or 8 corn sticks.
"The hot pan is the secret of the golden crust!"

Spoon Bread
(Courtesy of Hotel Roanoke, Roanoke, Virginia)

1½ cups corn meal
1 teaspoon sugar
1⅓ teaspoons salt
1½ cups boiling water

¼ cup butter
5 eggs
2 cups milk
1 tablespoon baking powder

Preheat oven to 350. Mix corn meal, salt and sugar together. Scald with boiling water. Add melted butter. Beat eggs; add milk. Combine mixtures. Add baking powder. Pour into oiled 9x13 baking pan and bake 30-40 minutes . Makes about 10 servings.
"One of the most famous Southern dishes originating from Indian porridge, Suppawn, which retains the consistency of porridge or pudding."

Westover

This home was originally owned by William Byrd II, a leading Virginia gentleman of his time. A planter of considerable intellect, he maintained and enjoyed a splendid library. Visitors to the home are told stories of Byrd's daughter, Evelyn, who died of a broken heart at the age of 27. Her ghost is said to be seen wandering the gardens during Indian Summer. A brick home laid in Flemish bond, Westover is an exquisite example of a formal Georgian mansion. Unlike many James River plantations, Westover's main entrance faces the land rather than the water. This superb structure located near Williamsburg remains very much the same as in 1730 when it was completed.

173

Hush Puppies

1 cup corn meal
1 teaspoon baking powder
1 1/2 teaspoons salt
dash of sugar

2 eggs
2 cups shoe peg corn (drained
   and pureed in the blender)
1 small onion, chopped

Mix all ingredients and drop by tablespoonsful into deep hot cooking oil. Cook until golden brown. Serves 6.

"Hunters sitting around camp fires, many years ago, were said to have quieted their dogs by throwing them left over bits of corn patties with the command, 'Hush, puppies!' Today they are a must served with fresh fish."

Popovers

1 cup flour
1 cup milk
3 tablespoons salad oil

1/2 teaspoon salt
3 eggs

Preheat oven to 400. Put all ingredients in blender and blend well. Place greased muffin tins in oven for 10 minutes. Pour batter into HOT muffin tins, filling each 2/3 full. Bake for 15 minutes; reduce heat to 350 and continue cooking 30 minutes. DO NOT OPEN oven door until cooking time is finished. Yields 8-10 popovers.

The Sebastian
(Courtesy of Williamsburg Lodge, Williamsburg, Virginia)

12 ounces ham, thinly sliced
6 ounces Cheddar cheese, sliced
3 cups cabbage, shredded
12 tablespoons mayonnaise
3 teaspoons curry powder

6 tablespoons chutney
salt to taste
12 slices rye bread
12 ounces butter

Make chutney cole slaw by combining the curry powder with the mayonnaise, chutney (medium chop), salt and cabbage. Spread both slices of rye bread with butter. Place 2 ounces ham, 1/2 cup cole slaw, 1 ounce Cheddar cheese on one slice, and top with other slice of buttered bread. Spread outside of the two slices of bread with 1 ounce of butter each. Place on a flat surface grill and toast until golden brown. Serves 6.

Note: Recipe can be prepared in any quantity.

Virginia Hostess
(Courtesy of Mount Vernon Inn, Alexandria, Virginia)

Corn Bread:

3 cups flour	*3 teaspoons baking powder*
1 1/2 cups cornmeal	*3 eggs, beaten*
dash of salt	*3 cups milk*
1/2 cup sugar	*1 ounce butter*

Preheat oven to 400. Thoroughly mix first 5 ingredients. Beat eggs well; add milk and butter, mixing thoroughly. Add liquids to dry ingredients; mix well. Spread mixture over a 12x30 sheet pan and bake for 10 minutes.

Hostess Sauce:

1 quart milk	*sherry to taste*
1 cup light cream	*6 ounces mushrooms*
1 cup cornstarch (more if needed)	

Put milk and cream in 2 quart saucepan and bring to boil. Remove from heat; stir in cornstarch. Stir in mushrooms and sherry. To serve: Split one piece of corn bread and place on a plate. Top with a slice of ham and a slice of turkey. Pour Hostess Sauce over all; sprinkle with Parmesan or sharp cheese. Garnish plate.
Note: Soften cornstarch in small amount of water before adding to milk.
"A delicious meal made of cornbread topped with ham, turkey and sauce."

Quick Sally Lunn

2 eggs, separated	*1/2 teaspoon salt*
1/2 cup sugar	*3/4 cup milk*
2 cups flour, sifted	*2 tablespoons butter, melted*
3 teaspoons baking powder	*1/4 cup sugar*

Preheat oven to 350. Beat egg yolks with sugar. Mix flour, baking powder and salt. Add dry ingredients to sugar mixture, alternately with milk. Add melted butter. Beat egg whites until stiff and fold into batter. Pour into greased loaf pan. Sprinkle sugar on top. Bake 40-45 minutes.
"Try this quick version with Brunswick Stew and salad."

Penn-Daw Cornsticks
(Courtesy of Gunston Hall)

3½ pounds sifted flour
8 pounds sifted cornmeal
½ pound sugar
5 ounces salt
½ pound baking powder

2 quarts buttermilk
1 pint water
3 pounds shortening, melted
8 eggs

Preheat oven to 425. Sift together flour, cornmeal, sugar, salt and baking powder. Add buttermilk, water and melted shortening to dry ingredients. Beat eggs until light and add to batter. Put in greased cornstick pans and bake 15-20 minutes. Makes approximately 11½ dozen cornsticks.

Banana Muffins

5 large ripe bananas, mashed
1 egg
½ teaspoon salt
1 teaspoon soda
1 cup sugar

1 teaspoon baking powder
¼ cup butter or margarine,
  softened
1 cup pecans or walnuts, chopped
1½ cups flour

Preheat oven to 375. Mix all ingredients except flour. Gradually add flour, stirring lightly. Pour into greased muffin tins and bake 15-20 minutes or until golden brown. Yields 2 dozen large muffins.
Note: Overripe bananas can be frozen in skins ready to use as needed in banana breads or muffins.

Blueberry Muffins

2 cups flour
3 teaspoons baking powder
½ teaspoon salt
2 tablespoons sugar*

1-2 eggs
1 cup milk
4 tablespoons butter, melted
1 cup FRESH blueberries

Preheat oven to 400. Sift flour; reserve ¼ cup to dredge berries. Mix and sift dry ingredients. Beat egg until light; add milk and butter. Add to dry mixture all at once and stir only enough to completely moisten dry ingredients. Dredge blueberries in reserved flour and carefully stir into batter. Drop by spoonfuls into well-greased muffin tins. Bake 15-20 minutes. Yields 12-15 large muffins.
*Up to ½ cup sugar can be added according to taste.

Bill Credle

Gunston Hall

Gunston Hall is the home of George Mason, author of the Virginia "Declaration of Rights". It is noted for its interior which is among the most impressive of the Colonial period. The wood-work of the drawing room is perhaps unequalled in the United States. The Chippendale dining room was the first in the Colonies with Chinese accent. This beautiful home was the center of a 5,000 acre plantation, of which 556 acres now belong to the Common-wealth of Virginia. Still a center for hospitality, music, entertainment and intellectual pursuits, this gracious home and its gardens on the Potomac River are now open to the public each day except Christmas.

Bran Muffins

1 cup shortening
2 cups boiling water
3 cups sugar
4 eggs, well-beaten
2 teaspoons salt
2 cups All-Bran cereal

4 cups Bran Buds cereal
3 teaspoons vanilla (or maple)
  flavoring
5 cups flour
5 teaspoons baking soda
1 quart buttermilk

Dissolve shortening in water; add sugar and cool slightly. Add eggs, salt, cereals and flavoring. Add flour mixture alternately with buttermilk and mix well. Keeps 5-6 weeks in refrigerator. Bake as needed in well-greased muffin tins at 450 for 10-15 minutes. Yields about 100 muffins. Baked muffins can be frozen.

Marmalade Muffins

1 egg, beaten
¼ cup orange juice
2 tablespoons sugar

1 tablespoon salad oil
1 cup Bisquick
¼ cup orange marmalade

Preheat oven to 400. Combine egg, juice, sugar and oil. Add Bisquick and beat 30 seconds. Stir in marmalade. Fill greased muffin tins ⅔ full and bake 15-20 minutes. Yields 6-8 large muffins.
"Instant success!"

Pumpkin Muffins

2 cups Bisquick
½ cup sugar
½ teaspoon cinnamon
¼ teaspoon nutmeg
¼ teaspoon cloves

1 egg
¾ cup milk
2 tablespoons salad oil
½ cup cooked pumpkin

Preheat oven to 400. Mix dry ingredients together. Add remaining ingredients and mix. Pour into greased muffin tins and bake 20 minutes. Yields 16 muffins.
"Great tasting and easy to prepare!"

"For quick breakfast buns, push canned biscuits into greased muffin tins; make an indentation with your thumb; fill with a dab of butter and jelly or preserves. Bake as directed."

French Apple Bread

2 cups sifted flour
½ teaspoon baking soda
1 teaspoon baking powder
1 teaspoon salt
¾ cup butter or margarine,
   melted
⅔ cup sugar

3 eggs, slightly beaten
¼ cup applesauce
1 cup apple, peeled and finely diced
½ cup sharp cheese, grated
¼ cup walnuts, chopped
1-3 pats butter or margarine
1 teaspoon cinnamon sugar

Preheat oven to 375. Sift dry ingredients. Combine melted butter and sugar; stir until thoroughly blended. Add eggs, applesauce, apples, cheese and nuts. Stir in dry ingredients and mix well. Spoon into well-greased loaf pan. Bake 50 minutes or until loaf tests done. Remove from oven, place butter pats on top and sprinkle with cinnamon sugar. Return to oven 5-8 minutes.
"This is not a sweet bread. It is good as a brunch or morning coffee bread."

Apricot Bread

1 cup dried apricots
1 cup boiling water
2 eggs
1 cup sugar
2¼ cups flour

3 teaspoons baking powder
½ teaspoon baking soda
½ teaspoon salt
1 cup pecans, chopped

Preheat oven to 350. Cut apricots into small pieces; cover with boiling water. Cool. Beat eggs well, in separate bowl, then add sugar and blend well. Sift together flour, baking powder, soda and salt. Add this to the egg mixture with the apricots. Stir until blended. Add nuts. Bake in greased and floured loaf pan for 1 hour.
"Spread with cream cheese while warm."

Banana Walnut Bread

¾ cup sugar
¼ cup shortening
2 eggs
1 cup mashed ripe banana
   (best done in blender)

2 cups flour
¼ teaspoon baking soda
2 teaspoons baking powder
1 cup black walnuts, chopped

179

Preheat oven to 350. Combine sugar and shortening and beat well. Add eggs, one at a time, beating well after each. Beat batter until light. Add mashed banana and stir. Sift dry ingredients together 3 times, stir into batter, beating until smooth. Add walnuts. Pour into greased loaf pan and bake 60-70 minutes. Cool in pan 5 minutes, turn onto rack to cool. This slices nicely when warm. It can be stored in refrigerator or freezer.

"This will make several small loaves if you prefer, as a nice gift size for teachers."

Bishop's Bread

1½ cups sifted flour
½ teaspoon baking powder
¼ teaspoon salt
⅔ cup chocolate chips
2 cups walnuts, chopped

1 cup dates, finely chopped
1 cup candied cherries, chopped
3 eggs
1 cup sugar

Preheat oven to 325. Line bottom of loaf pan with waxed paper. Grease paper and sides of pan. Sift flour, baking powder and salt together. Stir in chocolate chips, walnuts, dates and cherries until well coated with flour. In large bowl, beat eggs well; gradually beat in all sugar. Fold in flour mixture and pour into loaf pan. Bake 1½ hours or until well done. Cool in pan. Remove when cool and wrap in foil to store. Even people who HATE fruit cake LOVE this!

"This allegedly goes back to Colonial times when the Bishop made his visits on horseback and on a very uncertain schedule. The good wives, wanting something special to serve with tea, came up with this recipe which had wonderful lasting qualities and could be made up when the general time for the Bishop's visit rolled around, yet could be kept on hand until he arrived."

Heirloom Brown Bread

2 cups graham or whole wheat flour
½ cup flour
2 teaspoons baking soda
1 teaspoon salt

2 cups buttermilk
½ cup molasses
1 cup seedless raisins

Preheat oven to 350. Combine all ingredients and mix well. Spoon into 3 well-greased 1 pound tin cans. Let stand for ½ hour. Bake 45-50 minutes or until a cake tester comes out clean.

Note: Serve with cream cheese.

"Save your empty coffee cans to prepare this delicious bread."

Christmas Cranberry Bread

2 cups flour
3/4 cup sugar
1 1/2 teaspoons baking powder
1 teaspoon salt
1/2 teaspoon soda
1/2 cup nuts, chopped

1 cup fresh or frozen cranberries,
  chopped
1 egg, beaten
3/4 cup orange juice
2 tablespoons salad oil

Preheat oven to 350. Sift dry ingredients together. Stir in nuts and cranberries. Add remaining ingredients and blend until thoroughly moistened. Bake in greased, floured loaf pan 50 minutes or until golden brown.

Date-Nut Bread

1 1/2 cups dates, chopped
1 1/2 cups boiling water
1 1/2 cups sugar
2 tablespoons shortening
1 teaspoon salt
1 egg

3 cups flour
1 teaspoon baking soda
1 teaspoon cream of tartar
1 cup English walnuts or pecans,
  chopped
1/2 teaspoon vanilla

Preheat oven to 350. Pour boiling water over dates. Add sugar, shortening and salt. WHEN COOL, add egg and flour which has been sifted with soda and cream of tartar. Add nuts and vanilla; beat well. Pour into greased loaf pan and bake 55-65 minutes, or until it tests done.
"A nice gift for friends or neighbors at Christmas."

Pumpkin Bread

3 1/2 cups flour
3 cups sugar
1 teaspoon nutmeg
1 teaspoon cinnamon
1 teaspoon allspice
1/2 teaspoon baking powder
2 teaspoons baking soda

1 1/2 teaspoons salt
1 cup salad oil
4 eggs
2 cups canned pumpkin
1/2 cup walnuts, chopped (optional)
1/2 cup raisins (optional)

Preheat oven to 350. Mix all dry ingredients; add remaining ingredients and mix well. Bake in 2 well-greased loaf pans 50-60 minutes.

Blueberry Buckle

¼ cup butter
¾ cup sugar
1 egg
2 cups sifted flour
2 teaspoons baking powder
½ teaspoon salt
½ cup milk
2 cups fresh blueberries

Crumb Topping:

¼ cup butter, softened
½ cup sugar
⅓ cup flour
½ teaspoon cinnamon

Preheat oven to 375. Cream butter, add sugar and beat until light. Add egg and beat well. Add sifted dry ingredients alternately with milk, beating until smooth. Fold the berries into the batter and pour into greased 9 inch square pan. Sprinkle with blended crumb topping and bake 35 minutes. Cut into 6 or 9 squares.

Wellesley Coffee Cake

1 cup butter
2 cups sugar
2 eggs
1 cup sour cream
½ teaspoon vanilla
½ teaspoon almond extract

2 cups sifted flour
1 teaspoon baking powder
¼ teaspoon salt
4 teaspoons sugar
1 cup pecans, chopped
1 teaspoon cinnamon

Preheat oven to 350. Cream butter and sugar. Add eggs, one at a time, beating with each addition. Add sour cream, vanilla and almond extract; beat well. Combine flour, baking powder and salt. Add to mixture and beat. In separate bowl, combine sugar, pecans and cinnamon for filling. Place ⅓ batter in well-greased and floured tube pan. Sprinkle with ¾ of filling mixture. Spoon in rest of batter and sprinkle with remaining filling. Bake 1 hour.
"This cake can be frozen."

Feather Pancakes

1 egg, slightly beaten
1 cup milk
2 tablespoons salad oil
1 cup sifted flour

½ teaspoon salt
2 tablespoons baking powder
2 tablespoons sugar

Combine egg, milk and oil. Add sifted dry ingredients. Beat until smooth. Bake on hot griddle. Makes 8 5-inch cakes.
Note: For those in doubt, 2 tablespoons baking powder is correct.

Cream Waffles

2 eggs
1 3/4 cups milk
1/2 cup butter, melted
2 cups sifted flour

4 teaspoons baking powder
1/2 teaspoon salt
1 tablespoon sugar

Beat eggs; add remaining ingredients and continue beating until smooth. Bake in heated waffle iron. Do not stir batter between bakings.
Note: For variation, add chopped pecans to the batter.

Cinnamon Cream Syrup

1 cup sugar
1/2 cup light corn syrup
1/4 cup water

1/2 - 3/4 teaspoon cinnamon
1/2 cup evaporated milk

In a small saucepan, combine sugar, syrup, water and cinnamon. Bring to boiling over medium heat, stirring constantly. Cook and stir 2 minutes. Remove from heat; cool 5 minutes. Stir in milk. Serve warm over pancakes, waffles or French toast. Leftover syrup can be reheated.

Danish Pastry

1 1/2 cups corn oil margarine
4 cups flour
2 packages dry yeast
1/4 cup warm water

1/3 cup sugar
1 cup milk
1 egg, slightly beaten
jelly and preserves

Cut margarine into 1/2 cup flour and roll into 6x12 rectangle. Chill. Dissolve yeast in water, add sugar, milk and egg. Stir in 2 cups flour; mix well. Add remaining flour, beat until smooth and elastic. Turn onto a floured board; roll into a 14 inch square. Place margarine mixture on half of this dough, fold over other half and seal edges. Roll into a 12x14 rectangle. Fold 1/3 of dough over center, then fold remaining 1/3 over center and roll. Repeat twice more. Chill at least 1 hour; roll dough to 1/8 inch thickness. Shape and fill as desired. It is best to work with only 1/3 of the dough at a time and leave rest refrigerated.

Crescents: Cut dough into 3 inch triangle, place preserves on base and roll towards point. Bend dough into crescent shape.

Cockscombs: Cut dough lengthwise in 5 inch strips. Spread preserves down the center of each strip, then fold sides to center. slightly overlaping. Slash one edge of each 4 times and spread slightly.

Twists: Cut pastry in ½ inch strips and twist lengthwise. Shape into pin wheels, pretzels or S shapes. Fill centers with preserves.

Place pastries on greased baking sheets. Let rise 1 hour; bake at 400 for 10 minutes. Frost.

Almond Frosting:

3 cups confectioners' sugar   *1½ teaspoons almond extract*
3 tablespoons water

Combine all ingredients, mix well and spread on pastries when removed from oven.

Cinnamon Buns

½ cup warm water
2 packages dry yeast
1½ cups lukewarm milk
½ cup sugar
2 teaspoons salt
2 eggs

½ cup shortening
7-7½ cups flour, sifted
melted butter or margarine
½ cup sugar
2-2½ teaspoons cinnamon

Add yeast, milk and sugar to warm water in mixing bowl, stirring to dissolve. Stir in salt, eggs, shortening and half the flour. For light, flaky buns, keep dough as soft as possible, almost sticky, just so you are able to handle it. Mix with wooden spoon until smooth. Add enough remaining flour to handle easily. Mix with hands. Turn onto lightly floured board; knead until smooth and elastic (about 5 minutes). Round dough up in well-greased large bowl, greased side up. Cover with damp cloth, let rise in warm place until double in bulk (about 1½ hours). Punch down; let rise again until almost double (about 30 minutes). Roll out a portion of dough at a time about ⅜ inch thick, brush with melted butter; sprinkle with mixture of cinnamon and sugar. Roll dough "jelly-roll" fashion, to desired thickness and slice off buns ½ inch thick. Place in ungreased pans, close together; let rise. Bake at 375 for 20 minutes. When cool, ice with topping.

Topping:

2 cups confectioners' sugar   1 teaspoon vanilla
4 tablespoons milk

Yields 9-10 dozen.

All-Bran Rolls

1 cup shortening   2 eggs, well-beaten
¾ cup sugar   2 yeast cakes
1 cup All-Bran cereal   1 cup lukewarm water
1½ teaspoons salt   6½ cups flour
1 cup boiling water

Place shortening, sugar, All-Bran and salt in large mixing bowl; add boiling water gradually and stir until shortening is melted. Soften yeast in lukewarm water. Add eggs and yeast. Add half the flour and mix until smooth; add remainder of flour; mix thoroughly until smooth. Cover tightly and refrigerate until 2 hours before baking. Shape into Parker House or cloverleaf rolls. Place in greased muffin tins. Allow rolls to rise in warm room until double. Bake at 350 for 30 minutes. Yields 3½ dozen.

Twisted Rolls

1 yeast cake   ¼ cup sugar
½ cup lukewarm water   2 eggs, well beaten
1 cup milk, scalded   ½ cup butter, melted
1 teaspoon salt   4-4½ cups sifted flour

Dissolve yeast in warm water. Place milk in large mixing bowl; cool to room temperature and add softened yeast. Add salt, sugar, eggs, butter and enough flour to prevent sticking to bowl. Knead until smooth and elastic. Allow dough to rise in covered greased bowl until doubled in bulk. Roll. Cut in strips 4½ x ½ ; tie in knots. Let rise on greased baking sheets until very light. Preheat oven to 400 and bake 15-20 minutes. Yields 40 rolls.
"Lovely to look at, delightful to taste!"

Rolls
(Courtesy of Woodbourne)

1 package yeast	*1 ½ teaspoons salt*
¼ cup warm water	*½ cup shortening*
5 cups flour, sifted	*1 ¾ cups warm water*
3 tablespoons sugar	*butter or margarine, melted*

Dissolve yeast in warm water in large mixing bowl. Mix yeast, flour, sugar, salt and shortening. Add water and mix well. Knead until smooth. Let rise in a warm place until double or more in size. Shape into rolls and let rise again, about 1 hour. Cook at 400 until done. Use the melted butter or margarine when shaping dough into rolls. Also, brush the tops of the rolls with melted butter or margarine when starting to brown in oven.

Note: A treasured family recipe for rolls that melt in your mouth!

Dinner Rolls

½ cup shortening	*¼ cup lukewarm water*
½ cup sugar	*2 teaspoons salt*
3 eggs	*6 cups flour, sifted 3 times*
1 yeast cake	*1 cup milk, scalded*

Cream shortening and sugar. Add eggs, one at a time; mix well. Add yeast which has been dissolved in water. With a wooden spoon, stir in flour and salt alternately with milk until well mixed. Let rise in greased bowl covered with damp cloth until double in bulk. Make into cloverleaf rolls or Parker House rolls; place in greased muffin tins; cover and let rise again (about 30 minutes). Bake at 350 for 20 minutes or until brown. Yields 4-5 dozen.

Note: After the first rising, this dough will keep in the refrigerator for 4 or 5 days and can be used as needed.

Strawberry Butter

½ pound butter	*2 teaspoons confectioners' sugar*
½ teaspoon salt	*¾ cup strawberries*

Whip butter in blender for 1 minute. Add remaining ingredients and blend 2 more minutes. Refrigerate in a covered jar. Delicious for toast, pancakes or tea sandwiches.

Woodbourne

Woodbourne was originally a part of the Poplar Forest tract of approximately 4,000 acres of land which was inherited by Thomas Jefferson from his wife, Martha Wayles Skelton. Martha's father had owned the land in what is now Bedford County. Woodbourne was purchased from Thomas Jefferson by William Radford, an attorney and banker, in 1810 as a part of a tract of 942 acres. It is now owned and occupied by his great grandson, du Val Radford, and his family. This gorgeous home was constructed in three stages: the east wing in 1780; the central portion about 1811; and the west wing about 1820.

Egg Bread

2 packages dry yeast
1/2 cup warm water
1 1/2 cups lukewarm milk
1/4 cup sugar
1 tablespoon salt
3 eggs, slightly beaten

1/4 cup butter, softened
7 1/4 - 7 1/2 cups sifted flour

Glaze:
1 egg yolk
2 tablespoons water

Dissolve yeast in water in mixing bowl. Stir in milk, sugar and salt. Add eggs, butter and half the flour; mix well with wooden spoon. Add remaining flour, mix with hand. Turn onto lightly floured board. Knead until smooth and blistered (for about 8-10 minutes). Round up in a greased bowl; bring greased side up. Cover with a damp cloth and let rise in a warm place until doubled in bulk (1 1/2 -2 hours). Punch down, round up and let rise again until almost doubled in bulk (30 minutes). Divide dough into 9-12 equal parts, making each into a 14 inch long roll. Braid 3 rolls loosely, fastening ends. Repeat with additional rolls. Place on greased baking sheets, cover with damp cloth and let rise until almost doubled in bulk (50-60 minutes). Brush braids with glaze mixture. Bake at 425 for 30-35 minutes. Yields 3 or 4 loaves.
"Great way to spend a day at home."

French Bread

1 cup lukewarm water
1 package dry yeast
1 tablespoon sugar
1 1/2 teaspoons salt
2 tablespoons shortening, melted

3 cups flour
Topping:
1 egg white
1 tablespoon water
1 teaspoon salt

Place lukewarm water and yeast in large mixing bowl. Let stand for 5 minutes. Add sugar, salt and shortening; stir well. Add 1 cup of flour, and beat thoroughly with rotary beater or electric mixer. Add remaining flour. Sprinkle board with flour and place dough on board for 10 minutes. Knead well, let rise about an hour, punch down and let rise again about half an hour. Divide dough into 2 parts, roll each out to 1/4 inch with rolling pin. Roll up tightly, pinch edges to seal. Put loaves on greased cookie sheet that has been sprinkled with cornmeal. Cut slits along top of bread about 1 inch deep. Beat topping mixture and brush over tops of loaves. Let rise, uncovered, 1 hour. Put a large pan of boiling water on bottom oven rack with pan of bread on rack above. Bake at 425 for 10 minutes. Brush with egg mixture again, and bake at 375 for 25 minutes; or until bread sounds hollow when tapped. Cool on rack.

Herb-Buttered French Bread

1½ teaspoons chives
1½ teaspoons parsley
¼ teaspoon tarragon

¼ teaspoon chervil
4 tablespoons butter, melted
French bread, sliced

Mix ingredients. Spread on sliced bread, foil wrap, and bake at 350 for 20 minutes.
"Great with Italian dishes!"

Dilly Casserole Bread

1 package dry yeast
¼ cup warm water
1 egg
2 tablespoons sugar
1 cup creamed or small curd
  cottage cheese

1 tablespoon butter
1 tablespoon dried minced onions
2 teaspoons dill seed
1 teaspoon salt
2¼-2½ cups flour
¼ teaspoon baking soda

Dissolve yeast in water. Combine cottage cheese and butter, heating until butter melts. Mix all ingredients together in large bowl, using a wooden spoon. Let rise 50-60 minutes in covered bowl. Beat down and put batter in greased 1½ quart casserole. Cover and let rise 30-40 minutes. Bake at 350 for 40-50 minutes. Cool in casserole 5 minutes, and turn onto cake rack. May be frozen in foil.
Note: Dough is sticky, so oil hands before handling.

White Bread

½ cup margarine
2 cups milk, heated
¼ cup sugar
2 teaspoons salt

1 egg
1 package dry yeast
5½ cups flour

Heat margarine; add milk, sugar and salt. Beat egg in large bowl; add hot mixture. When milk mixture is comfortable to wrist (warmer than room temperature), add yeast and dissolve. Add half the flour and mix with wooden spoon. Add rest of flour and blend. Divide dough and place in 2 greased bowls. Grease tops of dough, cover and let rise in warm place for 2 hours. Knead vigorously, and place in 2 greased loaf pans to rise for ½ hour. Bake at 350 for 40-50 minutes. Cool on a trivet.

Wheat Bread

2 packages dry yeast
5 cups lukewarm water
2 tablespoons sugar
2 eggs, beaten
1 cup shortening, melted

5 teaspoons salt
1 cup sugar
12 cups flour, sifted
4 cups whole wheat flour, sifted
½ cup wheat germ

Dissolve yeast in 1 cup water, add 2 tablespoons sugar and let stand 45 minutes. Beat in eggs, shortening, remaining water, salt and sugar. Sift flours together. Add wheat germ. Stir some of the flour mixture gradually into other ingredients until a thick batter is formed. Pour dough onto floured board and knead in remaining flour (kneading 10 minutes). Place dough in well-greased bowl and let stand until doubled in size (about 1 hour). Punch down, knead edges in and let stand again until doubled. Punch down again; knead lightly. Cut dough into 6 pieces; cover with cloth. Grease 6 loaf pans. Shape dough into loaves; place in pans. Bake at 400 for 15 minutes, reduce heat to 375 and continue baking 25 minutes. Turn loaves onto racks and brush with melted butter.

Sally Lunn

1 package dry yeast
¼ cup warm water
2 tablespoons lard or soft butter
½ cup sugar

2 eggs
1 teaspoon salt
3½ cups flour
1 cup warm milk

Soften yeast in the warm water. In a mixing bowl, cream lard and sugar. Beat in eggs and salt, stir in 1½ cups of flour and beat vigorously. Stir in milk and softened yeast; mix well. Add remaining flour and beat vigorously. Cover, let rise in warm place until doubled (about 1 hour). Stir down batter and spoon evenly into greased tube or bundt pan. Cover and let rise again until doubled (30-45 minutes). Bake in preheated 325 oven for 10 minutes, increase temperature to 375 and continue baking for 20 minutes more. Remove from pan.

"Early Virginia settlers brought this recipe with them from England! It is legendarily attributed to the English girl who sold bread on the streets calling 'Sol et Lune', from the French for sun and moon, because the tops of the buns were golden and the bottoms white. In the colonies, it became 'Sally Lunn', a bread baked in a turk's head mold rather than buns."

Cookies and Candy

Colonial sweet breads labeled "biscuits" were the forerunners of the American cookie, and variations of the basic recipes were many. Almonds were a popular seasoning agent of the time; and spices, fruits, nuts and extracts of all kinds were employed to give variation and character to the biscuits.

Moreover, the "biscuit" dough could be shaped into any form desired on thin white paper or in tin molds; thin doughs could be beaten very light and dropped by spoonfuls on greased tin sheets. Basic classification of cookies stems from the six varieties of shape they might take: bars or squares, drop cookies, rolled cookies, pressed cookies, shaped or molded cookies, and refrigerator cookies.

Our American usage of the word "cookie" comes from the Dutch word "koekje" or "koekie," meaning small cake. In England, cookies are still referred to as biscuits.

Candy, a popular item since ancient times, takes many forms with sugar syrup forming the basic crystallization agent for a number of confections. Great favorites among the Virginia colonists were crystallized flower petals, nuts, roots, leaves and candied fruits. Legendary sugar plums, made of boiled sugar, delighted the children of colonial Virginia . . . as did other sweets such as marchpane, suckets, sweetmeats and caraway comfits. Marchpane was very similar to modern marzipan made of almond paste shaped into balls. Suckets and sweetmeats were fruits which had been preserved in thick syrup and dried. Caraway comfits, often used to decorate cakes, were caraway seeds dipped into a sugar syrup repeatedly until each seed had a thick coating of candy.

Most often the candy-making was the task of the druggist since candy drops containing peppermint, horehound and wintergreen were healing as well as rewarding to the palate. Left to their own devices, the children of colonial

Virginia relied upon honey, molasses, and jam to satisfy their cravings for sweets.

The first "real" candy on the American scene was made in the form of stick candy. Later on, during the nineteenth century, molasses candies, taffy, and caramels became popular, and a number of recipes for them appeared in the cookbooks of that era.

However, it has been the twentieth century that has produced the vast quantity of fudge and chocolate candy recipes in such demand today. America's appreciation of the sweeter things of life has promoted candy making into a domestic industry of great importance. Nevertheless, modern day housewives and their children still enjoy the satisfication and fun of making their own and basking in the nostalgia this pleasant chore brings about.

Brownies

1 cup margarine	*4 ounces unsweetened chocolate,*
2 cups sugar	*melted*
1 teaspoon vanilla	*1 cup sifted flour*
4 eggs	*1 cup nuts, finely chopped*

Preheat oven to 325. Cream margarine, sugar and vanilla; beat in eggs. Blend in chocolate. Stir in flour and nuts. Bake in greased 10 x 15 pan for 15 to 20 minutes. Cut while hot. Remove from pan immediately. Yields 5 dozen.

Mint Frosting for Brownies

2 tablespoons butter, softened	*1/8 teaspoon mint extract*
1 1/2 cups sifted confectioners'	*green food coloring*
sugar	*1 ounce semi-sweet chocolate*
2 tablespoons cream	

Combine butter and sugar; add cream gradually, beating to spreading consistency. Add mint extract and tint pale green with food coloring. Ice brownies. Drizzle melted chocolate on top. Cut into bars. Yields 1 cup; enough to ice 2 dozen brownies.

Chocolate Buttercream Squares

1 ounce unsweetened chocolate,
  melted
¼ cup butter
½ cup sugar

1 egg beaten
½ cup flour
¼ cup nuts (optional)

Cookie Layer:

Preheat oven to 350. Grease and flour an 8x8 pan. Cream butter, sugar and egg. Add melted chocolate, flour and nuts. Put in prepared pan and place in oven. Check after 10 minutes; it should be cooked. DO NOT OVERBAKE. Cool.

Filling Layer:

2 tablespoons margarine, softened
1 cup confectioners' sugar

1 tablespoon cream
½ teaspoon vanilla

Blend ingredients. Chill 10 minutes and spread over cookie layer.

Icing:

1 ounce unsweetened chocolate

1 tablespoon butter or margarine

Melt ingredients together and pour over filling. Chill in refrigerator. Cut into 24 small bars.
"These absolutely divine squares remind you of a brownie combined with buttercream candy. Cut into very small pieces since they are very rich."

English Short Bread

1¼ cups sugar
5 cups flour

2 cups unsalted butter, firm

Preheat oven to 325. Sift sugar and flour together 3 times. Break butter into bowl. Work in flour and sugar mixture until it resembles cornmeal. Turn dough onto floured board. Knead well, adding a little more flour until it begins to crack. (This may take ½-1 cup of flour.) Roll out ⅜ inch thick, cut into triangles. Put triangles on baking sheet. Bake for 20 minutes, until golden. DO NOT OVERBAKE. Yields about 100 3-inch triangles.
"Called Shortening Bread in the South—the kind best loved by Mammy's baby."

Graham Cracker Cookies

graham crackers
½ cup margarine
½ cup butter

1 cup brown sugar
1 cup nuts, chopped

Preheat oven to 350. Grease cookie sheet. Cover the entire cookie sheet with whole graham crackers. Blend together margarine, butter and brown sugar and boil over moderate heat for 2 minutes. Pour over graham crackers. Sprinkle nuts on top. Bake for 15 minutes. Cool and break into pieces. Yields 4-5 dozen. *"Children love these cookies and they are easy to make!"*

Lemon Squares

1 cup butter
2 cups sifted flour
½ cup confectioners' sugar
2 cups sugar
4 tablespoons flour

1 teaspoon baking powder
4 eggs
6 tablespoons lemon juice
pinch of salt

Preheat oven to 350. Melt butter; add sifted flour and confectioners' sugar. Mix well and pack into an ungreased 9 x 13 pan. Bake 15 minutes. Mix together sugar, flour and baking powder. Add eggs, one at a time, lemon juice and salt. Pour this mixture over hot crust and return to oven and bake 25-30 minutes. Cool and cut in small squares. Sprinkle confectioners' sugar on top. Yields 4 dozen.

Aunt Silence's Jumbles
(Courtesy of Scotchtown)

¾ pound flour
¾ pound sugar
1 cup butter

4 eggs
1 lemon, rind and part
of the juice

Preheat oven to 350. Very lightly beat all of the ingredients together. Drop from a teaspoon on buttered cookie sheets. Spread thin. Bake quickly until light brown. Makes 26.
Hint: An almond can be put on each one if desired.
"Two tablespoons of rosewater was the original flavoring for which lemon is now substituted."

Scotchtown

Scotchtown, built around 1719, was the home of Patrick Henry from 1771-1778. It is situated ten miles west of Ashland in upper Hanover County. This National Historic Landmark was also once the home of Henry's cousin Dolley Payne Madison, wife of President James Madison. The land around it was noted for its production of fine tobacco while the house itself was admired for its grace and beauty. A mansion which was saved from neglect and decay, Scotchtown is visited by an increasing number of people each year.

Date Nut Bars

1 cup butter	*2 cups flour*
2 cups confectioners' sugar	*1 pound pitted dates, chopped*
4 eggs	*2 cups nuts*

Preheat oven to 350. Cream butter and sugar and add beaten eggs one at a time. Add *one* cup of flour to mixture. Mix remaining cup of flour with dates and nuts. Add to mixture. Grease and flour a 9 x 13 x 2 pan and pour mixture into pan. Bake for 20 minutes. Cut and dip in confectioners' sugar. Yields 2-3 dozen.

Toffee Bars

1 cup butter	*1 teaspoon vanilla*
1 cup light brown sugar, packed	*6 ounces milk chocolate*
1 egg yolk	*1 cup nuts, chopped*
2 cups sifted flour	

Preheat oven to 350. Cream butter and sugar until light and fluffy. Mix in egg yolk. Add flour gradually, stirring only to blend. Add vanilla. Spread about ¼ inch thick in lightly buttered 10 x 15 jelly roll pan. Bake for 20-25 minutes or until golden brown. Remove from oven and while still hot distribute chocolate on top. When chocolate is soft, spread smoothly over surface. Sprinkle with nuts. While still warm, cut into bars. Yields 5 dozen.

Breakfast Cookies

½ pound bacon	*1 cup flour*
½ cup butter	*¼ teaspoon baking soda*
¾ cup sugar	*2 cups corn flakes*
1 egg	*½ cup raisins*

Preheat oven to 350. Cook bacon until very crisp, drain well. Break in ½ inch pieces. Beat together butter and sugar until fluffy; beat in egg. Combine flour and soda; stir into butter mixture. Stir in bacon, corn flakes and raisins. Drop by rounded tablespoons 2 inches apart on ungreased cookie sheets. Bake for 15 to 18 minutes. Cool one minute. Remove to racks to cool. Yields 2 dozen.
"These are good for a coffee or tea."

Butter Cookies

4 egg yolks
2 cups butter
1 1/2 cups sugar
2 teaspoons vanilla

4 cups flour
jelly, almonds, chocolate
    chips (optional)

Preheat oven to 350. Beat egg yolks until foamy and the color of lemon. Add butter, sugar and vanilla and mix well. Add flour gradually and combine thoroughly. Pinch off pieces of mixture the size of a marble and place on greased cookie sheet. OPTIONAL: Make a depression in each and fill with jelly, almond or chocolate chips. Bake for 10 minutes. Watch carefully, they will not turn brown. The bottom will get very light brown. Yields 4 dozen.

Chocolate Chip Meringues

2 egg whites (at room temperature)
1 teaspoon vanilla
1/8 teaspoon cream of tartar

3/4 cup sugar
1 cup chocolate chips
1/2 cup chopped nuts

Preheat oven to 300. Beat first 3 ingredients until soft peaks form, add sugar one teaspoonful at a time, beat until stiff peaks form. Fold in chocolate chips and nuts. Drop on brown paper-covered cookie sheets. Bake for 25 minutes. Yields 4 dozen.

Fruitcake Cookies

1 cup butter
1 1/8 cups brown sugar, packed
1 1/2 tablespoons milk
2 1/4 cups self-rising flour sifted
    with 1/2 teaspoon baking soda
1/2 teaspoon vanilla
1 to 2 eggs

6 slices candied pineapple
1/2 pound candied cherries
    (red and green)
1 pound dates
8 ounces pineapple preserves
1 1/2 pounds pecans, chopped

Mix first 6 ingredients in order, beating in one at a time. Dice pineapple, cherries and dates; flour well. (This can be done the night before.) Mix fruit with batter; then add preserves and pecans. Blend all ingredients together. Drop by teaspoonful on greased cookie sheets and bake at 325 for 12-15 minutes. Yields 160 cookies.

"These are great at Christmas and even fruitcake haters like these cookies!"

Barboursville Almond Macaroons

2 pounds almond paste
1 pound confectioners' sugar

1 teaspoon lemon juice
9 egg whites

Place almond paste, sugar and lemon juice in a mixing bowl; add 8 unbeaten egg whites and mix to form a soft dough. Add the remaining egg white only if neccessary. Using a teaspoon, drop the dough onto a buttered cookie sheet; bake in a preheated 375 degree oven for 15-20 minutes. Yields 5 dozen.

Benne Seed Wafers

³/₄ cup benne seed
 (sesame seed, toasted)
¹/₂ cup butter (no substitute)
2 cups brown sugar

1 egg, beaten
1 cup flour
¹/₂ teaspoon salt
1 teaspoon vanilla

Preheat oven to 350. Spread the benne seed on a cookie sheet and toast 3-4 minutes. Line cookie sheets with aluminum foil. Cream butter well, add brown sugar and beaten egg. Blend in flour and salt, and add vanilla. Fold in cooled benne seed. Drop by ¹/₂ teaspoonsful on ungreased foil-lined pans. Bake at 325 quickly—approximately 7-8 minutes. Allow to cool one minute and remove from foil. Yields 7 dozen.
"Always a great Southern favorite."

Ginger Cookies
(Courtesy of Stratford Hall)

1¹/₂ cups margarine, melted
¹/₂ cup molasses
2 cups sugar
2 eggs
4 cups flour

4 teaspoons soda
2 teaspoons cinnamon
1 teaspoon ginger
1 teaspoon cloves
sugar

Preheat oven to 350. Add molasses, sugar and eggs to the margarine. Beat well. Sift together and add to this mixture flour, soda and spices. Refrigerate the dough for several hours. Make into small balls. Roll in sugar. Bake until firm or brown, about 8-10 minutes.
Note: These are served in the Stratford kitchen.

Stratford Hall

Stratford Plantation is a 1544 acre working plantation on the Potomac River in Westmoreland County. The manor house, Stratford Hall, has undergone practically no structural changes since colonial times. It was purchased in 1929 by the Robert E. Lee Memorial Foundation and has since been preserved as a national shrine. Four generations of Lees lived at Stratford; Thomas Lee, who built it; his two sons, Richard Henry Lee and Francis Lightfoot Lee; Henry (Light Horse Harry) Lee and Robert Edward Lee. Today, operation of the estate resembles as authentically as possible the methods used during the lifetime of its early eighteenth century founder.

Chocolate Crinkle

4 ounces unsweetened chocolate
1/2 cup oil
2 cups sugar
4 eggs
2 teaspoons vanilla

2 cups flour
2 teaspoons baking powder
1/2 teaspoon salt
confectioners' sugar

Melt chocolate and mix with oil and sugar; add eggs, one at a time, and vanilla. Sift dry ingredients and blend into creamed mixture. Chill 2 hours and roll in balls. Roll in confectioners' sugar. Place on greased cookie sheet 2-3 inches apart. Bake at 350 for 10-12 minutes. Cool slightly; remove from pan. Yields 4 dozen.

Crisp Cookies

1 cup butter, softened
2 cups sugar
2 eggs
2 1/2 cups flour

1 teaspoon salt
2 teaspoons baking powder
2 teaspoons vanilla
cinnamon and sugar mixture

Cream butter and sugar; add eggs and beat well. Add sifted dry ingredients and vanilla. Shape into rolls; wrap in wax paper and chill overnight. Preheat oven to 350. Slice thin, sprinkle with mixture of cinnamon and sugar. Bake on well-greased cookie sheets until well-browned. Yields 10 dozen.

Note: Rolls of dough may be refrigerated and cookies sliced and baked when needed.

Nutty Fingers

1 cup butter
2/3 cup confectioners' sugar
2 cups flour
1/2 teaspoon salt

1 cup pecans, ground
2 teaspoons vanilla
confectioners' sugar

Cream butter. Add sugar and blend until light and fluffy. Add flour, salt, pecans and vanilla. Mix well. Chill dough. To shape cookies, take a teaspoon of dough and roll to finger shape. Bake on greased cookie sheet at 325 for 30 minutes. Remove from oven and roll in confectioners' sugar before cooling. Roll again when cooled. Yields 4 dozen.

Date-Nut Cheese Roll Ups

8 ounces cream cheese, softened
1/2 cup margarine, softened
1/2 cup butter, softened

2 cups flour
dates
pecan halves

Cream cheese, margarine and butter together; work in flour to form dough. Chill at least 5 hours. Roll half the dough out thinly on a generous layer of sugar mixed with a little flour. Cut into strips about 4-6 inches long and about 1 inch wide. Stuff date with pecan half and roll in cut strip of pastry. Roll in sugar. Repeat process with remaining dough. Bake 8-10 minutes until lightly browned in 400 oven. Yields 1 dozen.
"This is also a super dessert."

Ice Box Cookies

1 cup butter
2 cups light brown sugar
2 eggs
1 teaspoon vanilla

1 teaspoon soda
1/2 teaspoon salt
3 1/2 cups flour
1 cup nuts, chopped

Thoroughly cream butter and sugar; add eggs and vanilla and beat. Sift dry ingredients *3* times; add to creamed mixture. Stir in nuts. Shape dough into rolls. Wrap in waxed paper; chill overnight. Slice thinly. Bake on ungreased cookie sheet at 375 for 8 to 10 minutes. Yields 4 dozen.

Molasses Sugar Cookies

3/4 cup shortening or oil
1 cup sugar
1/4 cup molasses
1 egg
2 teaspoons baking soda

2 cups sifted flour
1/2 teaspoon cloves
1 teaspoon cinnamon
1/2 teaspoon salt

If using shortening instead of oil, melt it in a 3 or 4 quart saucepan over low heat; let cool. Add sugar, molasses and egg to shortening or oil. Beat well. Sift dry ingriedients together. Add to first mixture and mix well. Chill several hours. Form 1 inch balls, roll in sugar and place two inches apart on greased cookie sheets. Bake at 375 for 8-10 minutes. Yields 4-5 dozen.
"A fun cookie for children to help make."

Oatmeal Krispies

1 cup shortening	*1 teaspoon baking soda*
1 cup brown sugar	*1 teaspoon salt*
1 cup sugar	*1 teaspoon vanilla*
2 eggs	*3 cups regular rolled oats*
1½ cups flour	*1 cup nuts, chopped*

Cream shortening and sugar; add eggs and blend. Sift flour, soda and salt together. Mix into creamed mixture and add vanilla. Blend in oats and nuts. Shape into small rolls and chill overnight. Slice thinly and bake on greased cookie sheet at 375 for 10 minutes. Yields 8 dozen.

Walnut-Orange Crisps

1 cup walnuts, chopped fine	*½ cup sugar*
1 tablespoon orange rind, grated	*2 tablespoons orange juice*
2¾ cups sifted flour	*½ cup brown sugar, packed*
½ teaspoon baking soda	*1 egg, unbeaten*
½ teaspoon salt	*1 teaspoon vanilla*
1 cup shortening	

Sift flour with baking soda and salt. Cream shortening, sugar, orange juice, brown sugar, egg and vanilla until light and fluffy. At low speed, beat in flour mixture; then nuts until mixed. Chill until easy to handle. Preheat oven to 400. Form dough into ½ inch balls. Place on ungreased cookie sheet and flatten with bottom of a glass dipped in sugar. Top with more chopped nuts and orange rind. Yields 3 dozen. Bake 8-10 minutes . Yields 3 dozen.

Chocolate Nut Balls

6 ounces evaporated milk	*½ cup confectioners' sugar, sifted*
6 ounces chocolate chips	*1¼ cups walnuts or pecans, chopped*
2½ cups vanilla wafers, crushed	*⅓ cup brandy or orange juice*

In heavy 2 quart saucepan, cook milk and chocolate over medium heat; stir until chocolate is melted and the mixture is smooth. Remove from heat. Add remaining ingredients, using only ½ cup nuts. Mix well. Let stand at room temperature for 30 minutes. Shape into balls 1 inch in diameter. Roll in remaining nuts. Refrigerate 1 hour or until firm. Yields 4 dozen.

Norwegian Oatmeal Macaroons

1 cup sugar
1 1/2 cups quick-cooking rolled oats
1 cup flour
1 teaspoon baking powder

1/2 teaspoon salt
1 cup coconut
1 egg
1 cup margarine, melted

Preheat oven to 350. Mix together dry ingredients. Add egg and margarine. Blend. Roll dough into small balls the size of a walnut. Press very thin with a fork dipped in cold water on an ungreased cookie sheet. Bake for 10-15 minutes. Yields 4-5 dozen.

Snickerdoodles

1 cup soft shortening
1 1/2 cups sugar
2 eggs
2 3/4 cups sifted flour
2 teaspoons cream of tartar

1 teaspoon baking soda
1/2 teaspoon salt
2 tablespoons sugar
2 teaspoons cinnamon

Preheat oven to 400. Mix together thoroughly shortening, sugar and eggs. Sift together next 4 ingredients and stir into creamed mixture. Chill dough. Roll into balls the size of small walnuts. Roll in mixture of sugar and cinnamon. Place about 2 inches apart on ungreased cookie sheet. Bake for 8-10 minutes, until lightly browned, but still soft. These cookies puff up at first, then flatten out with crinkled tops. Yields 4 dozen.

Scotch Lace Wafers

4 ounces butterscotch pudding mix
2 cups quick-cooking rolled oats
1/2 cup pecans, chopped

1 cup butter, softened
1/2 cup sugar
1 teaspoon vanilla

Preheat oven to 350. Thoroughly blend together all ingredients with fingers. Shape into balls the size of small walnuts and place 6 inches apart on ungreased cookie sheets. Flatten balls slightly with fork. Bake 13-15 minutes. Cool on baking sheet before removing. Yields 3 dozen.
"Serve with ice cream or fruit."

Tea Time Tassies

3 ounces cream cheese   1 cup sifted flour
1/2 cup margarine

Let cream cheese and margarine soften at room temperature. Blend. Stir in flour. Chill about 1 hour. Shape into 2 dozen 1 inch balls; place in tiny ungreased 1 3/4 inch muffin tins. Press dough on bottom and sides of cups.

Pecan Filling:

1 egg   1 teaspoon vanilla
3/4 cup brown sugar   dash of salt
1 tablespoon margarine, softened   2/3 cup pecans, chopped

Preheat oven to 325. Beat together egg, sugar, margarine, vanilla and salt until smooth. Divide half the pecans among pastry-lined cups; add egg mixture and top with remaining pecans. Bake for 25 minutes or until filling sets. Cool before removing from pan. Yields 2 dozen.
"Guaranteed to melt in your mouth!"

Petit Orange Fruit Cakes

1/2 cup butter or margarine   1 cup dates, chopped
1 cup sugar   1 cup pecans, chopped
2 eggs   2/3 cup buttermilk
2 cups sifted flour   grated rind of 1 orange
1 teaspoon baking soda

Preheat oven to 375. Cream shortening and sugar until light. Add eggs, one at a time. Sift dry ingredients together, then add dates and nuts. Alternate dry mixture with buttermilk in adding to egg mixture. Blend in orange rind. Grease miniature muffin tins and fill 2/3 full. Bake for 10-15 minutes.

Topping:

3/4 cup sugar   1 tablespoon orange rind, grated
1/2 cup orange juice

Bring sugar, orange juice and rind to boil. Pour slowly over little cakes while they are still hot. Makes 5 dozen.

Glazed Cheesecake Puffs

16 ounces cream cheese
¾ cup sugar
2 eggs

1 teaspoon vanilla
24 vanilla wafers
22 ounces canned cherry pie filling

Preheat oven to 375. Place the cream cheese, sugar, eggs and vanilla in a large bowl and beat with electric mixer until smooth. Line muffin tins with paper liners and put one vanilla wafer in the bottom of each liner. Fill ¾ full with cheese mixture. Bake for 10 minutes and cool. Cover with pie filling. Chill. Yields 24.

Chocolate Reese Cups

1 pound confectioners' sugar
1 cup butter
1 cup peanut butter

12 ounces chocolate chips
2 tablespoons butter
½ block paraffin

Mix sugar, butter and peanut butter with a mixer until well-blended. Shape into balls and chill. Melt chocolate chips, butter and paraffin. Dip the chilled balls with toothpicks in chocolate mixture. Yields 50.

King's Arms Confections
(Courtesy of King's Arms Tavern, Williamsburg, Virginia)

½ cup egg whites
1 ¾ cups brown sugar
1 teaspoon lemon juice, fresh

2 tablespoons bread flour, sifted
½ cup pecans, chopped

Preheat oven to 200. Beat egg whites until stiff. Fold in brown sugar while beating egg whites. Add the lemon juice; fold in the sifted flour and pecans. Place mixture in a pastry bag. On a cookie tray or small sheet tray, place a piece of baking paper. Pipe approximately 1 tablespoon for each confection. Place tray in oven and bake for 25-30 minutes.

205

Never Fail Fudge

3 cups sugar
⅓ cup white corn syrup
¾ cup milk
almost ½ cup margarine, cut
    into pieces

3 ounces unsweetened chocolate,
    cut into pieces
1 teaspoon vanilla
1 cup nuts, chopped (optional)

Combine all ingredients, except vanilla and nuts, in a saucepan. Stir over low heat until all is melted. Turn heat to high; bring to *full* boil, stirring constantly, and cook *one* minute only. Remove from heat and add vanilla. Beat with mixer until mixture loses its shine to attain proper hardening consistency. Add nuts if desired. Pour into buttered 9x12 pan and cut into one-inch squares when firm. Yields approximately nine dozen pieces.
"Delicious, smooth and creamy!"

Easy Nut Fudge

1 pound confectioners' sugar
½ cup cocoa
¼ teaspoon salt
6 tablespoons butter or margarine

4 tablespoons milk
1 tablespoon vanilla
1 cup nuts, chopped

Combine all ingredients except nuts in top of double boiler. Place over hot water and stir until smooth. Add nuts and stir. Spread candy in buttered 9x5 pan. Cool and cut into squares. Yields 2 dozen pieces.

Walnut Fudge

4½ cups sugar
14½ ounces evaporated milk
18 ounces chocolate chips
1 cup butter

3 teaspoons vanilla
2 cups black walnuts, broken
pinch of salt

In a heavy saucepan combine sugar and milk. Cook over medium heat to soft ball stage, stirring frequently. Remove from heat; add remaining ingredients. Beat until mixture begins to thicken. Pour onto a greased cookie sheet. Let set for three hours or more. Cut into one-inch squares. Yields approximately eight dozen pieces.

Rum Balls

3 cups vanilla wafers, crushed
1 cup confectioners' sugar
1½ cups nuts, finely chopped
1½ tablespoons cocoa

2 tablespoons light corn syrup
½ cup rum
confectioners' sugar

Combine all ingredients and mix thoroughly. Form into small balls and roll in confectioners' sugar. Wrap in wax paper. They freeze well. Yields 50.
"Allow flavor to mellow a few days."

Stuffed Dates

pitted dates
marshmallows
pecan halves

bourbon
confectioners' sugar

Open date and stuff with ½ marshmallow and ½ pecan; press closed. Dip stuffed date in bowl of bourbon. Leave in long enough to get plenty of flavor! Roll in confectioners' sugar. Set on waxed paper to dry slightly, then store in tin cans or cake tins. They last well.
"These are nice for elegant holiday entertaining. Simple to do!"

Strawberry Candies

15 ounces sweetened condensed milk
1 pound coconut (finely ground type)
6 ounces strawberry gelatin
1 cup finely ground almonds
1 tablespoon sugar

1 teaspoon vanilla
½ teaspoon almond extract
green candied cherries or
    green tinted frosting

Combine condensed milk, coconut, 3 ounces dry gelatin, almonds, sugar and flavorings. Mix well. Shape to form strawberries. Roll berries in remaining gelatin to coat thoroughly. Allow to dry before storing. To make stem, use a piece of candied cherry or any kind of green frosting piped through a pastry tube. At Christmas time you may also use a holly leaf for the stem. These confections do not need refrigeration. Yields 4½ dozen.
"Delicious served as candy or to garnish fruit, salad or tea trays."

207

Spiced Nuts

¹/₄ cup sugar
1 tablespoon cinnamon
¹/₈ teaspoon ground cloves

¹/₈ teaspoon nutmeg
1 cup pecans
1 egg white, slightly beaten

Mix spices and sugar in a small bowl. Add nut meats, a few at a time, to the egg white and rub between fingers to coat thoroughly. Toss nuts in bowl of sugar and spices, coating completely. Place coated nuts on buttered cookie sheet. Bake in preheated 300 oven for 30 minutes.

Walnut Brittle

2 cups sugar
1 cup maple syrup
¹/₂ cup sherry
1 teaspoon salt

2 tablespoons margarine
3 cups walnuts, coarsely chopped
2 teaspoons baking soda

Combine sugar, syrup, sherry, salt and margarine. Cook over moderate heat, stirring until sugar is dissolved. Cover and simmer 5 minutes to wash crystals of sugar down from sides of pan. Uncover and boil to hard crack stage (300⁰ on candy thermometer). Meanwhile, turn walnuts into shallow pan and toast lightly in oven at 300. When candy reaches the hard crack stage, quickly stir in warm walnuts and baking soda. Turn at once onto oiled jelly roll pan or cookie sheet (10 x 15), and spread evenly. Let stand until cold. Break in pieces. Makes about 2 pounds.

Sugar Walnuts

1¹/₂ cups light brown sugar
1 teaspoon light corn syrup
¹/₂ teaspoon cinnamon

¹/₂ cup sherry
¹/₄ teaspoon salt
2-3 cups English walnut halves

Cook all ingredients, except nuts, to soft ball stage. Remove from heat and add walnuts. Stir gently and turn out on wax paper. Separate at once, using two spoons or forks. Yields 2 dozen.

Cakes

The dessert-loving colonists must have suffered during the first few years of the Jamestown settlement when neither ingredients nor equipment for baking cakes was available. Although the colony was well-stocked with milk, cheese, eggs and butter by 1624, it was not until late in the century that sugar and molasses were imported to Virginia from the West Indies. Even then, sugar was so costly that only the gentry used it, while the poor families sweetened their food with molasses. Cakes were scarce and even the wealthy reserved them for holidays and special occasions.

Cake making in colonial days was a tedious, all-day feat since everything was done by hand. Cone-shaped loaves of sugar had to be broken into hunks to be pulverized and sifted to the exact amounts. Flour had to be put before the open fire to dry, the butter washed free of salt, and whole spices had to be powdered by putting them in a mortar and pounding them or putting them through a spice mill. So important a task was this that regardless how large her staff of servants, the mistress of the house always attended to the preparation of cakes personally.

Cakes played such a prominent role in the family and social life of colonial times that there was a special cake for every happy or sad occasion—bridescake for weddings, rich fruit cakes for Christmas, pancakes for St. Valentine's Day, Twelfth Night cakes, and even funeral cakes. One of the best known special-occasion cake recipes to be passed down is that of Martha Washington's "Great Cake" . . . outstanding for both its enormous proportions and delicious flavor.

A less complicated but equally popular cake to span more than 200 years of Virginia cookery is the tipsy cake (modeled after the English trifle), often served as a traditional Christmas dessert. Another favorite to withstand the whims of two centuries is the pound cake, so named because its ingredients are

209

conveniently measured in quantities of one pound. Similarly, a small cake enjoyed then as now is the cupcake, appropriately measured in quantities of the cup. A dessert long associated with the colonial south is that of floating minature cakes on Syllabub (curdled or whipped milk with wine, sugar and other flavorings).

Cheesecake and its many derivatives were well liked in the seventeenth and eighteenth centuries as they are today. One particularly interesting eighteenth century recipe for "Cheesecake Without Curd" points out the "fine careless-ness" of naming recipes in early Virginia cookbooks. Apparently, the author did not care for cheese and simply omitted it from her original recipe without re-naming the dish.

Time has not diminished the Virginian's enjoyment of cakes, large or small. Though "great cakes" are seldom demanded by the large and steady stream of dinnertime visitors that characterized colonial times, trimmed down versions still are used to celebrate special occasions when family and friends are brought together.

Chocolate Filled Angel Cake

1 large angel food cake
8 ounces semi-sweet chocolate
4 tablespoons sugar
4 tablespoons water

4 eggs separated
1 pint heavy cream, whipped
  and sweetened

Combine chocolate, sugar and water; melt. Slowly add small amount of melted chocolate to beaten yolks. Stir warmed yolk mixture into remainder of choco-late. Beat egg whites into stiff peaks and fold into chocolate mixture. Prepare a narrow channel in the cake by cutting around the top of the cake 1 inch from each side. DO NOT cut through to bottom. Lift out section. Fill with chocolate mixture. Replace section. Ice exterior with cream. Garnish with shaved choco-late. Chill for several hours.

"Aluminum baking pans give best results for cakes; glass is better for pies."

Frozen Strawberry Angel Cake

16 ounces frozen strawberries
1 pint heavy cream
1 cup sugar

16 ounces cream cheese, softened
1 large angel food cake, cubed
10-20 fresh strawberries, sweetened

Thaw strawberries, drain and reserve ½ cup syrup. Whip ½ pint cream with ¼ cup sugar. Reserve. In large bowl, combine cream cheese and ½ cup sugar at low speed, then beat at high speed for 3 minutes or until smooth and creamy. Add reserved syrup. Beat 1 minute at low speed. Gently fold in strawberries, reserved cream and cake. Spoon mixture into oiled tube pan. Cover with foil and freeze. Remove from pan by dipping in hot water and loosening edge with knife. Refrigerate immediately. Allow to chill several hours. Before serving, whip remaining cream and sugar for icing. Decorate with fresh berries.
Note: A ready-made cake is fine to use. Fresh, sweetened berries may be used.

Apple Cake

2 cups flour
2 cups sugar
2 teaspoons baking soda
1 teaspoon cinnamon
½ teaspoon nutmeg
½ teaspoon salt

4 cups apples, peeled and
    finely diced
½ cup walnuts, chopped
½ cup butter, softened
2 eggs, slightly beaten

Preheat oven to 325. Grease a 9 x 13 baking dish. Sift dry ingredients into bowl. Add remaining ingredients and beat until JUST combined. Batter will be thick. Spread evenly in pan. Cook for 1 hour or until done.
"Delicious when served warm topped with ice cream or whipped cream."

Applesauce Cake

2 cups golden raisins
2 cups pecans, chopped
4 cups flour, sifted
2 teaspoons cinnamon
2 teaspoons cloves
2 teaspoons allspice
2 teaspoons baking soda

1 cup butter or margarine, softened
2⅔ cups sugar
2 eggs
2 cups applesauce
¼ cup hot water
¼ cup apricot brandy

211

Preheat oven to 350. Cover the raisins with some warm water for a few minutes, then drain and discard water. Dredge raisins and nuts with a little of the sifted flour. Resift flour with cinnamon, cloves, allspice and soda. Beat butter and sugar until creamy. Add eggs; beat. Add applesauce; beat. Add flour, nuts, raisins, water and brandy. Beat well. Pour into a greased and floured tube pan. Bake 1 hour.

"Keeps well in refrigerator or freezer and is best made the day before."

Blueberry Cake

1 cup butter, softened	1/2 teaspoon salt
2 cups sugar	1 teaspoon baking powder
4 eggs	1 pint fresh blueberries or
1 teaspoon vanilla	2 cups canned blueberries,
3 cups flour	drained and rinsed

Preheat oven to 325. Cream butter and sugar. Add eggs, one at a time and beat until fluffy. Add vanilla. Sift dry ingredients together. Reserve 1 cup flour mixture. Add remaining flour to batter; beat well. Dredge berries in reserved flour. Fold gently into batter. Spoon into greased and floured tube pan. Bake for 1 1/4 hours.

Note: Grease pan with butter and "flour" with sugar.

Carrot Cake

2 cups flour	4 eggs
2 cups sugar	3 cups carrots, shredded
2 teaspoons baking soda	1 teaspoon vanilla
2 teaspoons cinnamon	1 cup nuts, chopped (optional)
1 teaspoon salt	8 ounces crushed pineapple,
1 cup salad oil	drained (optional)

Preheat oven to 350. Sift dry ingredients together. Add the oil and eggs, one at a time. Beat until thoroughly mixed. Add carrots and vanilla. Mix well. Pour into greased and floured 9x13 pan, and bake for 45 minutes.

Icing:

1/2 cup butter, softened	1 teaspoon vanilla
1 pound confectioners' sugar	1 cup nuts, chopped
8 ounces cream cheese, softened	

Mix all ingredients together. Spread on the top and sides of the cake.

Centennial Cheddar Cheesecake

Crust:

1½ cups sifted flour
¼ cup plus 2 tablespoons sugar
1½ teaspoons lemon rind, grated

¾ cup margarine, softened
1½ egg yolks
½ teaspoon vanilla

Preheat oven to 400. Mix flour, sugar and lemon rind. Cut in margarine. Add egg yolks and vanilla. Mix with hands until dough is formed. Press ⅓ of dough evenly into bottom of a spring-form pan. Bake 10 minutes or until golden brown. Cool. Press remaining dough around sides of pan to within ½ inch of top.

Filling:

32 ounces cream cheese, softened
1 cup medium sharp Cheddar
    cheese, finely grated
1¾ cups sugar
¼ teaspoon vanilla
½ teaspoon orange rind, grated

½ teaspoon lemon rind, grated
4 eggs
2 egg yolks
¼ cup beer
¼ cup heavy cream

Preheat oven to 500. Beat cream cheese until fluffy. Add grated cheese; beat until well blended. Combine sugar, vanilla and grated fruit rinds. Add gradually to cheese mixture, beating until smooth. Add eggs and egg yolks, one at a time, beating after each. Stir in beer and cream. Pour in dough-lined pan and bake 8-10 minutes until top is golden. Reduce heat to 250. Bake 1 hour (cake tester should come out clean). Cool on rack, then chill. Remove sides of pan when ready to serve.

Strawberry Glaze:

2-3 cups fresh strawberries
1 cup water
1½ tablespoons cornstarch

¾ cup sugar
red food coloring

Crush 1 cup strawberries, add water and cook for two minutes. Strain. Mix cornstarch with sugar and stir into hot berry mixture. Bring to a boil, then cook, stirring constantly, until thick and clear. Add a few drops of red food coloring and cool. Serve with the cheesecake by slicing fresh strawberries on each slice and spooning glaze on top.

Village Cheese Cake

24 single graham crackers, crushed
6 tablespoons butter
24 ounces cream cheese, softened
1 cup sugar
1 tablespoon vanilla

rind of 1 orange, grated
rind of ½ lemon, grated
3 eggs, beaten
16 ounces sour cream
3 tablespoons sugar

Reserve 2 tablespoons crumbs for topping. Combine remaining crumbs with butter and press in bottom of 10 inch spring-form pan. Preheat oven to 325. Using mixer, blend cheese, sugar, rinds and vanilla slightly. Add eggs and beat ONLY until mixed. Pour over crumbs; bake 35-40 minutes. Cool at room temperature for 1 hour. Preheat oven to 425. Combine sour cream and sugar; spread over cheese cake. Top with reserved crumbs; bake 5 minutes. Cool at room temperature for 30 minutes. Chill 24 hours before serving. Serves 12-14.
"Your guests will remember you forever if you serve this dessert."

Dreamy Chocolate Fudge Cake

Cake:

½ cup butter
1 cup sugar
4 eggs

16 ounces chocolate syrup
1 cup self-rising flour, sifted
1 teaspoon vanilla

Preheat oven to 350. Cream butter and sugar. Add other ingredients and mix well. Pour into a greased and floured 9 x 13 pan. Bake about 40 minutes. Have topping ready to pour over cake when it comes from oven.

Topping:

2 ounces unsweetened chocolate
½ cup butter
1 cup evaporated milk

1 pound confectioners' sugar
1 teaspoon vanilla

Melt chocolate and butter. Add milk, sugar and vanilla. Blend over low heat until smooth. Pour over cake and return to oven for about 20 minutes or until it bubbles all over.
"Best if it sits one day before being cut."

Chocolate Chip Cake

1 teaspoon baking soda
1 cup dates, chopped
1 cup hot water
1 cup sugar
1 cup butter
1 ²/₃ cups flour

2 eggs, beaten
2 tablespoons cocoa
1 teaspoon vanilla
1 cup chocolate chips
½ cup nuts, chopped

Preheat oven to 350. Add soda to dates and pour hot water over them; let stand until cool. Cream sugar and butter. Combine with dates, flour, eggs, cocoa and vanilla. Add chocolate chips. Place in greased and floured 9x13 pan. Sprinkle with remainder of chips and nuts. Bake approximately 40 minutes.
"You don't know the dates are there—but you wonder why it is so moist!"

Chocolate Cookie Sheet Cake

2 cups flour
2 cups sugar
½ teaspoon salt
½ cup margarine
1 cup water
½ cup shortening

4 tablespoons cocoa
3 eggs, beaten
1 teaspoon baking soda
½ cup buttermilk
1 teaspoon vanilla

Preheat oven to 350. Grease and flour an 11x17 cookie sheet. Sift together flour, sugar and salt; set aside. In a saucepan, combine margarine, water, shortening and cocoa and bring to a boil; pour over flour mixture. Mix well. In another bowl, beat eggs, add soda, buttermilk and vanilla. Stir well and add to first mixture. Mix well. Bake for 20-25 minutes. Start icing during last 5 minutes of baking.

Icing:

½ cup margarine
4 tablespoons cocoa
1 pound confectioners' sugar
1 teaspoon vanilla

pinch of salt
6 tablespoons buttermilk
½ cup nuts, chopped (optional)

In a saucepan, melt margarine and cocoa, but DON'T BOIL. Take from heat and add remaining ingredients. Ice cake while hot. Yields 35 squares.

Fresh Coconut Cake

6 eggs	2½ cups flour, sifted
2 cups sugar	1 teaspoon vanilla
½ cup butter or margarine	3 teaspoons baking powder
1 cup hot milk	½ cup black walnuts, chopped

Preheat oven to 350. Separate eggs. Reserve 4 whites for icing. Beat egg yolks, 2 egg whites and sugar at medium-high speed on electric mixer until light and fluffy, at least 5 minutes. Melt butter in hot milk. Add ½ cup flour to eggs and sugar mixture, beating slowly. Add half of the hot milk mixture, 1 cup flour and remaining hot milk. Then add the rest of the flour, vanilla, baking powder and nuts. Pour into three 9-inch greased or lined cake pans. Bake 20 minutes. Cool slightly before removing from pans.

Icing:

1½ cups sugar	½ teaspoon cream of tartar
½ cup water	1 teaspoon vanilla
4 egg whites	2 cups fresh coconut, shredded

Boil sugar and water for 2 minutes. Beat egg whites and cream of tartar until eggs stand up in stiff peaks, but are not dry. Pour boiling syrup into egg whites, beating at highest speed on mixer. When icing becomes stiff enough to spread (2-4 minutes), add vanilla. Spread between layers, on top and sides of cake. Sprinkle with coconut.

"This is an old family recipe handed down for 4 generations."

Kenmore

Kenmore was built around 1752 by Colonel Fielding Lewis for his bride, the only sister of George Washington. The plain exterior of this red brick house and its detached wings contrasts vividly with the elaborate ceilings and ornamental panels of the interior. Through the work of such organizations as the Kenmore Association and The Garden Club of Virginia, Kenmore has become one of the most outstanding national museums with a fine array of authentic eighteenth century furniture, china, silver and glass.

Kenmore Ginger Bread
(Courtesy of Kenmore)

½ cup butter
½ cup brown sugar
1 cup West India molasses
½ cup warm milk
2 tablespoons ground ginger
1 heaping teaspoon cinnamon
1 heaping teaspoon mace
1 heaping teaspoon nutmeg

2-3 ounces brandy
3 eggs
3 cups flour
1 teaspoon cream of tartar
1 large orange, juiced and
    rind grated
1 teaspoon soda
1 cup raisins (optional)

Preheat oven to 350. Cut up in a pan the butter and brown sugar; beat to a cream with a paddle. Add molasses and warm milk, ginger, cinnamon, mace and nutmeg; add brandy. Beat eggs till very light and thick. Flour and cream of tartar should be sifted, then stirred alternately with the beaten eggs into the batter. Mix in the juice and grated rind of the orange. Dissolve soda in a little warm water, and stir in. Beat until very light. Raisins are a good addition. Bake in a loaf, sheet or patty pans for about 30 minutes.

Japanese Fruitcake

1 cup butter, softened
2 cups sugar
6 egg yolks, beaten
3 cups self-rising flour
2 tablespoons cocoa
1 teaspoon nutmeg

1 teaspoon cinnamon
1 teaspoon allspice
1/2 pound shredded coconut
1 cup nuts, chopped
1 pound seedless raisins

Preheat oven to 350. Cream butter and sugar. Add eggs and mix well. Sift flour, cocoa and spices together; add to egg mixture. Add coconut, nuts and raisins. Mix well. Use hands to mix thoroughly. Spoon batter in 4 greased and floured 9 inch layer pans. Bake for 25 minutes.

Filling:

2 cups sugar
2 large oranges, ground
2 large lemons, ground

4 tablespoons flour
1 cup hot water
1/2 pound shredded coconut

Mix sugar, oranges, lemons, flour and water together. Place in pan and boil until thick. Add coconut and mix well. Put filling between layers, on top, and on sides of cake. Wrap and store cake in refrigerator for at least 1 week before serving. Cut in thin slices.

White Fruitcake

12 eggs, separated
2 cups sugar
1 pound butter, softened
1 pound flour
2 pounds white raisins
2 pounds almonds and pecans,
    chopped
1 pound candied pineapple

1/4 pound candied orange peel
1/4 pound candied lemon peel
1/2 pound candied citron
1/2 pound candied cherries
1 teaspoon baking powder
1 tablespoon milk
1/2 teaspoon salt

Preheat oven to 250. Grease and flour pans. Number of cakes depends on size of pans used. Beat egg yolks and sugar together until light. Cream butter and flour until creamy, then mix. Save a little flour for the fruit. Mix all fruit and flour, and add to batter. Dissolve baking powder in milk. Add salt to egg whites and beat until stiff. Mix well into dough. Fill pans 3/4 full. Bake for 3 hours. Wrap in cheesecloth moistened with brandy.
"This old Virginia fruitcake uses traditional measurements."

Virginia Cherry Filbert Cake

1 1/2 cups butter, softened
2 cups sugar
6 eggs, separated
3/4 cup milk
1/4 cup cognac
3 1/2 cups sifted flour

1/2 teaspoon cream of tartar
1/4 teaspoon salt
3 cups toasted filberts, chopped
1 cup red candied cherries, halved
confectioners' sugar

Preheat oven to 275. Cream butter and gradually beat in sugar. Add egg yolks, one at a time, beating until light and fluffy. Combine milk and cognac, and add with flour to creamed mixture. Beat egg whites with cream of tartar and salt until stiff. Fold in the filberts and cherries, then fold egg whites into batter. Spoon into greased and waxed paper-lined tube pan and bake for 2 hours and 15 mintues. Peel off paper and sprinkle with confectioners' sugar. Cake keeps well; wrap well and store in a cool place.

Christmas Cake

2 cups butter, softened
1 pound light brown sugar
6 eggs
4 cups flour
1 teaspoon baking powder

2 teaspoons nutmeg
1 cup brandy
1 pound seedless raisins
3 cups pecans, chopped

Preheat oven to 325. Cream butter and sugar. Add eggs, one at a time and beat well after each. Sift together the dry ingredients and add gradually to the creamed mixture. Beat until well blended. Stir in brandy; fold in raisins and pecans. Pour mixture into a greased and floured tube pan. Bake for 1 hour and 40 minutes. Cool; wrap and store for one week.
"Like a fruitcake without all the extra fruit."

Hermit Cake

2 cups butter
3 cups brown sugar
6 eggs
5 cups sifted flour
4 teaspoons baking powder
1/4 teaspoon salt

2 teaspoons cinnamon
1 pound dates, chopped
1 pound nuts, chopped
1 lemon, juiced
4 teaspoons vanilla

Preheat oven to 275. Cream butter and sugar. Add well-beaten eggs. Gradually add sifted dry ingredients, reserving some to "flour" dates and nuts. Add well-floured dates, nuts, lemon juice and vanilla. Bake for 3 hours in greased large tube or bundt pan.

Note: This recipe must use butter.

Nut Cake

3 cups sifted cake flour
1 ¾ cups sugar
2 teaspoons baking powder
1 ½ teaspoons salt
1 cup shortening

¾ cup milk
2 teaspoons vanilla
4 eggs
1 cup nuts, finely chopped

Preheat oven to 375. Sift dry ingredients into mixing bowl. Add shortening, milk, vanilla and 2 eggs. Beat exactly 300 strokes by hand or 2 minutes at medium speed on mixer. Add remaining eggs, beat exactly 2 minutes more. Fold in nuts. Turn into greased and floured 9 inch tube pan and bake for 1 hour. Leave in pan on rack 10-15 minutes before removing from pan.

Frosting:

2 cups sugar
⅛ teaspoon cream of tartar
1 cup hot water

½ teaspoon vanilla
confectioners' sugar

Cook sugar, cream of tartar and water to a thin syrup (226 degrees). Cool to lukewarm (110 degrees). Add vanilla and then sifted confectioners' sugar until frosting is of consistency to pour. Drizzle frosting over cake.

Banana Nut Cake

½ cup butter or margarine
1 ½ cups sugar
2 eggs, added one at a time
2 cups sifted flour

1 teaspoon baking soda
½ teaspoon salt
3 large bananas, mashed
1 cup nuts, chopped

Preheat oven to 350. Cream butter and sugar. Add rest of ingredients. Pour into a greased tube pan. Bake for 50-60 minutes.

"This cake freezes very well."

Hot Milk Cake

½ cup butter
1 cup milk
4 eggs
2 cups sugar

1 teaspoon vanilla
2 cups flour
½ teaspoon salt
1 teaspoon baking powder

Preheat oven to 325. Combine butter and milk in saucepan, bring to just a boil (DO NOT BOIL). Beat eggs and gradually add sugar, beating constantly. Add vanilla. Sift flour and salt; add to egg mixture. Beat until smooth. Gradually add the milk and butter mixture and beat well. Add baking powder and beat again. Pour into well-greased and floured tube pan. Bake for 1 hour. Cool for 10 minutes before removing from pan.

Note: This cake is very good warm with berries and whipped cream. Also you can halve the recipe and bake in an 8 or 9 inch square pan about 30 minutes.

"A good all-purpose cake."

Oatmeal Cake

1¼ cups boiling water
1 cup quick-cooking rolled oats
½ cup margarine
1 cup light brown sugar
1 cup sugar
2 eggs, well beaten

1⅓ cups sifted flour
1 teaspoon baking soda
1 teaspoon cinnamon
½ teaspoon salt
1 teaspoon vanilla

Preheat oven to 350. Pour boiling water over oats and let stand for 20 minutes. Cream margarine and all sugar thoroughly, and add eggs. Sift together flour, soda, cinnamon and salt, and add to creamed mixture; add oat mixture and vanilla. Bake in greased and floured 9 inch square pan for 45-55 minutes.

Icing:

3 tablespoons margarine, melted
10 tablespoons sugar
2 tablespoons cream

⅛ teaspoon salt
½ cup shredded coconut
   or nut meats

Mix ingredients and spread over warm cake. Place cake on low oven shelf and broil until icing bubbles over surface. DO NOT SCORCH.

221

Glazed Orange Cake

1 cup butter or margarine, softened
2 cups sugar
½ teaspoon vanilla
2 tablespoons orange rind, grated
5 eggs

3 cups cake flour
1 tablespoon baking powder
pinch of salt
¾ cup milk

Preheat oven to 350. Cream butter or margarine and sugar until light and fluffy. Add vanilla and orange rind. Add eggs, one at a time, beating well after each. Combine and sift cake flour, baking powder and salt TWICE. Add dry ingredients to the creamed mixture gradually, alternating with the milk and ending with flour, beating well after each addition. Spoon into buttered and floured tube pan and bake one hour or until cake springs back when touched. Cool 15 minutes.

Glaze:

¼ cup butter or margarine
⅓ cup orange juice

⅔ cup sugar

Heat ingredients in saucepan until sugar is dissolved. Pour evenly over cake in pan while cake is still warm. Allow cake to cool thoroughly in the pan before removing.

"Overmixing causes cake failure."

Old Fashion Jelly Roll
(Courtesy of Mount Gilead)

3 eggs
1 cup sugar
3 tablespoons cold water
1 cup flour

⅓ teaspoon salt
1 teaspoon baking powder
sugar
jam or jelly

Beat eggs and sugar until creamy and thick. Add water. Sift flour, salt and baking powder twice; add to eggs. Line jelly roll pan with greased waxed paper. Pour cake batter into pan. Bake at 400 for 12 minutes. Turn out on cloth that is sprinkled with sugar as soon as you take it from the oven. Quickly and gently roll up cake with cloth being part of the rolling. Unfold it. Spread with jam or jelly. Roll up quickly.
Note: Secret is to roll while warm.

222

Mount Gilead

Mount Gilead, a Lee family home, was built in 1794 by George R. L. Turburville on land granted by the King of England. Turburville, one of the founders of Phi Beta Kappa, married Henrietta Lee, daughter of Richard Henry Lee and spent happy years in this eight room frame house. Distinguishing features of this splendid home in Centreville are a beautiful staircase, three chimneys, six fireplaces with original mantels and much of the original flooring.

Buttermilk Pound Cake

1 cup butter, softened
3 cups sugar
4 eggs
¼ teaspoon baking soda

1 teaspoon vanilla
3 cups flour
1 cup buttermilk

Preheat oven to 350. Cream butter and sugar. Add eggs, one at a time. Add soda and vanilla. Add flour alternately with buttermilk. Bake in a greased and floured tube pan for 1 hour.

"Have butter, eggs and milk at room temperature before mixing cakes."

Chocolate Pound Cake

3 cups sugar
1 cup butter, softened
½ cup shortening
5 eggs
3 cups flour

8 tablespoons cocoa
½ teaspoon baking powder
¼ teaspoon salt
1 cup milk
1 teaspoon vanilla

Preheat oven to 275. Cream sugar with butter and shortening. Add eggs, one at a time, beating thoroughly after each. Add sifted dry ingredients alternately with milk. Add vanilla. Pour into greased and floured tube pan. Bake 1 hour; then an additional hour at 300.

Icing:

¼ cup butter
2 ounces unsweetened chocolate
1 pound confectioners' sugar

1 teaspoon vanilla
evaporated milk

Melt butter and chocolate over hot water. Add to sugar and vanilla. Add milk to desired consistency, beating continuously. Drizzle over warm cake.

Virginia-North Carolina Pound Cake

1 pound butter, softened (2 cups)
1 pound sugar (2 cups)
10 eggs, separated
1 pound flour (4 cups)

1 teaspoon almond extract
1 teaspoon lemon extract
1 teaspoon vanilla extract
1 teaspoon baking powder

224

Preheat oven to 350. Cream butter and add sugar. Add beaten egg yolks, one at a time. Add flour, flavorings and baking powder. Fold in stiffly beaten egg whites. Bake for 1 hour in a greased and floured tube pan.

"This traditional pound cake, using a pound of everything, has been a family speciality since 1800 when the kitchen in which it was prepared was divided by the Virginia-Carolina state line."

Sour Cream Pound Cake

1 cup butter, softened
3 cups sugar
6 eggs
1 cup sour cream
¼ teaspoon baking soda

¼ teaspoon baking powder
¼ teaspoon salt
3 cups sifted flour
1½ teaspoons lemon extract
1½ teaspoons almond extract

Preheat oven to 300. Cream butter. Add sugar, 1 cup at a time. Beat at high speed after each addition. Add whole eggs, 1 at a time, beating well at medium speed. Add sour cream, beating well. Add soda, baking powder and salt to flour. Then add dry ingredients, 1 cup at a time, mixing well after each addition. Add flavorings. Pour into well-greased tube pan. Bake for 1½ hours. Let stand 10 minutes before removing from pan.

Sweet Potato Pound Cake

1 cup butter, softened
2 cups sugar
2½ cups sweet potatoes,
  cooked and mashed
4 eggs
3 cups flour

¼ teaspoon salt
2 teaspoons baking powder
1 teaspoon baking soda
½ teaspoon nutmeg
1 teaspoon cinnamon
1 teaspoon vanilla

Preheat oven to 350. Cream butter and sugar. Add potatoes and beat until light and fluffy. Add eggs separately and beat well after each addition. Combine dry ingredients and add to creamed mixture slowly. Add vanilla and beat well. Pour into greased and floured tube pan. Bake for 1¼ hours.

Note: Warm cake can be spread with orange glaze if desired: 1 cup confectioners' sugar and 2-3 tablespoons orange juice.

"This is a delightful addition to the winter holidays."

Spice Cake

2 cups self-rising flour
2 cups sugar
1 teaspoon nutmeg
1 teaspoon allspice

1 cup salad oil
3 eggs
7¾ ounces baby food prunes
1 cup nuts, chopped (optional)

Preheat oven to 300. Combine flour, sugar and spices. Add oil, eggs and prunes; mix well. Pour into greased and floured tube pan and bake 1 hour.
Note: Other fruits may be substituted.

Icing (Optional):

1 cup sugar
½ cup buttermilk
½ cup margarine

1 tablespoon light corn syrup
½ teaspoon baking soda
½ teaspoon vanilla

Mix and boil for 2 minutes. Pour over warm cake.

Huguenot Torte

4 eggs
2 cups sugar
8 tablespoons flour
5 teaspoons baking powder
2 teaspoons vanilla
2 cups nuts, chopped

3 cups apples, chopped and sprinkled
    with a dash of lemon juice
¼ teaspoon salt
butter or margarine
whipped cream

Preheat oven to 350. Beat eggs, add sugar and other ingredients. Pour into well-buttered 9 x 13 pan. Bake for 30 minutes. Cut in squares. Top with whipped cream.
"Delicious for luncheon or dinner party."

Pineapple Torte

Batter:

2 cups flour
1 tablespoon baking powder
½ teaspoon salt
½ cup shortening

1⅓ cups sugar
1 teaspoon vanilla
1 cup pineapple juice
3 egg whites

Sift flour, baking powder and salt together. Cream shortening and sugar; beat until light and fluffy. Add sifted ingredients alternately with flavoring and pineapple juice. Beat well. Beat egg whites until stiff but not dry; fold into batter. Pour into 2 9-inch cake pans which have been greased, floured and completely lined with waxed paper. Cover batter with meringue.

Meringue:

3 egg whites
¼ teaspoon salt
⅔ cup sugar

1 teaspoon vanilla
¾ cup nuts, chopped

Preheat oven to 350. Beat egg whites and salt until stiff but not dry. Add sugar gradually; beating and folding in. Add flavoring and nuts. Bake approximately 35-40 minutes or until cake springs back when touched; cool.

Frosting:

½ pint heavy cream
2 tablespoons confectioners' sugar

1 cup crushed pineapple, drained

Whip cream; fold in sugar and pineapple. Spread between layers of cake. Refrigerate until ready to serve.

Note: Torte may be refrigerated several hours before serving.

Vanilla Wafer Cake

1 cup butter, softened
2 cups sugar
6 eggs
12 ounces vanilla wafers,
  crumbled fine

½ cup milk
1 cup nuts, chopped
7 ounces shredded coconut
½ teaspoon vanilla

Preheat oven to 325. Cream butter and sugar; add eggs. Add crumbs and milk alternately to mixture. Add nuts, coconut and vanilla. Put in well greased and floured tube pan and bake for 1½ hours.

Note: After placing cake batter in pan, tap pan firmly on counter top to release air bubbles.

"Better the second day."

227

Virginia Whiskey Cake
(Courtesy of Evans Farm Inn, McLean, Virginia)

1 cup sugar	*½ teaspoon baking powder*
1 cup brown sugar, packed	*½ teaspoon mace*
1 cup butter, softened	*1 cup 100 proof bourbon whiskey*
3 eggs	*2 cups pecans, chopped*
3 cups sifted cake flour	

Preheat oven to 250. Combine the sugars and cream with butter. Add well-beaten eggs. Sift flour. baking powder and mace; add alternately with whiskey. Add nuts. Bake in well greased or paper-lined tube pan for 2½-3 hours. The cake should have a moist, crumbly texture similar to a macaroon. Wrap in foil and store in a cool place. (Do not freeze.) The cake cuts easier when cold, but should be served at room temperature. It will keep for 2 weeks or longer. Slices about ½ inch thick are best. Save the crumbs for parfaits or sundae topping.

Note: For added flavor, add one tablespoon of WHISKEY SAUCE (½ cup light corn syrup, 1 tablespoon rum, 2 tablespoons whiskey) to cake about half an hour before serving. Whipped cream topping is optional.

Buttercream Frosting

3 egg whites	*⅓ cup cocoa*
1½ cups confectioners' sugar, sifted	*½ teaspoon vanilla*
	almonds or pecans
8 ounces sweet whipped butter	

Beat egg whites to form soft peaks. Gradually add ¾ cup sugar, beating until stiff peaks form. Set meringue aside. Beat butter until creamy. Mix remainder of sugar with cocoa and gradually beat into butter. Fold in vanilla and meringue until well-blended. Use to fill and frost cooled cake. Decorate with nuts.

Quick Chocolate Glaze

2 teaspoons cocoa	*1 tablespoon light corn syrup*
1 tablespoon plus 1 teaspoon water	*1 cup confectioners' sugar, sifted*
1 tablespoon salad oil	

Mix all ingredients except sugar in small saucepan. Stir over medium heat until blended. Remove from heat and stir in sugar. Drizzle over cake.

Foolproof Caramel Icing

1 cup dark brown sugar
½ cup butter
¼ cup milk

1½-2 cups confectioners' sugar
1 teaspoon vinegar

Cook brown sugar and butter for 2 minutes. Remove from heat and add milk. Cook a few minutes. Remove from heat and beat in confectioners' sugar and vinegar. Beat until smooth and thick. Frosts top and sides of three 9 inch layers.

Cherry Fluff Frosting

2 egg whites
1½ cups sugar
3 tablespoons maraschino cherry syrup

3 tablespoons water
¼ teaspoon cream of tartar
dash of salt
1 teaspoon vanilla

Place above ingredients in top of double boiler. Beat 1 minute with mixer to blend. Place over boiling water, beating constantly until frosting forms peaks, about 7 minutes. Remove from water. Add vanilla and beat until of spreading consistency, about 2 minutes.

Cream Cheese Frosting

3 ounces cream cheese, softened
1 tablespoon butter, softened

1 teaspoon vanilla
2 cups confectioners' sugar, sifted

Beat cream cheese, butter and vanilla until smooth and fluffy. Gradually add sugar, beating at medium speed until fluffy.
Note: Orange juice may be substituted for vanilla.

Easy White Frosting

1 egg white, unbeaten
¾ cup sugar
¼ teaspoon cream of tartar

1 teaspoon vanilla
¼ cup boiling water

Mix first 4 ingredients in small, deep bowl. Add boiling water and beat to stiff peaks. Spread between layers and on top and sides of 2 8-inch cake layers. Decorate with coconut or any other suitable decoration.

Pies

So significant were pies and pastries to the American diet that by 1830 a special cabinet called the pie safe was manufactured to protect the mouth-watering goodies from flies, insects and mice. This simple wooden cabinet had perforated tin doors for ventilation and was usually kept on the back porch; it remained in vogue until the invention of the first true ice box.

Favorites since colonial times, sweet pies traditionally required two crusts and were filled with fruits or mincement. The abundance of fresh fruit at her finger-tips gave the Virginia housewife of yesteryear an endless variety of pies to place before her family: apple, pear, plum, apricot, quince, peach and cherry. Lemon- and orange-flavored pies were also popular. During the winter months when fresh fruit was scarce, the enterprising cook reverted to preserved fruits and berries to make sweetmeat tarts.

Custard pies must have also been in great demand judging from the number of colonial puddings which were baked in a "coffin"—the equivalent to our modern pastry shell. Even as late as the early twentieth century, Virginia cook-books had more recipes for puddings baked in pastry than for actual pies. The pastry for early Virginia pies and related delicacies was a "puff-paste" so fore-boding that few modern day cooks are willing to attempt it. This "lighter-than-air" pastry calls for cold ingredients, frequent chilling of the paste and skillful handling. Nevertheless, colonial and subsequent cooks somehow managed to achieve the perfection of this light, flaky crust even before the days of refrig-eration and temperature-sure ovens. Part of their success is attributed to the cool marble slab upon which the pastry was prepared and rolled.

Mincemeat pie, which is associated most often with Thanksgiving and Christ-mas desserts, was generally made of equal quantities of veal and beef suet, apples, raisins, currants, candied orange and lemon peel, citron, almonds, sugar, spices, rosewater and wine. Even today there has been no improvement upon eighteenth-century mincemeat recipes.

Cheesecakes or pies borrowed from English cookbooks or from favorite family recipes were often enjoyed by the early cooks also, but the best and most delicious pies in colonial Virginia were the ingenious adaptations developed from the native foodstuff of the area such as sweet potatoes, pumpkins, pecans and fox grapes.

Advanced technology has relegated the old-fashioned pie safe to the category of collector's items, but the role of pies in Virginia cookery has not diminished in the least through the years!

Brown Sugar Apple Pie

6 cooking apples, pared and sliced
⅔ cup sugar
butter
cinnamon
½ cup butter, softened

½ cup brown sugar
1 cup flour
pinch of salt
whipped cream

Preheat oven to 325. Butter a 9 inch pie plate. Pile apples in plate and sprinkle with sugar, butter and cinnamon. Next cream butter and sugar; add flour and salt. Press this crumbly mixture firmly over apples. Bake for 45 minutes or until apples are tender. Serve garnished with whipped cream.

Note: For variation, substitute fresh peaches for apples.

Brown Sugar Pie

2 eggs, well-beaten
½ cup brown sugar, packed
1 teaspoon vanilla
4 tablespoons water

3 tablespoons butter, melted
¾-1 cup pecans, chopped
8 inch pastry shell, unbaked

Preheat oven to 375. Combine all ingredients in order. Pour into pastry shell and bake for 45 minutes or until firm.

Blueberry Strata Pie

1 pound canned blueberries
8 3/4 ounces canned crushed
  pineapple
8 ounces cream cheese, softened
3 tablespoons sugar
1 tablespoon milk
1/2 teaspoon vanilla

9 inch pastry shell, baked
1/4 cup sugar
2 tablespoons cornstarch
1/4 teaspoon salt
1 teaspoon lemon juice
1/2 cup whipping cream, whipped

Drain fruits, reserving syrups. Blend cream cheese, sugar, milk and vanilla. Set aside 2 tablespoons pineapple; stir remaining into cheese mixture. Spread over bottom of pastry shell; chill. Blend sugar, cornstarch and salt. Combine syrups and measure 1 1/2 cups; blend into the cornstarch mixture. Cook and stir until thickened. Add blueberries and lemon juice; stir and cool. Pour over cheese layer and chill. Top with whipped cream and reserved pineapple.

Brandy Alexander Pie

1 tablespoon gelatin
1/2 cup cold water
2/3 cup sugar
1/8 teaspoon salt
3 eggs, separated

1/4 cup brandy
1/4 cup creme de cacao
1 cup heavy cream, whipped
1-10 inch or 2-8 inch graham cracker
  pie shells

Sprinkle gelatin over cold water in saucepan. Add 1/3 cup sugar, salt, egg yolks; stir to blend. Cook over low heat, stirring until gelatin dissolves and mixture thickens. DO NOT BOIL. Remove from heat, stir in brandy and creme de cacao. Chill until the mixture mounds slightly (approximately 1/2 hour). Beat egg whites until stiff and gradually add remaining sugar; fold into the thickened mixture. Fold in the whipped cream and turn into the pie shell(s). Chill overnight and garnish with chocolate shavings.

Butter Nut Brown Pie

20 saltine crackers, crushed
1 cup pecans, finely chopped
2 teaspoons baking powder

3 large egg whites
1/2 cup sugar
1/2 cup brown sugar

232

Preheat oven to 350. Mix crackers, pecans and baking powder. Beat egg whites until they are very stiff. Add sugar, a teaspoon at a time and then the brown sugar. Fold in the cracker mixture and place in a buttered pie plate. Bake for 25 minutes. Cool and top with whipped cream, if desired.

Cheesecake Pie

Crust:

1 ¼ cup vanilla wafer crumbs	*2 ounces butter, melted*

Combine the above and press into a buttered 8 inch pie plate, building up sides.

Filling:

8 ounces cream cheese, softened	*½ teaspoon vanilla*
½ cup sugar	*dash of salt*
1 tablespoon lemon juice	*2 eggs*

Preheat oven to 325. Beat cream cheese until fluffy. Gradually blend in sugar, lemon juice, vanilla and salt. Add eggs, one at a time, beating after each. Pour into crust and bake for 25-30 minutes or until set.

Topping:

1 cup sour cream	*2 tablespoons sugar*
(at room temperature)	*½ teaspoon vanilla*

Combine ingredients and spoon over top of pie as soon as you remove from oven and return immediately for 10 more minutes. Cool. Chill several hours.
Note: You can grate the rind of the lemon and use along with the lemon juice.

Chocolate Chess Pie

½ cup butter	*1 ⅞ cups sugar*
3 ounces unsweetened chocolate	*1 ½ teaspoons vanilla*
1 tablespoon flour	*6 ounces evaporated milk*
3 eggs, beaten	*1 pastry shell, baked*

Preheat oven to 375. Melt butter and chocolate in a saucepan. Add remaining ingredients to chocolate and cook for 5 minutes. Pour into pastry shell and bake for 25 minutes. Garnish with whipped cream or meringue, if desired.
Note: Fills one extra-large or two 8 inch pastry shells.

Chocolate Angel Pie

Shell:

2 eggs, separated	1/2 cup sugar
1/8 teaspoon salt	1/2 cup pecans, chopped
1/8 teaspoon cream of tartar	1/2 teaspoon vanilla

Preheat oven to 275. Combine egg whites, salt and cream of tartar in a mixing bowl. Beat until foamy throughout. Add sugar (2 tablespoons at a time), beating after each addition until sugar is blended. Continue beating until mixture will stand in very stiff peaks. Fold in nuts and vanilla. Spoon into a lightly buttered 9 inch pie plate, building sides to 1/2 inch above edge of plate. Bake 50-55 minutes. Cool.

Filling:

4 ounces sweet cooking chocolate	1 cup whipping cream
3 tablespoons water	1 tablespoon confectioners' sugar
2 egg yolks, beaten	1/8 teaspoon cinnamon

Place chocolate and water in a saucepan over low heat. Stir until chocolate is melted. Remove from heat. Gradually stir the egg yolks into the chocolate mixture. Return the saucepan to low heat and cook for 1 minute, stirring constantly; cool. Combine whipping cream, sugar and cinnamon in a chilled bowl. Beat until cream holds its shape (do not overbeat). Spread about 1 cup of the whipped cream in the bottom of the meringue shell. Fold the remaining whipped cream into the chocolate mixture and spread evenly over the cream filling in the shell. Chill for several hours or overnight. Garnish with additional whipped cream and pecans.

German Chocolate Pie

1 cup sugar	3 tablespoons butter, melted
1 tablespoon cornstarch	2/3 cup milk
1 tablespoon flour	3/4 cup shredded coconut
2 tablespoons cocoa	1/2 cup pecans, chopped
pinch of salt	1 teaspoon vanilla
2 eggs	9 inch pastry shell, unbaked

Preheat oven to 400. Combine sugar, cornstarch, flour, cocoa and salt. Add eggs, butter and milk; then coconut, nuts and vanilla. Pour into pastry shell and bake for 35-40 minutes. Top will be crusty and firm.

Chocolate Rum Pie

¾ cup sugar
1 tablespoon gelatin
dash of salt
1 cup milk
2 eggs, separated

6 ounces semisweet chocolate bits
⅓ cup rum
½ pint whipping cream
1 teaspoon vanilla
10 inch pastry shell, baked

In a heavy saucepan, combine ½ cup sugar, gelatin and salt. Stir in milk and beaten egg yolks. Cook and stir over low heat until mixture is slightly thickened. Remove from heat; add chocolate; and stir until melted. Add rum and chill until partially set. Beat egg whites until soft peaks form; gradually add remaining sugar, and beat until stiff. Fold meringue into chocolate mixture. Whip cream with vanilla. Pour ½ of chocolate mixture into pastry shell. Layer whipped cream evenly across top, reserving some for topping. Pour remaining chocolate mixture on top of cream layer. Swirl the rest of the whipped cream in chocolate. Chill until set.

Blender Chocolate Fudge Pie

2½ cups sugar
7 tablespoons cocoa
4 eggs
1¼ cups evaporated milk

1 tablespoon vanilla
1 stick margarine, melted
2-8 inch pie shells

Preheat oven to 350. Put first 6 ingredients in blender and mix well. Pour into pie shells and bake for 35-40 minutes. Remove from oven while center is still shaky.

Double Fudge Pie

½ cup butter
3 ounces unsweetened chocolate
3 eggs, beaten
1½ cups sugar

¼ cup flour
½ teaspoon vanilla
½ teaspoon salt
1 teaspoon milk

Preheat oven to 325. Melt butter and chocolate and cool slightly. Gradually mix into eggs. Add remaining ingredients and stir until just mixed. Spread into a buttered 9 inch pie plate and bake for precisely 40 minutes. Center will be soft and moist when taken from oven, but firms a little when cooling. Best served warm with vanilla ice cream.
"So easy since there's no crust!"

Christmas Cheer Pie

1¼ cups chocolate wafer crumbs
¾ cup sugar
⅓ cup butter, melted
1 tablespoon gelatin
⅛ teaspoon salt
3 eggs, separated

½ cup cold water
¼ cup green creme de menthe
¼ cup white creme de cacao
1½ cups heavy cream
pistachio nuts, chopped
red cherries, chopped

Mix crumbs, ¼ cup sugar and butter, press into a 9 inch pie plate. Bake at 400 for 5 minutes, cool. Combine gelatin, ¼ cup sugar and salt in a medium-sized saucepan. Beat egg yolks and water together; stir into gelatin mixture. Cook over low heat, stirring constantly, for 3-5 minutes or until gelatin dissolves and mixture thickens. Remove from heat, stir in creme de menthe and creme de cacao. Chill, stirring occasionally until mixture is the consistency of unbeaten egg whites. Beat egg whites until stiff, but not dry. Add remaining sugar gradually to egg whites; beat until very stiff. Fold into the gelatin mixture and chill. Whip 1 cup of cream until stiff and fold into the gelatin mixture. Pour into pie shell and chill until firm. Whip remaining cream until stiff and place on pie in the shape of a wreath. Sprinkle with nuts and cherries.
"A lovely holiday dessert—light, but rich."

Holiday Pie

4 eggs
1 cup butter, melted
2 cups sugar
2 tablespoons vinegar
2 teaspoons vanilla

1 cup shredded coconut
1 cup pecans, chopped
1 cup white raisins
9 inch pastry shell, unbaked

Preheat oven to 350. Beat eggs and add butter. Add remaining ingredients and mix. Pour into pie crust and bake for 30-40 minutes.
"Try this as a change for Thanksgiving or Christmas!"

Coconut Pie

2 eggs
1½ cups sugar
pinch of salt
½ cup butter, softened

¼ cup flour
½ cup milk
1 cup shredded coconut
9 inch pastry shell, unbaked

Preheat oven to 325. Beat eggs and gradually add sugar and salt; beat until thick and lemon colored. Blend in butter; then flour and milk. Add coconut. Spoon into pastry shell and bake for 45 minutes to 1 hour or until set and slightly browned.

Great-Grandmother's Custard Pie

2 tablespoons flour
1 1/2 cups sugar
2/3 cup butter
3 eggs
2/3 cup evaporated milk

2/3 cup water
2 teaspoons vanilla
2-9 inch pastry shells,
    unbaked

Preheat oven to 350. Mix flour and sugar. Add butter and eggs; beat well. Add milk and water. Mix well; add vanilla. Bake 1 hour or until firm and golden.
Note: Before cooking, it will have a curdly appearance; afterwards it will appear golden.

Lemon Chess Pie
(Courtesy of The Carriage House, Norfolk, Virginia)

3 eggs, beaten until light
1 1/2 cups sugar
1 1/2 lemons, juiced
grated rind of 1 lemon

3 tablespoons butter, melted
1/2 teaspoon salt
1 pastry shell, unbaked

Preheat oven to 350. Combine first 6 ingredients and pour into the pastry shell. Bake for 25-30 minutes.

Lovely Lemon Pie

4 eggs, separated
14 ounces sweetened condensed milk
2 tablespoons butter, melted
1/2 cup lemon juice

1/2 cup sugar
1/4 teaspoon vanilla
9 inch pastry shell, baked

Preheat oven to 325. Beat egg yolks and milk; mix in butter and then lemon juice. In a separate bowl, beat the egg whites until stiff. Add sugar and vanilla. Fold 4 tablespoons of egg whites into lemon mixture; pour into pastry shell. Use remaining egg whites for meringue. Bake for 20 minutes.

237

Double Crust Lemon Pie

3 eggs
1¼ cups sugar
2 tablespoons flour
⅛ teaspoon salt
¼ cup butter, softened

1 whole lemon
juice of ½ lemon
½ cup water
9 inch double pastry, unbaked
egg white, cinnamon, and sugar

Preheat oven to 400. Beat eggs, add sugar, flour, salt and butter. Grate rind of a lemon; peel and slice paper-thin. Blend lemon juice, rind and slices into mixture. Add water, mix and pour into pastry shell. Cover with crust and brush with egg whites; sprinkle with cinnamon and sugar. Bake for 30 minutes.

"Always have egg whites at room temperature before making meringues or beating egg whites."

Lemonade Meringue Pie

1 cup sour cream
3 eggs, separated
4½ ounces vanilla pudding mix
⅓ cup frozen lemonade concentrate
   thawed

1¼ cups milk
9 inch pastry shell, baked
½ teaspoon vanilla
¼ teaspoon cream of tartar
6 tablespoons sugar

Preheat oven to 350. Combine sour cream and slightly-beaten egg yolks in saucepan. Stir in pudding mix, lemonade and milk. Cook and stir until mixture thickens and boils. Remove from heat and spoon into pastry shell. Beat egg whites, vanilla and cream of tartar until soft peaks form. Gradually add sugar, beating to stiff peaks. Spread on top of hot filling, sealing meringue to the edges of the pastry. Bake for 12-15 minutes. Cool and chill.

Note: Meringues—how to make them perfect.
1. Separate eggs while cold.
2. Use a deep, narrow bowl and electric mixer.
3. Add salt and cream of tartar when foamy.
4. Add sugar when whites hold soft peaks.
5. Bake on highest rack in oven.
6. Cool baked meringue at room temperature, then refrigerate if necessary.

The Sheild House

The Sheild House, the oldest house in Yorktown, was built in 1692 by Thomas Sessions and passed through many ownerships before becoming the property of the Sheild family in 1901. The front door is said to be the largest single door opening of any old house in Virginia. This lovely home with its large central hall displays original seventeenth and eighteenth century woodwork. This singular landmark has been visited by many famous personages, including five Presidents of the United States.

Lemon Chess Pie
(Courtesy of The Sheild House)

1 cup butter or margarine	*½ teaspoon salt*
2 cups sugar	*3 lemons, juice and rind*
6 eggs	

Preheat oven to 400. Cream butter with sugar. Add eggs, one by one. To this, add salt and the juice and rind of lemons. Pour into 2 unbaked pie shells. Cook until browned.

Lemon Chess Pie

¼ cup butter
1½ cups sugar
juice of 1 lemon

3 eggs, beaten
9 inch pastry shell, unbaked

Preheat oven to 325. Blend all ingredients in blender. Pour into pastry shell and bake for 45 minutes.

Creamy Lime Pie

1 cup shredded coconut
2 tablespoons flour
2 tablespoons butter
1 tablespoon gelatin
¼ cup cold water
3 eggs, separated
¾ cup water

¾ cup sugar
16 ounces cream cheese, softened
¼ cup lime juice
1 teaspoon grated lime rind
2-3 drops green food coloring
1 cup heavy cream, whipped

Preheat oven to 350. Combine coconut, flour and butter. Press mixture into one 9 inch pie plate. Bake for 12-15 minutes. Soften gelatin in cold water. Combine egg yolks, water and sugar in saucepan; stir over medium heat for 5 minutes. Add gelatin and stir until it dissolves. Place cream cheese in large bowl and gradually add gelatin mixture; mix until blended. Add lime juice, rind and food coloring; stir. Fold in whipped cream and stiffly-beaten egg whites. Pour into shells and chill. Garnish with lime slices.

Ice Cream Pie

1 cup flour
¼ cup brown sugar
½ cup pecans, chopped

½ cup butter, melted
1 quart French vanilla ice cream

Preheat oven to 325. Mix together flour, sugar and pecans. Add butter and mix well. Reserve approximately ¼ of mixture for topping. Pat remaining mixture on sides and bottom of a 9 inch pie plate. Bake 20-30 minutes or until brown, cool. Crumble reserved mixture in a shallow pan; bake slowly until brown. Slightly soften ice cream and spread on crust. Sprinkle on topping and freeze. Serves 8.
"Keeps several weeks."

Pecan Pie
(Courtesy of the Wayside Inn, Middletown, Virginia)

3 eggs, beaten
1 cup maple syrup
1 cup brown sugar
1 tablespoon vanilla

2 tablespoons butter
2 cups pecans, broken pieces
1 pastry shell, unbaked

Preheat oven to 325. Beat the first 3 ingredients and then add the next 3. Pour into the pastry shell and bake for 45 minutes.

Pecan Pie

1 cup light corn syrup
1 cup "white" sugar
1 cup milk
1 cup pecans, chopped
2 eggs, beaten

3 tablespoons flour
1 teaspoon vanilla
dash of salt
9 inch pastry shell, unbaked

Preheat oven to 400. Mix all ingredients well. Pour into pastry shell and bake for 10 minutes. Reduce heat to 300 and bake for 30 minutes or until firm in the middle.
"You'll love the praline flavoring of this pie."

Pumpkin Pie

1½ cups evaporated milk or
*   half and half*
1 tablespoon butter
2 eggs, slightly beaten
1 heaping cup cooked pumpkin
1 cup sugar

pinch of salt
pinch of cloves
pinch of nutmeg
¼ teaspoon ginger
1 teaspoon cinnamon
10 inch pastry shell, unbaked

Preheat oven to 350. Scald milk with butter, combine with eggs and pumpkin. Mix dry ingredients and add to pumpkin mixture. Pour into pastry shell and bake for 1 hour or until knife comes clean. Top with whipped cream, if desired.

Frosty Pumpkin Pie

1 cup pumpkin, cooked or canned
1/2 cup brown sugar
1/4 teaspoon salt
1/2 teaspoon cinnamon
1/2 teaspoon nutmeg
1 quart vanilla ice cream,
   slightly softened
9 inch graham cracker pie crust

Combine pumpkin, sugar, salt and spices. Add pumpkin mixture to ice cream and blend well. Pour into pie shell and freeze until firm. Garnish with whipped cream or slivered almonds.

Rum Chiffon Pie

2 tablespoons gelatin
1/2 cup cold water
2 cups milk
3/4 cup sugar
pinch of salt
3 teaspoons cornstarch
1/4 cup cold milk
1 pint vanilla ice cream
1 pint heavy cream, whipped
3 tablespoons rum
2-9 inch graham cracker pie shells

Soak gelatin in water. Combine milk, sugar and salt and heat to boiling. Dissolve cornstarch in the milk and add to hot mixture; cook and stir until thickened. Pour over gelatin and stir well. Immediately add ice cream, slightly softened, and stir until melted. Chill until mixture begins to thicken; fold in whipped cream. Stir in rum and pour into pie shells; refrigerate overnight. Garnish with chocolate curls.

"Chill beaters, bowl and cream for perfect whipped cream."

Rum Cream Pie

2 tablespoons gelatin
1 cup cold water
6 egg yolks
3/4 cup sugar
1 3/4 cups whipping cream
1/4 cup dark rum
10 inch graham cracker pie shell

Soak gelatin in cold water; put over low heat and stir until dissolved. Beat egg yolks until light and add sugar. Pour gelatin over egg mixture, stirring briskly. Whip cream until stiff and fold into egg mixture. Add rum and cool until filling begins to set (about 15-30 minutes). Pour into pie shell and chill until firm. Garnish with chocolate curls.

Toffee-Coffee Pie

Shell:

5 ounces packaged pie crust mix	*1 ounce unsweetened chocolate, grated*
¼ cup brown sugar	*1 tablespoon water*
¾ cup walnuts, chopped	*1 teaspoon vanilla*

Preheat oven to 375. Combine mix with brown sugar, walnuts and grated chocolate. Add water and vanilla; mix until well-blended. Spread into a well-greased pie plate, pressing firmly. Bake for 15 minutes and cool.

Filling:

½ cup butter, softened	*2 teaspoons instant coffee*
¾ cup sugar	*2 eggs*
1 ounce unsweetened chocolate, melted	

Beat butter until creamy and gradually add sugar; beat until light. Blend in chocolate and coffee. Add 1 egg and beat 5 minutes; add second egg and again beat 5 minutes. Turn into pastry shell, cover and refrigerate overnight.

Topping:

2 cups heavy cream	*½ cup confectioners' sugar*
2 tablespoons instant coffee	*chocolate curls*

Combine cream, coffee and sugar; refrigerate for one hour. After chilled, beat until mixture is stiff. Cover filling with topping and sprinkle with chocolate curls. Refrigerate at least 2 hours before serving.

Strawberry Pie

1 quart strawberries	*½ cup water*
1 cup sugar	*9 inch pastry shell, baked*
pinch of salt	*8 ounces whipping cream, whipped*
4 tablespoons cornstarch	

Mash ½ of the berries and combine with sugar, salt, cornstarch and water. Cook until mixture is clear. Cool and fold in remaining berries. Pour into pastry shell and chill. Garnish with whipped cream.

Note: For an added treat, spread pie crust with a thin layer of softened cream cheese before filling with strawberry mixture.

Sweet Potato Pie

3 eggs
1 cup sugar
1 cup cooked sweet potato,
 beaten or strained
¾ cup evaporated milk

¼ cup milk
¼ cup butter, melted
2 teaspoons vanilla
10 inch pie shell, unbaked

Preheat oven to 400. Beat together eggs, sugar and sweet potatoes. Add milk, butter and vanilla. Pour into pastry shell and bake at 400 for 10 minutes; then at 325 for 30 minutes more. When knife inserted comes out clean, the pie is done.
"Serve with vanilla ice cream."

Flaky Pie Shells

1 egg
2 tablespoons vinegar
iced water

5 cups flour
2 teaspoons salt
1 pound shortening

Preheat oven to 425. Put egg and vinegar in a measuring cup. Fill to 1 cup with iced water and mix with a fork. Mix flour, salt and shortening to a consistency of small crumbs. Add egg mixture to dry ingredients. Roll out into six 9 inch shells. Use one and freeze the others. Bake for 8 minutes.
Hint: When rolling pastry use 2 sheets of waxed paper; wet bottom sheet to prevent slipping on counter.

Perfect Pastry

1 cup flour, sifted
½ teaspoon salt

½ cup shortening
3 tablespoons iced water

Preheat oven to 450. Combine flour and salt, and sift again. Using a pastry blender or 2 knives, cut the shortening into the flour mixture until lumps become the size of small peas. Add the water, a small amount at a time, to an unmoistened spot. When dough is pressed lightly and balls together, form into a ball and chill for 15 minutes. Roll out on a pastry cloth or a lightly-floured board to fit a 9 inch pie plate. Line plate with pastry, placing another plate on top to hold pastry in place. Bake for 10 minutes; remove top plate and bake 5 minutes.

Three Pastry Shells

1 1/4 cup shortening
3 cups flour
1 teaspoon salt

1 egg, beaten
1 teaspoon lemon juice
5 tablespoons cold water

Preheat oven to 425-450. Cut shortening into flour and salt. Mix egg, lemon juice and water; add to dry ingredients. Roll out into three 9 inch shells or three balls. The raw pastry freezes beautifully. Shells can be baked without filling for 15-20 minutes. Be sure to prick pastry thoroughly.

Note: Frozen Pie Crust Hint

For an unbaked crust: Brush edge with salad oil and the bottom with beaten egg white; bake at 350 for 7 minutes; cool, fill and bake according to recipe.

For a baked crust: Follow the above directions and bake at 400 for 10-12 minutes; cool and fill according to directions.
"Gives you a pie with a golden edge and a flaky bottom crust."

Graham Cracker Crust

1 1/4 cups graham cracker crumbs
2 tablespoons sugar

1/3 cup butter, melted

Preheat oven to 375. Mix all ingredients and press into 9 inch pie plate. Bake 6 minutes. Cool before filling.

Variations: Follow the directions above with the following ingredients.

Gingersnap Crust

1 1/4 cups gingersnap crumbs
3 tablespoons sugar

1/4 cup butter, melted

Chocolate or Vanilla Wafer Crust

1 1/4 cups wafer crumbs
2 tablespoons sugar

1/4 cup butter, melted

Zwieback Crust

1 1/4 cups zwieback crumbs
2 tablespoons sugar

1/3 cup butter, melted

Desserts

In keeping with fine English tradition, the early Virginians were immensely fond of desserts; and elegantly set tables frequently became groaning boards under the weight of the lavishly spread "sweet course."

The dessert course in colonial times consisted of a vast assortment of available fresh fruits, which was supplemented with puddings, pies, custards, fritters, cakes, cookies, sweetmeats, jellies and preserves as needed, to create an artistic design for the table. Eye appeal was of extreme importance to a proper hostess, and elaborated flummeries, blanc manges and mousses were imaginatively molded and exuberantly decorated. It mattered not that the green froth smacked smartly of spinach or that the red delight was dominated by the flavor of beets!

Ingenuity with the natural resources of the young colony knew no bounds; and vegetables, meats and herbs might as easily appear in the dessert course as elsewhere in the meal. For instance, one old recipe called for a handful of tansy, a handful of sorrel, and spinach. Another dessert recipe passed down through the years was for parsnip fritters, flavored with wine and rosewater and served in a sweet wine sauce.

For many years puddings were the most prominent dessert, especially in the early-and mid-seventeenth century. Their limitless variety ranged from plum and fruit puddings to bread puddings to meat and blood puddings. There were also baked puddings, boiled puddings and hasty puddings. Equally impressive in number and variety were the names given to this popular dessert . . . some of which were far from appetizing!

Typical ingredients of the much-hailed pudding included the basic elements of milk, flour, eggs, butter and sugar with the addition of minced meat, suet, vegetables, spices, stewed fruits, dried currants, raisins and plums. Plum pudding, a favorite of olden times, has survived through the years and is still a popular traditional dessert. The early variety of puddings were coarse due to the use of bread crumbs, cracker meal or oatmeal in their preparation; but when flour became more available the desserts became lighter and finer in texture.

The early introduction of French delicacies to the colonial dessert board was brought about by none other than Thomas Jefferson. Fortunately for the Virginia housewife . . . and for the nation . . . Jefferson's appreciation of the French confections during the time he was in Paris as American minister motivated him to investigate the mysteries of French dessert. It was Jefferson who brought back the vanilla bean from France as well as ice cream, blanc mange, charlotte russe, wine jelly, macaroons and meringues. Later, when he became President of the United States, Jefferson set culinary standards at the White House which never since have been matched, and one of the most successful unions of all times—that of Virginia and French cooking—was brought about.

Melon Bowls With Honey Dressing

½ cup sour cream
¼ teaspoon dry mustard
1½-2 tablespoons honey
½ teaspoon orange peel, grated
dash of salt
1 tablespoon orange juice

1 teaspoon lemon juice
2 honeydew melons or
  2 cantelopes, halved and seeded
1 pint fresh blueberries
1 pint fresh strawberries
2 bananas, sliced

Make dressing of sour cream, mustard and honey. Beat well. Add orange peel and salt. Slowly beat in fruit juices. Chill at least 1 hour. At serving time, arrange berries and bananas in melon bowls, and spoon dressing over all. Serves 8. *"An excellent summer dessert! Easy to prepare."*

"In the eighteenth century floral arrangements were not used in the center of the table. Instead an epergne was laden with fruits, candies, nuts and raisins; and the guests nibbled at the centerpiece at the end of the meal."

Apple Crisp

4 large apples, peeled and sliced
1 cup sugar
nutmeg and cinnamon to taste

4 tablespoons water
½ cup margarine
1 cup flour, sifted

Preheat oven to 350. Sprinkle apples with nutmeg, cinnamon and ½ cup of sugar; add water. Place in a 9 inch square baking dish. Cream margarine and remaining sugar. Add flour and mix well. Pat this mixture over apples and bake 30-45 minutes. Serves 6.
"Delicious served warm with vanilla ice cream."

Chocolate Fondue

6 tablespoons cream
12 ounces sweet baking chocolate

⅛ teaspoon cinnamon
2 tablespoons brandy

Heat cream over low heat in 1½ cup fondue pot. Break chocolate into pieces and add to cream, stirring until smooth. Stir in cinnamon and brandy.
"Arrange a variety of fruit sections and cubes of pound cake on a large tray surrounding fondue."

Mincemeat Coffee Ring

¾ cup mincemeat
½ cup hot milk
1 egg
⅓ cup shortening

¾ cup sugar
2½ teaspoons baking powder
½ teaspoon salt
2 cups sifted flour

Preheat oven to 375. Combine mincemeat and milk; add egg, shortening and dry ingredients. Mix only until flour is moistened. Turn into a buttered and floured 6 cup ring mold. Bake 30-35 minutes.

Icing:

1 cup confectioners' sugar
2 tablespoons butter

3 tablespoons milk, hot
⅛ teaspoon salt

Mix all ingredients and pour over cake that has been removed from mold, but is still warm. Serves 6-8.

Peach Cobbler

3 cups fresh peaches, sliced
1 tablespoon lemon juice
1/4 teaspoon almond extract
1 cup sifted flour

1 cup sugar
1/2 teaspoon salt
1 egg, beaten
6 tablespoons margarine, melted

Preheat oven to 375. Butter 10x6 baking dish. Place peaches on bottom. Sprinkle with lemon juice and extract. Sift together dry ingredients. Add egg and mix with fork or hands until crumbly. Sprinkle over peaches. Drizzle with melted margarine. Bake 35 to 40 minutes.
Note: Also excellent made with blueberries or other fresh fruit.
"Top with ice cream."

Peach Macaroon Dessert

20 peach halves
2 1/4 cups sweet sherry
20 almond macaroons, crumbled

2 1/2 tablespoons grated orange and
   lemon rind, mixed
1 1/2 tablespoons lemon juice
   whipped cream

Preheat oven to 350. Drain peach halves and place in baking dish, cavity sides up. Mix macaroons with fruit rind and juice; spoon into each peach. Pour sherry over peaches and heat in oven for 7-10 minutes. Serve hot or cold, spooning some of the sherry onto each. Top with whipped cream. Serves 10.

American Pudding

3 cups blueberries
1 cup brown sugar
6 tablespoons butter
1 cup sugar
2/3 cup butter, softened
dash of vanilla
2 eggs

1 1/2 cups flour
2 teaspoons baking powder
1/2 teaspoon salt
2 teaspoons orange rind, grated
3/4 cup orange juice
2 cups heavy cream
6 tablespoons Grand Marnier

Preheat oven to 350. Simmer blueberries in brown sugar and 6 tablespoons butter. Cream sugar, 2/3 cup butter and vanilla. Add eggs and beat. Sift flour, baking powder and salt into mixture. Add orange rind and juice. Place blueberry mixture in bottom of 3 quart baking dish. Pour batter over berries. Bake 45 minutes. Whip cream and add Grand Marnier. Serve as topping for each serving. Serves 10-12.

Bread Pudding

4 cups milk
2 cups fresh bread cubes, packed
1 1/4 cups sugar
1/4 teaspoon salt

4 eggs, beaten
1 teaspoon vanilla
1/4 teaspoon nutmeg
raisins or coconut (optional)

Preheat oven to 325-350. Scald milk; add bread cubes, sugar and salt. Allow to stand 5 minutes. Slowly pour mixture into bowl of beaten eggs, stirring constantly. Add vanilla, and raisins or coconut if desired. Place mixture in well-buttered 2 quart casserole and sprinkle with nutmeg. Bake in pan of hot water for 1 hour, or until firm and knife inserted comes out clean. Don't rush or have oven too hot as it will make pudding watery. Serves 8-10.

Creamy Rice Pudding

3 eggs
1 cup sugar
2 cups milk
1 1/2 teaspoons cornstarch

1/2 teaspoon vanilla
1/3 cup rice, cooked
1/2-1 cup raisins (optional)
nutmeg to taste

Preheat oven to 325. Beat eggs, add sugar and beat well. Add milk, cornstarch and vanilla; mix well. Stir in rice, raisins and nutmeg. Pour in 8 inch square baking dish and set in a pan containing 1 inch of water. Bake for 2 hours. Serves 8-10.
Note: A good way to use one cup of left-over rice.

Date and Walnut Torte
(Courtesy of Poplar Hall)

16 ounces dates, pitted
1 cup walnuts or pecans
1 teaspoon vanilla

1 1/2 cups sugar
4 tablespoons flour
4 eggs

Preheat oven to 325. Line a 9 inch square pan with waxed paper. Cut dates into small pieces. Mix with nuts. Add vanilla, sugar and flour. Stir in eggs. DO NOT BEAT EGGS. Spoon mixture into pan. It will be too thick to pour. Bake. When done, about 25 minutes, remove from oven and allow to cool for 10 minutes. Turn upside down on platter and waxed paper will pull off easily. Cut into squares. Serve with ice cream.
Note: Will keep well in cake tin for weeks if not discovered by family!

Poplar Hall

Poplar Hall, located on Norfolk's Broad Creek in old Princess Anne County, was built in the mid 1700's and had what is thought to be the first shipyard in America. The house sustained no damage during the Revolutionary War or the War Between the States and retains many legends. A favorite tells of a lady house guest, who on hearing the grandfather clock chime thirteen at midnight, immediately arose from bed, packed her bag and refused to stay where any clock struck thirteen. However, this gracious Georgian home with its brick laid in Flemish Bond and its original floors, mantels, paneling and many hand-blown glass panes, has delighted numerous other guests.

Cranberry Torte

2¼ cups flour
¼ teaspoon salt
1 teaspoon baking powder
1 teaspoon baking soda
1 cup sugar
1 cup walnuts, chopped
1 cup dates, diced
1 cup fresh cranberries, diced

rind of 2 oranges, grated
2 eggs, well beaten
1 cup buttermilk
¾ cup oil

Glaze:
1 cup orange juice
1 cup sugar

Preheat oven to 350. Sift together first 4 ingredients. Stir in sugar, nuts, dates, cranberries and rind. Combine eggs, milk and oil. Add to fruit mixture and stir well. Pour into well-greased tube pan. Bake 1 hour. Cool until lukewarm. Place on rack with pan underneath. Pour glaze over torte, then repeat with drippings. Serves 10-12.

Pumpkin Date Torte

½ cup dates, chopped
½ cup walnuts, chopped
2 tablespoons flour
¼ cup butter or margarine
1 cup brown sugar
⅔ cup pumpkin, cooked
1 teaspoon vanilla
2 eggs

½ cup sifted flour
½ teaspoon baking powder
½ teaspoon cinnamon
½ teaspoon nutmeg
¼ teaspoon ginger
¼ teaspoon baking soda
whipped cream

Preheat oven to 350. Mix dates, nuts and flour; set aside. Melt butter over low heat; blend in sugar. Remove from heat; stir in pumpkin and vanilla. Beat in eggs one at a time. Sift together remaining dry ingredients; add to pumpkin mixture, mixing thoroughly. Stir in floured dates and nuts. Turn into greased 9 inch cake pan. Bake for 20-25 minutes. Serve warm with whipped cream topping. Serves 8.

Baked Caramel Custard

4 eggs
½ cup sugar
¼ teaspoon salt
1 cup milk

½ pint heavy cream
1 teaspoon vanilla
¼ teaspoon nutmeg

Preheat oven to 300. Beat eggs until fluffy. Add ¼ cup sugar and salt; beat until thick and lemon-colored. Add milk, cream, vanilla and nutmeg; beat thoroughly. In a skillet over medium heat, melt remaining sugar, stirring constantly until it becomes caramel-like syrup. Pour immediately into a buttered 1 quart casserole. Slowly pour custard into casserole. Place in baking pan filled with hot water to within ¾ inch from top of casserole. Bake for 1¼ hours or until inserted knife comes out clean. Cool and refrigerate until cold. Unmold. Caramel becomes a sauce over custard.

Charlotte Russe

1 tablespoon gelatin
1½ cups milk
½ cup sugar
1 egg, separated

½ cup sherry
½ pint heavy cream, whipped
½ teaspoon vanilla
9 ladyfingers, split

Soak gelatin in ½ cup milk. Combine remaining milk, sugar and egg yolk in double boiler. Prepare a custard. Add gelatin mixture to custard and cool. Fold in stiffly beaten egg white, sherry, whipped cream and vanilla to cooled mixture. Line a bowl with ladyfingers and pour in custard. Chill several hours before serving. Serves 6-8.

Chocolate Mousse Ice Box Cake

48 ladyfingers, split
18 ounces chocolate chips
1 cup sugar
⅓ cup water

1 teaspoon vanilla
8 eggs, separated
confectioners' sugar

Line sides and bottom of springform pan with about ¼ of the ladyfingers, split side in. Set aside. In medium saucepan, combine chocolate, sugar and water. Stir constantly over low heat until melted. Remove and add vanilla. Beat and let cool. In a large bowl, beat egg yolks. Add chocolate mixture, beating constantly until thick. Beat egg whites until stiff. Combine mixtures with whisk. Spread ¼ of chocolate over ladyfingers, cover with layer of ladyfingers and repeat 3 times. Refrigerate for 4 hours and gently remove sides of pan. Sprinkle liberally with confectioners' sugar. Serves 12.

"Sounds lengthy but can be whipped up in a jiffy!"

Chocolate Angel Delight

12 ounces chocolate chips
2 tablespoons water
3 eggs, separated
pinch of salt
3 tablespoons sugar

1 1/2 cups heavy cream
1 teaspoon vanilla
13 ounces angel food cake
vanilla ice cream

Melt chocolate in water on top of double boiler; cool. Stir in yolks and salt. Beat egg whites until stiff; add sugar and stir into cooled chocolate mixture, blending well. Whip cream; add vanilla; fold into chocolate mixture. Break cake (fresh or stale) into bite-sized chunks. Place in 9x13 pan. Cover with chocolate mixture. Chill at least 6 hours before serving. Cut into squares and top with ice cream. Serves 16-18.

Chocolate Torte Royale

Cinnamon Meringue Shell:

2 egg whites
1/4 teaspoon salt
1/2 teaspoon vinegar

1/2 cup sugar
1/4 teaspoon cinnamon

Preheat oven to 275. Cover a cookie sheet with brown paper, draw an 8 inch circle in the center. Beat egg whites, salt and vinegar until soft peaks form. Blend sugar and cinnamon; gradually add to whites, beating until very stiff peaks form and all sugar has dissolved. Spread within circle making bottom 1/2 inch thick and mounding around edge to 1 3/4 inches. For trim, form ridges on outside with back of teaspoon. Bake for 1 hour. Turn off heat and let shell dry in oven with door closed about 2 hours. Peel off paper.

Filling:

6 ounces chocolate chips
2 egg yolks, beaten
1/4 cup water

1 cup heavy cream
1/4 cup sugar
1/4 teaspoon cinnamon

Melt chocolate over hot water. Cool slightly; then spread 2 tablespoons of chocolate over bottom of meringue shell. To rest of chocolate, add egg yolks, water and blend. Chill until mixture is thick. Combine cream, sugar and cinnamon; whip until stiff. Spread half over chocolate in shell, fold remainder into egg mixture and spread on top. Chill for several hours or overnight. Garnish with whipped cream and pecans. Serves 6-8.

French Silk

1 cup brown sugar, loosely packed
1 cup flour

½ cup pecans, chopped
¼ cup butter, softened

Preheat oven to 400. Mix all ingredients and spread on bottom of buttered 9x13 baking dish. Bake for 15 minutes. Remove from oven, STIR, pat smooth and chill.

Filling:

1 cup butter, softened
1½ cups sugar
2 teaspoons vanilla

3 ounces unsweetened chocolate,
  melted
4 eggs

Cream butter and sugar. Add vanilla, chocolate and eggs, one at a time. Beat 5 minutes after each egg. Fill crust and chill several hours. May be topped with whipped cream. Serves 10-12.

Pots De Creme

2 eggs
6 ounces chocolate chips

1 teaspoon vanilla
1 cup milk, scalded

Mix eggs, chocolate and vanilla in blender until smooth. Slowly add milk and continue mixing until blended. Pour into demitasse or pot de creme cups. Chill at least 2 hours before serving. May add a dash of whipped cream or grated chocolate. Serves 4.
Note: A very simplified version of the traditional French dessert.

Coffee Bavarian Cream

2 tablespoons gelatin
1 cup milk
1 cup coffee, very strong
1 cup sugar

2 egg whites
⅛ teaspoon salt
2 cups heavy cream
crushed peanut brittle

Soak gelatin in milk. Dissolve gelatin in boiling coffee, add sugar. Chill these ingredients until about to set. DO NOT SET! Whip until light. Whip egg whites and salt until stiff. Fold into gelatin mixture. Whip cream until stiff. Fold lightly into mixture. Chill until set. Serve with crushed peanut brittle on top. Serves 8-10.

Bristol Ice Box Cake

¼ cup butter, melted
2 cups crushed pineapple, drained
½ cup sugar

½ cup pecans, chopped
3 cups vanilla wafer crumbs
½ pint heavy cream, whipped

Mix first 4 ingredients. Line a 1 quart dish with a layer of crumbs, then a layer of mixture. Repeat the process, ending with crumbs. Refrigerate 3-4 hours or overnight. To serve, garnish with whipped cream. Serves 8.

Lemon Sponge Dessert

2 tablespoons butter, softened
1 cup sugar
4 tablespoons flour
⅛ teaspoon salt

5 tablespoons lemon juice
rind of 1 lemon, grated
3 eggs, separated
1½ cups milk

Preheat oven to 325. Cream butter; add sugar, flour, salt, lemon juice and rind. Beat egg yolks, stir in milk and add to lemon mixture. Fold into stiffly beaten egg whites. Turn into a 2 quart baking dish set in a pan of water; bake 45 minutes or until inserted knife comes out clean. Refrigerate before serving. Serves 8. *"A good light dessert to accompany any menu! Garnish with whipped cream if desired."*

Meringue on a Cloud

6 egg whites
2 cups sugar
1 teaspoon white vinegar
½ teaspoon vanilla
⅛ teaspoon salt

48 ounces peaches, frozen or
  canned
1 pint heavy cream
slivered almonds, toasted

Preheat oven to 275. Beat egg whites until frothy. Add sugar, 2 tablespoons at a time. Add vinegar and vanilla; beat for 10 minutes. Cut 2 9-inch circles of brown paper and spread meringue over each. Bake on cookie sheet for 1 hour. Let cool in oven. Thoroughly drain peaches on paper towels. Whip cream; spread half on 1 meringue layer and top with half the peaches. Add second meringue layer, remaining whipped cream and peaches. Sprinkle with almonds. Serves 12.
Note: Fresh, sweetened peaches or other fruits may be substituted.

Crushed Candy Meringue

6 egg whites
2 teaspoons vanilla
1/2 teaspoon cream of tartar
dash of salt

2 cups sugar
6 Heath bars, chilled and crushed
dash of salt
2 cups heavy cream, whipped

Preheat oven to 275. Have egg whites at room temperature, add vanilla, cream of tartar and salt. Beat to soft peaks, gradually add sugar, beating until very stiff peaks are formed. Cover 2 cookie sheets with plain brown paper. Draw a 9 inch circle on each and spread meringue evenly within the circle. Bake 1 hour. Turn off heat; let dry in oven with door closed for at least 2 hours. Fold crushed candy and dash of salt into whipped cream. Spread between layers and on top and sides of meringue (ice like 2 layer cake). Chill at least 8 hours. Top with additional crushed candy. Serves 16.

"Never clean off a beater by tapping on the edge of the bowl after beating egg whites or the whites will drop."

Grand Marnier Meringue With Lemon Ice

Meringues:

2 egg whites
1/2 teaspoon vanilla

1/2 teaspoon vinegar
1/2 cup sugar

Preheat oven to 450. Beat whites, vanilla and vinegar until stiff; add sugar slowly and whip until mixture stands in stiff peaks. Drop by tablespoons onto brown paper-lined cookie sheet. Hollow out centers for ice cream. Place in oven. Turn oven OFF. Leave for several hours. Yields 10.

Filling:

Grand Marnier

1 quart lemon ice, molded

Pour 2 tablespoons of Grand Marnier on a plate and set meringues in it. See that they absorb some of the liquid. On a platter place a melon mold of lemon ice. Surround it with meringues. Pass a cruet of Grand Marnier to splash over the dessert!!

257

Elegant Rum Dessert

3¾ ounces instant lemon
   pudding mix
1½ cups milk
¼ cup rum
grated rind of 1 orange

12 ounces frozen pound cake, cubed
½ cup apricot or peach preserves
½ pint heavy cream
¼ cup confectioners' sugar
⅓ cup slivered almonds, toasted

Prepare pudding using 1½ cups of milk. Fold in rum, orange rind and cake cubes. Pack this mixture back in pound cake tin. Chill several hours; loosen edges, unmold on platter, spread top and sides with preserves. Whip cream with confectioners' sugar and spread over top. Sprinkle with almonds. Chill. Serves 6-8.

Rum Mousse
(Courtesy of Snowden House)

2½ dozen almond macaroons,
   broken
½ cup butter, softened
1 cup rum
2 tablespoons gelatin
3 tablespoons cold water

6 egg yolks
1½ cups sugar
2 egg whites
1 pint heavy cream
2 tablespoons sugar

Crust:

Toast macaroons in the oven at 300. Brown lightly, turning often. Cool and dry thoroughly. Place on flat surface and roll fine with rolling pin. Place crumbs in bowl and mix with butter. Reserve some crumbs to sprinkle on top of the mousse when it is unmolded. Place mixture in bundt pan or mold. Press to cover bottom and midway up the sides. Return to 300 oven and brown lightly. Remove and cool.

Filling:

Put one cup of rum in double boiler and heat carefully over low heat. Soften gelatin in water. Add gelatin to rum and stir. Cool. Beat egg yolks well; add ½ cup sugar. Add cooled rum and mix well. Whip ½ pint of cream, adding ½ cup sugar. Beat the egg whites until stiff, adding ½ cup sugar. Fold whites into whipped cream. Fold in egg yolk mixture. Place mixture in crust and chill over night. Before serving, whip the remaining cream; add rum to flavor and remaining sugar. Unmold on a silver tray and top with whipped cream. Sprinkle with reserved crumbs.
Note: Should be made a day in advance!

Snowden House

This Alexandria home, built around 1790, has had numerous owners. It was named for Edgar Snowden, an early resident whose father owned and edited the *Alexandria Gazette*. This paper is said to be the oldest daily newspaper continuously printed in this country. It has been a truly lived-in and loved home where thousands have been entertained, including members of the Supreme Court and Presidents Truman and Johnson. Much remodeling was done by Justice Hugo Black and his wife Josephine who bought it in 1939 and cut windows in the "flounder" side of the house to give more light to the beautifully proportioned hallway with its classic keystone arch. They also added a tennis court and had the garden landscaped to enhance the joy of those who live in and visit Snowden House.

Rum Mold

2 tablespoons gelatin
1/4 cup water
4 eggs, separated
2 cups milk
1 cup sugar
2 tablespoons flour
1 pint heavy cream, whipped and
   sweetened

1/2-3/4 cup light rum
1 small angel food cake

Topping:

1/2 pint heavy cream, whipped
sugar to taste
light rum to taste

Soften gelatin in water. Beat egg yolks, milk, sugar and flour. Cook in double boiler until thickened. Add gelatin mixture. Cool; fold in stiffly-beaten egg whites and whipped cream. Flavor with rum to taste. Layer bottom of torte or springform pan with some custard. Break angel food cake into pieces and push some well into custard. Alternate custard and cake until all is used. Refrigerate overnight. Turn onto platter and garnish with whipped cream topping. Serves 14-16.

Surprise Torte

4 egg whites
1 1/2 cups sugar
1 teaspoon baking powder
16 soda crackers, finely crushed

1 cup pecans or walnuts, chopped
1/2 pint heavy cream, whipped and
   sweetened

Preheat oven to 350. Beat egg whites until stiff. Add sugar and baking powder slowly while continuing to beat. Fold in crackers and nuts. Pour into a buttered 8 or 9 inch pie plate, lined with waxed paper and bake 45-50 minutes. Allow to cool. Spread with cream and refrigerate for 24 hours before serving. Serves 6-8.

French Pudding

3/4 cup butter, softened
2 1/4 cups confectioners' sugar
3 eggs, beaten
3/4 pound vanilla wafers, crushed

20 ounces frozen strawberries,
   slightly drained
1 1/2 cups pecans, chopped
1 pint heavy cream, whipped

Cream butter and sugar; add beaten eggs. Butter a springform pan and line with a layer of wafer crumbs. Add a layer of batter, a layer of fruit, a layer of nuts and whipped cream. Repeat layers, reserving some whipped cream and nuts for topping. Refrigerate 24 hours before serving. Serves 10-12.

Strawberry Parfait

1 tablespoon gelatin
1 tablespoon flour
¾ cup sugar
1 quart heavy cream
5 egg yolks

1 teaspoon vanilla
grated peel of 1 orange
1½ ounces brandy or Kirsch
½ pint strawberries, puréed
1 pint strawberries, whole

In a large saucepan, mix gelatin, flour and sugar. Beat 3 cups of cream and yolks together and add to gelatin mixture, stirring constantly with a wire whisk. Cook over medium heat for 10 minutes. Remove from heat; add vanilla. Pour into large bowl and stir in grated peel and brandy. Chill briefly until mixture is thickened slightly. Mix together the puréed and the whole berries, reserving 6 for garnish. Whip 1 cup cream, fold into berries, fold into lightly thickened, chilled cream mixture. Spoon into glasses and chill until firm. Garnish with reserved berries. Serves 6-8.

Note: Raspberries may be used, blend with 1 tablespoon sugar to sweeten.

Strawberry Roll

¾ cup flour
1 teaspoon baking powder
¼ teaspoon soda
4 eggs, separated
¾ cup sugar

1 teaspoon vanilla
2 teaspoons water
6 tablespoons confectioners' sugar
1½ cups heavy cream
3 cups strawberries

Preheat oven to 375. Sift flour, add baking powder and salt and sift again. Beat egg whites until stiff, but not dry. Gradually beat in half the sugar, 2 tablespoons at a time. Beat egg yolks until thick and lemon-colored, add remaining sugar, vanilla and water, continuing beating until very thick. Gently fold in beaten whites. Fold in flour mixture gradually, about ¼ cup at a time. Pour mixture into a shallow 10x15 pan lined with waxed paper. Bake for 15-20 minutes. Remove cake from pan and turn out on a clean cloth. Strip off waxed paper, roll up cake like a jelly roll quickly. Wrap in cloth and cool on a rack. Just before serving combine confectioners' sugar and cream. Whip until stiff. Unroll cake, cover with half the cream and layer of strawberries. Roll and spread outside with remaining cream. Top with strawberries. Serves 10.

Cherry Trifle
(Courtesy of the Cascades Restaurant, Williamsburg, Virginia)

lady fingers
strawberry or raspberry jelly
grated lemon rind
½ pint Kirschwasser
canned tart red cherries, drained

crushed macaroons
1 pint custard
slivered almonds
heavy cream, whipped

Place ladyfingers in bottom of 8 inch crystal bowl. Coat with jelly and grated lemon rind. Soak with Kirschwasser. Cover with layer of cherries and crushed macaroons. Coat with thick custard, allow to set. Repeat the above procedure for second layer. Top with whipped cream and slivered almonds. Serves 6-8.
Note: A little gelatin may be added to custard to help it set more quickly.

Trifle

4 eggs
½ cup sugar
2 cups milk
⅛ teaspoon salt
24 lady fingers

1 cup apricot jam
½ cup muscatel
½ pint heavy cream,
    whipped and sweetened
½ cup sliced almonds, toasted

Beat eggs slightly; combine with sugar, milk and salt in double boiler. Cook over hot, not boiling, water, stirring constantly until mixture thickens slightly and coats spoon. Cool. Split ladyfingers and sandwich together with apricot jam. Place in serving dish, making 2 layers; sprinkle each layer with muscatel. Pour custard over and chill several hours or overnight. Before serving, top with cream; sprinkle with almonds. Serves 8-10.
"Tipsy cake or English Trifle has been popular with Virginians for 200 years. It is served today most often during the Christmas season. The ingredients have been traditionally ladyfingers, fruit, custard and sherry."

Wine Jelly

2 cups sugar
1 pint water
3 tablespoons gelatin

1 pint Burgundy
1 lemon, juiced
whipped cream, sweetened

Dissolve sugar in 1¾ cups hot water. Dissolve gelatin in ¼ cup water. Add to hot sugar water; stir well. Add wine and lemon, chill until firm. Serve topped with sweetened whipped cream. Top with crushed brown-edge wafers. Serves 12-16.

Apricot Ice

3½ cups canned peeled apricots
1 lemon, juiced
12 macaroons

1 pint heavy cream
½ teaspoon almond extract
½ cup confectioners' sugar

Mix apricots and juice in blender. Line a loaf pan with waxed paper. Pour in apricot mixture and freeze. Heat macaroons in oven until dry and crumb in blender. Whip cream, adding flavoring and sugar. Combine with macaroons. Spread on apricot mixture and return to freezer. Remove from freezer 15 minutes before serving. (Pull waxed paper for easier removal.) Slice. Serves 8.

Old Fashioned Frozen Fruit

1 cup sugar
2 cups water
1 teaspoon gelatin
¾ cup water

8 ounces crushed pineapple
2 large bananas, mashed
15 maraschino cherries, quartered
juice of 2 large lemons

Add sugar to 2 cups water. Bring to a boil, then simmer for 20 minutes. Dissolve gelatin in ¾ cup water. Add syrup to softened gelatin, then cool. To cooled syrup, add fruits and juice. Freeze in refrigerator trays or a 9x13 pan. Cut into small squares to serve. Serves 8-10.
Note: This can be served as an appetizer or a dessert.

Mother's Ice Cream

4 tablespoons cornstarch
3 cups sugar
½ teaspoon salt
2 quarts milk
3 eggs

3 egg yolks
4 tablespoons vanilla
1 quart fresh or canned fruit,
    sweetened as desired

Mix cornstarch, sugar and salt. Add milk slowly. Cook and stir in large, heavy pan 10 minutes or until it begins to thicken. Beat all eggs slightly; add some of cooked mixture to eggs until hot. Return all to milk mixture and cook 2 minutes. Cool. Add flavoring and fruit and freeze in electric ice cream freezer.

Triple Treat Ice Cream

3 bananas
3 lemons, juiced
3 oranges, juiced
3 cups sugar

3 cups milk
3 cups heavy cream or
   3 pints half and half in place
   of milk <u>and</u> cream

Mash bananas in blender, add juice of lemons and oranges. Add remaining ingredients and stir well. Freeze in ice cream freezer. For variety, you may substitute other fruits in place of bananas—peaches, strawberries, etc. Serves 8-10.

Old Virginia Ice Cream

1 quart milk
1 quart half and half
10 eggs
2 cups sugar
1 ½ tablespoons cornstarch

½ teaspoon salt
2 teaspoons vanilla
1 quart fresh fruit, chilled
   sweetened and crushed
   (optional)

Heat milk and half and half in top of double boiler. Beat eggs; add sugar, cornstarch and salt. Slowly stir egg mixture into rest of milk which is near boiling point. Stir until mixture coats metal spoon. Add vanilla and fruit if desired. Freeze in electric ice cream freezer.

Note: This recipe is excellent with peaches. Custard should be made ahead and chilled before freezing.

Black Walnut Ice Cream Dessert

½ cup butter (no substitute)
1 cup light brown sugar
1 cup very fine coconut

1 cup Rice Krispies
2 quarts French vanilla ice cream
1 cup black walnuts

Melt butter; add sugar, coconut and Rice Krispies. Line the bottom of a 9 x 13 pan with half of the mixture. Place the ice cream on top, and cover with remaining mixture. Top with walnuts. Keep in freezer until time to serve. Serves 12.

Note: Make several days ahead. Will keep frozen for three weeks.

Frozen Lemon Dessert

3 eggs, separated
1/2 cup sugar
dash of salt
3 tablespoons lemon juice

1/2 pint heavy cream, whipped
vanilla wafer or
   graham cracker crumbs

Beat yolks until light; add sugar, salt and lemon juice. Cook over hot water until thick. Beat whites stiff; add to yellow mixture. Add whipped cream. Butter and line refrigerator tray with crumbs. Pour in mixture. Cover with crumbs. Freeze. Serves 8-10.

Kahlua Mousse

16 marshmallows
1 cup heavy cream

1 1/2 ounces Kahlua

Heat marshmallows in 1/3 cup cream until softened, fluffy and smooth. Stir in Kahlua. Whip 2/3 cup cream and fold into marshmallow mixture. Freeze in refrigerator tray without stirring. Serves 6-8.

Raspberry Mousse

20 ounces frozen raspberries, thawed
1/2 pint heavy cream
2/3 cup confectioners' sugar

1/8 teaspoon salt
whipped cream

Save 3 berries for garnish, press remaining through sieve or blend. In separate bowl, beat cream until foamy; add sugar and salt, beat until stiff. Fold in raspberries and spoon into refrigerator tray. Freeze until crystals form around edge; stir until smooth. Spoon into 4 cup mold or individual molds; freeze until firm. Unmold and garnish with whipped cream and berries. Serves 8.

Butterscotch Sauce

1 1/2 cups light brown sugar
3/4 cup light corn syrup

4 tablespoons butter
1/2 cup light cream

Cook sugar, syrup and butter in double boiler to soft ball stage. Add cream and continue to cook for a few more minutes. Before serving, add toasted almonds, if desired. Yields 1 1/2 cups.

Chocolate Sauce

½ cup butter
4 ounces unsweetened chocolate
3 cups sugar

¼ teaspoon salt
1¾ cups evaporated milk
1 teaspoon vanilla

Melt butter and chocolate over low heat. Remove from heat, stir in sugar (about ¼ at a time). Add salt, then return to heat and add milk. Cook 7 minutes. stirring constantly. Remove; add vanilla.
"A delicious topping for ice cream or pound cake. Leftovers can be stored in a jar in the refrigerator."

Bittersweet Chocolate Sauce

8 ounces unsweetened chocolate
2 cups sugar
13 ounces evaporated milk

2 tablespoons coffee, strong
dash of salt
1 teaspoon vanilla

Melt chocolate in double boiler. Add sugar, mix well, cover and cook over boiling water for ½ hour. Add milk, coffee, salt and vanilla. Beat until smooth and thick. Cool and refrigerate.
Note: This will keep several weeks. Reheat over boiling water to serve.

Lemon Sauce

1 cup sugar
1 tablespoon flour
¼ teaspoon salt
1 cup boiling water

1 tablespoon butter
3 tablespoons lemon juice
3 teaspoons lemon rind, grated

Blend sugar, flour and salt. Add boiling water and stir until smooth. Boil 3 minutes. Add butter, lemon juice and lemon rind.
"Especially good over gingerbread or fruit cake."

Pickles and Preserves

Judging from the number of preserving kettles, stone or earthenware vessels, jelly glasses and pickle dishes carried in the inventories of colonial estates, one might suspect that our American ancestors were great fanciers and connoisseurs of condiments and preserves. Pickles, preserves, jellies, sweetmeats, conserves and relishes were in fact staple delicacies in those times. Every type of food, from cucumbers to fish, was pickled to avoid spoilage and to substitute in some measures for the fresh vegetables and fruits missing from winter menus.

In addition to the pickled products which are still popular today, our colonial forefathers enjoyed such exotic pickled items as blossoms from sassafras and redbud trees, nasturtium buds, barberries and currants, certain herbs and pods from the "aerial" radish. Some fruits such as mango melons, small green apples, peaches, apricots, plums and grapes were also pickled. Even lemons were pickled and used to season sauces.

Catsups were also popular among the colonists for preserving flavors and seasoning dishes. In addition to tomato catsup, which has persisted until the present day as a favorite seasoning aid, mushroom and walnut catsups were in great demand 200 years ago.

Old cookbooks give detailed instructions on the best manner of pickling and preserving; porcelain or agate lined kettles were generally considered the best for such purposes. Bell-metal kettles could also be used, but the authors stressed that they be "bright and clean" before pickling, and cooks were cautioned that "under no circumstances should a brass or copper kettle be tolerated." However, some over color-conscious cooks risked ptomaine poisoning and continued to use the copper pickling kettles because of the brilliant green they produced.

Tin kettles were sometimes used in the preparation of preserves, but cooks were cautioned that the use of tin in cooking fruit would discolor the fruit, and acid fruits would eat away the coating from the tin.

Until the invention of self-sealing jars in 1850, a number of measures were taken to make the jars of pickles and preserves airtight. Normally the jar was sealed with oil, butter or mutton fat and was then covered with leather, a bladder or several layers of coarse cloth which was then tied securely. In the case of delicate preserves, the recommended sealing method was to cut pieces of paper to fit the jars, dip them in brandy, alcohol or the the white of an egg, and press them closely on top of the preserves or jelly.

Today pickling and preserving need not be a tedious chore—and certainly nothing adds a more personal flair to any meal than a homemade condiment. Beware, however, of an old saying which warns that the flavor of a homemade pickle will take on the personality of the person preparing it. Perhaps the wise cook, now as then, might check the sweetness of her disposition before undertaking the rewarding and pleasant culinary adventure of pickling!

Bread and Butter Pickles

1 gallon cucumbers
8 small onions
2 green peppers
1/2 cup salt
cracked ice
5 cups sugar

1/2 teaspoon turmeric
1/2 teaspoon ground cloves
2 tablespoons mustard seed
2 tablespoons celery seed
5 cups vinegar

Slice cucumbers, onions and peppers into very thin slices. Cover with salt. Cover completely with ice and stir. Top with weighted lid. Allow to stand for 3 hours. Drain, DO NOT RINSE. Combine sugar and spices with vinegar, and cook until the sugar dissolves. Pour over drained cucumber mixture. Bring to a boil. Place in jars while hot and seal. Yields 6-8 pints.

Four Day Cucumber Pickles

7 pounds cucumbers
2 gallons water
¼ ounce slaked lime
1 tablespoon salt

8 cups cider vinegar
14 cups sugar
1 teaspoon celery seed
1 tablespoon pickling spice

On the first day, slice cucumbers into ¼ inch slices. Put water and lime into a crock. Let stand for 1 hour to dissolve lime. Stir well. Add cucumber slices and weight down with a plate. Let stand for 24 hours. During the second day, change the water 3 times. On the third day, drain the cucumbers well. Cook salt, vinegar, sugar, celery seed and pickling spice until the sugar is completely dissolved. Pour this mixture over the cucumbers, let stand overnight. On the fourth day, transfer the mixture to a cooking pot and boil hard for 15 minutes. Put in glass jars and seal hot. Yields 10-12 pints.

Pickled Okra

6 garlic cloves
6 hot red peppers
40-50 small okra
6 teaspoons dill seed

1 quart vinegar
1 cup water
½ cup salt

Sterilize 6 pint jars. Place 1 garlic clove and 1 red pepper in each jar. Pack firmly with okra. Add 1 teaspoon dill seed to each jar. Boil vinegar, water and salt. Simmer for 5 minutes and pour immediately over the okra. Seal.

Quick Pickled Peaches

4 pounds canned peach halves,
*   drain and reserve juice*
¾ cup brown sugar, packed

½ cup cider vinegar
3 sticks cinnamon
1 tablespoon whole cloves

Drain peaches. Place juice and remaining ingredients in saucepan and simmer for 5 minutes. Place peach halves in sterilized jars, cover with hot syrup. Keep refrigerated until used. Use within a few days. Yields 3 pints.

Note: Pineapple chunks may be substituted for peach halves.

269

Pickled Squash

2 cups yellow or zucchini squash,
   sliced thin
salt
1 green pepper, diced
2 cups cider vinegar

3 cups sugar
2 teaspoons mustard seed
2 teaspoons celery seed
1 cup onions, sliced into rings

Put squash in a bowl, cover well with salt and let stand for an hour. Rinse lightly with a cup of water to remove some salt. Combine green pepper, vinegar, sugar, mustard and celery seeds, and bring to a boil. Boil for 2 minutes; add squash and onions and return to a boil. Remove from heat and pack while hot into sterilized jars; seal. Yields 2 pints.

Iced Green Tomato Pickles

2 gallons water
3 cups garden lime
7 pounds small green tomatoes,
   sliced
5 pounds sugar

3 pints vinegar
7 tablespoons pickling spice
1 tablespoon whole cloves
2 tablespoons stick cinnamon, broken

Mix water and lime together. Soak the tomatoes in the lime water for 24 hours. Drain. Soak in fresh water for 4 hours, changing the water every ½ hour. Drain well. Make a syrup of the sugar and vinegar. Add spices. Bring syrup to a boil and pour over the tomatoes. Let stand overnight. Next morning, boil for 1 hour. Seal in jars while hot. Yields 11-12 pints.

Green Tomato Pickle Relish

2 gallons green tomatoes
½ gallon white onions
3 green peppers
3 sweet red peppers
½ cup salt

2 quarts white vinegar
3½ pounds sugar
4 tablespoons mustard seed
4 tablespoons celery seed
2-3 tablespoons turmeric

Slice tomatoes, onions and pepper into very thin slices. Sprinkle with salt. Cover and let stand overnight. Drain. Add vinegar, sugar, mustard seed and celery seed. Cook mixture for 3 hours until tender. Add turmeric just before removing from heat. Put into hot, sterilized jars. Place on lids but do not tighten until partially cooled. Yields 14-16 pints.

Virginia Watermelon Pickle

10 pounds watermelon rind
  (2 large melons)
1/4 ounce slaked lime
2 gallons water
3/4 cup salt
10 pounds sugar

7 cups white vinegar
1 cup water
2-3 tablespoons whole cloves
2-3 tablespoons whole allspice
2-3 tablespoons cinnamon sticks,
  broken

Peel and cut rind into small pieces. Mix lime with 1 gallon water. Add rind, cover with a heavy plate to keep the rind covered in liquid. Soak overnight, drain and wash 4 times. Squeeze all the rind by hand to remove most of the water. Boil rind 20 minutes in remainder of water mixed with salt. Drain and wash 3 times in clear, cool water. Drain and squeeze water from rind. Make a syrup of remaining ingredients, cook until sugar dissolves. Add rind and cook 1 hour. Cool slightly. Pack jars with rind, cover with syrup and seal. Yields 12 pints.

Hot Dog Relish

4 cups onion, coarsely ground
4 cups cabbage, coarsely ground
4 cups green tomatoes, coarsely
  ground
12 green peppers, seeded and minced
6 sweet red peppers, seeded and
  minced

1/2 cup salt
6 cups sugar
1 tablespoon celery seed
2 tablespoons mustard seed
1 1/2 teaspoons turmeric
4 cups cider vinegar
2 cups water

Combine vegetables, sprinkle with salt, and let stand overnight. Rinse well and drain. Combine remaining ingredients and pour over vegetables; mixing well. Heat to the boiling point, then simmer for 3 minutes. Pour into sterilized jars and seal. Yields 8 pints.

Pepper Relish

1 dozen green peppers
1 dozen sweet red peppers
7 medium onions
2 tablespoons salt

2 tablespoons mustard seed
3 cups vinegar
3 cups sugar

Grind peppers and onions coarsely. Reserve the liquid. Combine liquid with all other ingredients and boil for 30 minutes. Put in sterilized jars and seal. Yields 12 pints.

Corn Relish
(Courtesy of Lisburne)

5-6 ears corn
3 peppers, chopped
¾ cup sweet red pepper
1 cup ripe cucumber,
   peeled and chopped
½ cup celery, diced
1 cup onions, chopped
3 cups ripe tomatoes,
   seeded and diced

1½ cups vinegar
1 cup sugar
2½ teaspoons salt
1 teaspoon mustard seed
¾ teaspoon turmeric
2 teaspoons celery seed
¼ teaspoon dry mustard

Wash and drain all vegetables. Cut corn from cob, scraping well. Combine all vegetables except tomatoes. Turn into colander to drain thoroughly. Add tomatoes. Combine with remaining ingredients in 3 quart pot, heat to boiling. Reduce heat and simmer for 40 minutes until vegetables are just tender. Pour at once into hot sterilized jars. Seal. Yields 4 pints.

Note: Delicious served on fresh greens or as part of a relish tray.

Dilled Carrot Sticks

3 pounds carrots
2 tablespoons pickling spice
2 tablespoons dill seed
1 quart white vinegar

1½ cups sugar
1 garlic clove, chopped
6-8 dill sprigs or
   ¾ teaspoon dried dill

Peel and slice carrots into strips. Cook until tender. Drain carrots; cool and place in a bowl. Tie the pickling spice and dill seed in a cheese cloth bag. Place in a medium saucepan with vinegar and sugar. Bring to a boil, stirring constantly. Reduce heat and simmer for 5 minutes. Remove the spice bag. Pour hot syrup over carrots and refrigerate, covered, overnight. Remove carrots from syrup and pack into sterilized jars. Boil syrup for 1 minute and pour over carrots. Divide garlic and dill evenly in each jar. Yields 3-4 pints.

Southern Red Pepper Sauce

2-3 hot red peppers

1 cup cider vinegar

Combine and allow to stand in a cruet until good and spicy. Drizzle over fresh greens, sliced pork or barbecue.

Lisburne

Lisburne and its original dependencies were built about 1810. The present owners, Mr. and Mrs. David Peebles, began restoration and additions in 1964. They have also restored the gardens and added a formal boxwood garden at the front of the house. An English basement is included in the four floors of this lovely Gloucester home. The luxurious setting amid stately old trees has been admired and envied by many who have visited this gracious home either as guests or on tours.

Green Tomato Dills

6 pounds small, hard green tomatoes
24-28 ribs celery, cut in strips
2-3 large green peppers, cut in strips
12-14 garlic cloves
pickling spice

1 gallon vinegar
5 quarts water
2½ cups salt
2 boxes dill seed or
12 fresh dill heads

Fill each sterilized jar with tomatoes, 2 ribs celery, 1 strip green pepper, 1 clove garlic and a pinch of pickling spice. Pack the jars compactly. Boil the remaining ingredients for 5 minutes. Fill each jar to the rim with hot vinegar mixture. Seal and store for 6 weeks before serving. Chill before serving. Yields 12-14 pints.

Note: If using fresh dill, stuff a large bunch in each jar with tomatoes.

Burgundy Wine Jelly

3 cups sugar
2 cups Burgundy wine

3 ounces Certo

Combine sugar and wine. Bring to a rolling boil. Add Certo and reboil. Remove from heat and pour into sterilized jelly glasses. Yields 5.
"Simple to make, yet oh so good! Serve on hot bread."

Pepper Jelly

½ cup vinegar
½-¾ cup hot red peppers,
   seeded and chopped
1 green pepper, seeded and chopped
6½ cups sugar

1¼ cups vinegar
6 ounces Certo
⅓ ounce red food
   coloring

Place vinegar and peppers in blender and blend well. Make a syrup of sugar and vinegar, and bring to a slow boil. Cook until sugar dissolves. Add the pepper mixture and stir while cooking for 5 minutes. Remove from heat, add Certo and food coloring. Pour into jars and seal with wax. Yields 3-3½ pints.
"Use this jelly to 'ice' a large cake of cream cheese and serve with crackers."

Mint Jelly

2 cups mint leaves
1 1/2 cups white vinegar
1/2 cup water
1 tablespoon lemon juice

2-3 drops green food coloring
3 1/2 cups sugar
3 ounces Certo

Place mint, vinegar and water in a blender and blend well. Place in pan and bring to boil. Cover, remove from heat, and let stand for 10 minutes. Strain out all but a few chopped leaves. Place 1 3/4 cups of the mixture in a large saucepan. Add lemon juice, food coloring and sugar; bring to a boil quickly, stirring constantly. Add Certo immediately. Bring to a rolling boil for 1 minute, stirring constantly. Pour into sterilized jars and cover with wax. Cool, cover with additional wax. Yields 2 pints.

Holiday Chutney

2 pounds crushed pineapple,
   undrained
1 cup cider vinegar
1 cup light brown sugar, packed
1/2 teaspoon salt
1/2 teaspoon ground ginger

1 clove garlic, minced
1/4 cup sliced almonds, lightly
   toasted
1/2 cup seedless raisins
1 small green pepper, minced

Cook pineapple, vinegar, brown sugar and salt for 30 minutes over low heat. Add ginger, garlic, almonds, raisins and pepper. Simmer until thickened, stirring frequently. Spoon into jars. Store in refrigerator. Yields 2 pints.
"Good with ham or pork roast."

Cranberry Conserve

4 cups fresh cranberries
2/3 cup cold water
1 orange, unpeeled and thinly
   sliced

1 cup raisins, chopped
3 cups sugar
1 cup chopped pecans

Wash and pick over cranberries. Cook in water until skins burst, about 15-20 minutes. Stir occasionally to keep from sticking. Add orange slices, raisins, and sugar. Simmer until thickened, about 20 minutes. Add nuts and put in jars. Store in the refrigerator. Yields 2 pints.
Note: Keeps 3-4 weeks.

Peach Conserve

4 cups peaches, fresh or frozen
½ cup maraschino cherries,
   with juice
1 cup orange marmalade
2 tablespoons lemon juice

8 cups sugar
6 ounces Certo
1 teaspoon almond extract
⅓ cup peach liqueur

Combine the peaches, cherries, marmalade, lemon juice and sugar. Bring to a rolling boil, stirring constantly. Boil for 2 minutes, remove from heat and add Certo, almond extract and liqueur. Pack in sterilized jelly jars. Cover with melted wax. Yields 10 half-pint jars.
"Delicious on toast or muffins."

The three recipes that follow are traditional ways of making preserves.
They have been handed down for generations in an old Virginia family.
The recipes may be prepared in any quantity.

Damson Preserves

1 pound damson plums

1 pound sugar

Stem and wash damsons. Coat with sugar and let stand for 12 hours. Bring mixture slowly to a boil. Stir frequently. Boil gently until the syrup drops bead by bead. Pour into shallow pan and skim off seeds. Let stand until cold. Pack into sterilized jars and seal with wax. Yields 2-3 pints.

Peach Preserves

1 pound peaches, peeled and sliced   1 pound sugar

Coat peaches with sugar, and let stand for 12 hours. Bring mixture slowly to a boil. Stir frequently. Boil gently until the fruit becomes clear and the syrup drops bead by bead. Let stand until cold. Skim off foam. Pack into sterilized jars and seal with wax. Yields 2-3 pints.

Note: Pears can also be used. Season to taste with lemon peel, ginger or cloves.

Strawberry Preserves

4 cups strawberries   4 cups sugar
1 cup water

Wash and cap berries. Combine water and sugar, and cook until it makes a thread (soft ball stage). Add strawberries and cook over high heat for 15 minutes. Skim off foam while cooking. Cool. Put in sterilized jars and seal with wax. Yields 2-3 pints.

Lemon Marmalade

5 large lemons   1 ³/₄ ounces Sure Jell
2 ¹/₂ cups water   4 cups sugar
¹/₈ teaspoon soda

Shave the yellow rind off the lemons and cut into strips. Remove the white rind and discard. Cut lemons into thin slices, remove all seeds, and cut into small pieces. Place the rind, water and soda in a covered saucepan and simmer for 20 minutes. Add lemon and simmer for 10 more minutes. Add Sure Jell and boil hard for 1 minute. Add all the sugar at one time, stirring constantly, and continue boiling for 1 minute. Remove from heat, skim, and let stand for 7 minutes. Pour into jelly glasses and cover with melted paraffin. Yields 6 glasses.
Note: For variation, use 2 oranges and 3 lemons.
"This very old Virginia receipt is good served with toast or muffins."

Note: Pickle and Preserving Pointers

1.   Never use copper, brass or zinc utensils in canning.

2.   Enamel may be used if not chipped, but glass or pottery is preferred.

3.   In order to prevent spoiling, use only regular canning jars which have been sterilized in boiling water for 10 minutes. Make sure seal is airtight.

4.   Store in a dark, cool place to prevent discoloration. Usually it is best to allow pickles to "set" several weeks before using to enhance the flavor.

5.   Use whole spices when possible; ground spices may darken the product.

6.   Use only non-iodized salt.

7.   Slaked lime, also called calcium hydroxide, is available at drugstores.

UNITS of MEASURE

1 tablespoon . . . . 3 teaspoons
4 tablespoons . . . . ¼ cup
8 tablespoons . . . . ½ cup
16 tablespoons . . . . 1 cup
1 fluid ounce . . . . 2 tablespoons
1 cup . . . . ½ pint (liquid)
2 cups . . . . 1 pint
2 pints (4 cups) . . . . 1 quart
4 quarts . . . . 1 gallon
8 quarts . . . . 1 peck (dry)
4 pecks . . . . 1 bushel
16 ounces . . . . 1 pound

METRIC EQUIVALENTS OF U.S. WEIGHTS AND MEASURES

WEIGHTS

5 grams	= 1 teaspoon (approx.)
28.35 grams	= 1 ounce
50 grams	= 1¾ ounces
100 grams	= 3½ ounces
227 grams	= 8 ounces
1000 grams	= 2 lbs. 3¼ ounces

FLUID MEASURES

1 deciliter	= 6 tablespoons and 2 teaspoons
¼ liter	= 1 cup and 2¼ teaspoons
½ liter	= 1 pint and 4½ teaspoons
1 liter	= 1 quart and 3 tablespoons
4 liters	= 1 gallon and ¾ cup
10 liters	= 2½ gallons and 1 pint

VIRGINIA HOMES highlighted in
Virginia Hospitality

Acknowledgments

The Junior League of Hampton Roads, Inc., wishes to express its appreciation to both the private owners and historical societies for allowing us to include their homes in our book, to our art-coordinator, Barclay Sheaks, for his assistance, and to the outstanding Virginia artists for their sketches. These artists include:

Betty Anglin	*Forrest Coile*	*Barbara Harvell*	*Betty Zoe Miller*
Ken Bowen	*Bill Credle*	*Allan Jones*	*Else Nethersole*
George Chavatel	*Cynthia Haack*	*Jean Craig Jones*	

The cover, by Barclay Sheaks, is in the style of an eighteenth-century woodcut and includes the cardinal, dogwood, and pineapple symbolic of the Commonwealth of Virginia.

FRP.INC

FRP creates successful connections between organizations and individuals through custom books.

 Favorite Recipes® Press

Favorite Recipes Press, an imprint of FRP, Inc., located in Nashville, Tennessee, is one of the nation's best-known and most-respected cookbook companies. Favorite Recipes Press began by publishing cookbooks for its parent company, Southwestern/Great American, in 1961. FRP, Inc., is now a wholly owned subsidiary of the Southwestern/Great American family of companies, and under the Favorite Recipes Press imprint has produced hundreds of custom cookbook titles for nonprofit organizations, companies, and individuals.

Other FRP, Inc., imprints include

Additional titles published by FRP, Inc., are

Favorite Recipes of Home Economics Teachers

| Cooking Up a Classic Christmas | Recipes Worth Sharing | More Recipes Worth Sharing | The Hunter's Table | The Vintner's Table |

Junior Leagues In the Kitchen with Kids: Everyday Recipes & Activities for Healthy Living

Almost Homemade

The Illustrated Encyclopedia of American Cooking

To learn more about custom books, visit our Web site, www.frpbooks.com.

Also by the Junior League of Hampton Roads, Inc.

My Mama Made That
Very Virginia
Children's Party Book

To learn more about the Junior League of Hampton Roads, Inc.,
visit their Web site at www.jlhr.org.

Classic JUNIOR LEAGUE® COOKBOOK COLLECTION

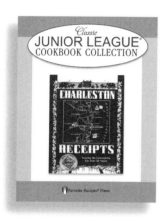  

This collection includes six of the most well known and respected Junior League cookbooks of all time; combined there are more than 2,000 pages with 4,000 regionally inspired, tried-and-true recipes. Collectively, over 2,000,000 copies of these cookbooks have sold over a span of 60 years.

 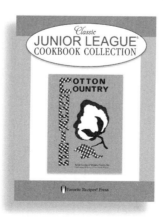 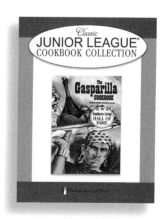